The Visitor's Guide
to
FRANCE: PROVENCE & COTE D'AZUR

FRANCE

Provence &
Côte d'Azur

THE VISITOR'S GUIDE TO FRANCE:
FRANCE:
PROVENCE
& COTE D'AZUR

NORMAN BRANGHAM
&
RICHARD SALE

MPC

HUNTER
PUBLISHING INC

Published by:
Moorland Publishing Co Ltd,
Moor Farm Road,
Airfield Estate,
Ashbourne,
Derbyshire DE6 1HD
England

1st edition published 1984
    (as *Visitor's Guide to South of
    France* by Norman Brangham).

Reprinted 1986

2nd edition revised and enlarged
by Richard Sale 1990

ISBN 0 86190 367 6 (paperback)
ISBN 0 86190 366 8 (hardback)

Colour and black & white
origination by:
Scantrans, Singapore

Printed in the UK by:
Richard Clay Ltd, Bungay, Suffolk

British Library Cataloguing in
Publication Data:
Brangham, A.N. (Arthur Norman),
1916-
    The visitor's guide to France:
    Provence and Cote D'Azur.
    -2nd ed., *Norman Brangham,
    Richard Sale.*
    1. France. Cote d'Azur &
    Provence. Visitor's guides
    I. Title II. Sale, Richard, *1946-*
    III. Brangham, A.N.
    (Arthur Norman), *1916-86*
    914.4904839

Cover photograph: *Menton*
(International Photobank).

Illustrations have been supplied as
follows: French Government
Tourist Office: pp 19, 111, 115, 170
(bottom), 182, 183, 186, 199
(bottom), 207; MPC Picture
Collection: pp 35, 179; Ron Scholes:
pp 107 (inset), 146, 147, 206
(bottom).

All other illustrations supplied by
R. Sale.

Published in the USA by:
Hunter Publishing Inc,
300 Raritan Center Parkway,
CN 94, Edison, NJ 08818
ISBN 1 55650 266 4 (USA)

10/1991

CONTENTS

Key to Symbols Used in Text Margin and on Maps

U Horse riding

π Archaeological site

Nature reserve/Animal interest

Birdlife

Garden

Sports facilities

Cave

Church/Ecclesiastical site

Building of interest

Castle/Fortification

Museum/Art gallery

Beautiful view/Scenery, Natural phenomenon

Other place of interest

Watersports

Interesting railway

Key to Maps

——— Main road

═══ Motorway

▪▪▪▪▪ Railway

～～ River

Town/City

● Town/Village

Lake

—·—·· Country Boundary

ACKNOWLEDGEMENTS

The author would like to thank Pauline Hallam of the French Government Tourist Office in London for her assistance during the preparation of this book.

He would also like to thank those people in Tourist Offices in the South of France who assisted him for their help and kindness. There are many such people, but it would be unfair not to thank Isabelle Roche and Veronique Seban of the Nice office personally for their help.

INTRODUCTION

For some people, the South of France is the whole French Mediterranean coast from the Italian to Spanish frontiers. For most, it is the south-east corner of France which encompasses Provence and the Côte d'Azur, two names with enticing associations. Provence suggests vines, olives and herbs, sun-filled open landscapes and a profusion of antique monuments. The Côte d'Azur is synonymous with luxury set in semi-tropical splendour. These stereotyped ideas are a little inaccurate but they are not entirely misleading since both areas share the Mediterranean's warmth and its brilliant light, so popular with artists.

The political map of France shows that Provence and the Côte d'Azur are made up of five *départements*. Each of these equates, very roughly, with a British county, although the head of a *département*, the *préfet*, is a powerful political figure, appointed by central government and responsible to the Minister of the Interior. The five *départements* are; in the north, Vaucluse (taking in the east bank of the Rhône), and, further east, the Alpes-de-Haute-Provence. South of these two are Bouches-du-Rhone, Var and Alpes-Maritimes, all of which border the sea.

To these is added here the southern strip of a sixth *département*, Drôme, that piece which totally surrounds a lopped-off bit of Vaucluse. Southern Drôme is part of the old province of Dauphiné, but it is essentially Provençal. There are the same terracotta curled roof tiles — which are like skeins of unravelled orange and yellow wool; the same heavy-shadowed, arcaded streets in clustered villages. Grignan, St Paul-Trois-Châteaux, Buis-les-Baronnies and Montbrun-les-Bains think of themselves as *La Dauphiné Provençal*.

The major town, conscious of its importance for tourists, proudly calls itself Nyons-la-Niçoise to emphasise — as do its olive groves — its climatic identity with the French Riviera.

Part of a seventh *département* must also be included. Just across the River Rhône is Gard whose Roman monuments link it to Provence. Finally, just to be sure that nothing the visitor is tempted by is excluded, there is an itinerary into the Ardèche Gorge, to good to be missed out just because a politically drawn line excludes it. It is, after all, normal for the French to include the Ardèche in Provence.

Geography

From the Rhône, which forms a natural frontier with neighbouring Languedoc, the distance to the Italian frontier is no more than 240km (150 miles) at the most. From Serre-Poncon in the north of Alpes-de-Haute-Provence to the islands south of Hyères, the southernmost islets off the Var mainland, is a distance of 160km (100 miles). It is not a vast territory, and is fully encompassed by Michelin 1:200,000 (1cm to 2km) No.245 which is more than adequate for most touring purposes, or by Michelins Nos. 84 and 81, with just a small part of Nos. 80 and 83, at the next larger scale.

Countless writers and artists have commented on how some part of Provence reminds them of one particular country or another. Katherine Mansfield was reminded of her native New Zealand by the mountains behind Menton. Vincent van Gogh saw in La Crau round Arles a replica of his Netherlands home. The centenarian explorer, Alexandra David-Neel, living in the arid hills of Digne, felt she was almost in the Tibet she had got to know so well, Roy Campbell, the flamboyant rancher-poet, saw the Natal of his youth recreated in the Camargue.

The drawing of such comparisons is a form of flattery, but they also show how much Provence is a landscape of many distinct characters. They can safely be termed, in French, *pays*. The word is hard to translate; 'country' or 'district' cannot convey the intimacy and rooted possessiveness implicit in its French meaning. Stemming from the Latin *pagus*, it rightly carries a flavour of Provence's human antiquity. The diversity of these *pays* throw into relief innumerable contrasts within Provence, making it an endlessly rich region to explore.

As with all lands, the geography of Provence is dependent upon the underlying geology and, in geological terms, the region is as varied as any other of comparable size. There are lush river valleys, though, as shall be seen, Provence is more usually associated with a less fertile vegetation. There are alluvial plains to the sides of the major rivers, especially the River Rhône, and there is that most dramatic of landscapes, the Camargue, a land where the normal boundary between land and sea has been blurred. In the Camargue, the visitor is never absolutely sure where the sea starts or stops, though gradual desalination of the salty lagoons is making the distinction a little easier with time. Hopefully though, the Camargue will be a curious in-between world for many years to come, a fascinating landscape made more so by the African nature of some of its wildlife.

Elsewhere in Provence, the meeting of water and land has allowed the limestone rock beneath the surface to be eaten away to form caves, the bigger and more accessible of these being among the best show caves in Europe. The rivers have also cut deeply into the limestone to form gorges, none more famous — and rightly so — than the Verdon Gorge which cuts its way through the limestone plateau of the Haute Provence.

It is interesting to note the contrast between the two great rivers of Provence. The broad Rhône is a fast-flowing frontier river, industrialised and impersonal, while its tributary, the Durance, once a seasonally destructive torrent but now tamed by dams, is still the true artery of Provence, as it coils snake-like and sluggishly past gravel islets along a broad valley.

West of the Verdon Gorge there are mountains, a complicated range where the Pyrennean and Alpine folds meet, and here is the 1,909m (6,260ft) Mont Ventoux, the highest peak in Provence, one that has featured prominently in the history of the Tour de France. How totally different are the green shadows and the cool, pyramidal hump of chalk-dusted Mont Ventoux, 'the giant of Provence', from the buckled, seemingly molten, ridges of Montagne Ste Victoire further south. To the east and north of the Verdon are other mountain ranges; the beautiful Provençal Ranges of Maures and Esterel, together with the mountain wall of the pre-Alps that separates this area from real Alpine France.

In Vaucluse, the yellow soil suffuses the buildings of whole villages while around Aix the intense iron-oxide soil glows a vivid crimson-brown, especially after rain. Even the olive trees of one district hardly look to be the same species as those in another. In the

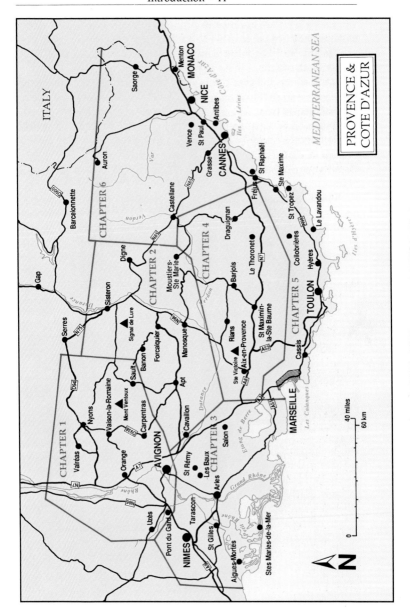

Rhône Valley they are mostly pruned low and round, but behind Menton they are left to grow to a full and majestic height.

Those who think only of a monotonous coastline when they think of the South of France must also be prepared for surprises, for, in its coastal scenery, the area offers almost as many contrasts as it does inland. East from the Camargue there are the Calanques, stretching out eastwards from Marseille, tight, beautiful bays with sculpted limestone cliffs. East again there are well-sheltered harbours near Toulon and, by way of contrast, the extraordinary feature of the Presqu'ile de Giens (*Presqu'ile* means nearly island). Occasionally, flamingoes can be viewed here against a background of the French Navy.

Next comes the Maures Coast, where those mountains meet the sea, and the wide bays around Antibes before the Riviera coast begins. There, with roads running along platforms cut out of the rock of the Alps, is a sea that really does live up to its name, the turquoise sea of the Côte d'Azur. The name was coined in the late nineteenth century by Stephen Liégard in a poem that, like its author, has not stood the test of time. Only that most descriptive phrase for the coast is now remembered.

Animal and Plant Life

The rich variety of scenery produces a diversity of habitats which makes the whole country fascinating to naturalists. They now come to Provence in much the same way as medieval monks used to travel here to gather herbs and samples. Europe's richest concentration of avifauna is in the Camargue which has had enough exposure on television to be well-known by most visitors. Millions of birds migrate across Provence, though they rarely catch the casual eye. Dawn choruses are uncommon; it is a question of adjusting to different seasonal sound-cycles. Instead of waking to the songs of garden and woodland birds, sleep is broken by choirs of nightingales in the thickets. Early spring is tree-frog belching time, high summer is when the cicada's sizzling song splits the hot daylight hours, while in late spring and autumn, both days and nights are filled with the melodies of crickets.

Zoologists can study beavers, boars, tortoises, reptiles, snakes — fortunately there are no adders below 1,000m (3,300ft) — and batracians. For botanists, hundreds of unfamiliar species and plant communities await identification. There is even an arctic flora clinging to the upper slopes of Mont Ventoux, despite the Mediterranean at its feet. The more serious horticulturist will want to make his own arrangements to visit some of the private and public gardens on the Côte d'Azur where exotic trees and plants from all the continents have been acclimatised.

As readers of J.H. Fabre will know, Provence is fascinating for entomolgists, but please refrain from cabinet collecting. Butterflies and moths appear in profusion but the survival of some species is precarious, and observation of habits must be considered pleasure enough. Large and showy insects attract the attention of every visitor; there are praying mantises, carpenter bees, locusts, scarab and capricorn beetles, as well as emperor moths, swallowtail butterflies, and the silent tracer-lights of fireflies.

Art and Architecture

Nature is one magnet, the art and architecture of man through the different epochs of his time in Provence is another. The creative vision of the artist and the celebrated monuments to the stonemason's craft are achievements which draw admirers from great distances. There are prehistoric relics, a plethora of Roman monuments — which are among the finest the Roman world has to offer — medieval churches, Renaissance mansions, art museums which emphasise the artist's long obsession with Provence, and the striking new coastal architecture. Off the beaten track, there are half-forgotten ruins, wayside shrines and Romanesque chapels. To stumble across them is the wanderer's delight, clearly remembered when better-known images have receded.

Like the contrasts in nature, the obvious and the obscure among human artefacts help complete an undertanding of Provence. There is certainly something for everyone to enjoy and discover in all these Provences.

Climate

It is tempting, with such a small area, to believe that it must be just a continuation of the France that you have crossed to reach it. Yet, however often it is repeated, an entry into Provence seems to be different. It is not because some administrative boundary has been crossed which identifies it, but because the physical features become different. A climatic frontier is crossed; the vegetation changes, and so does the quality of light. It is true that some man-made things change too, but Nature gives the chief clue as to why Provence, for all its undoubted Frenchness, is nonetheless a land apart. In place of soft, springy turf there is coarse hummocky grass, there are shrubs still but now there are tall succulents and palms, and the deciduous trees give way to evergreen. At first sight, the conifers are a surprise, but here the needle leaf is a protection against the heat, not the cold.

Provence obeys the rhythms of the Mediterranean climate. Seasons follow in abrupt succession. Sudden autumn rains end the panting heat of summer and there are few autumn tints to please the eye, except among the vines and highland fruit trees and along river banks where poplars grow. Winters are mild, particularly along the sheltered parts of the coast.

Spring produces the year's most sustained rainfall. Dormant plant life explodes into growth, flowers and seeds before the rising heat of summer introduces a punishing drought which can last for 3 months. For the tourist these are the picture-postcard days when the scent of resin and herbs fills the air. Yet summer is when local life is threatened by dehydration.

The naturalist might say that Provence begins where anthills cease, but this is not to be taken too literally. It illustrates that in the north nature harvests warmth and drains off excess moisture — which is what anthills do — while in the south living things ward off the heat and aridity by searching for moisture in hidden crevices, on cooler, shaded north-facing slopes and underground where the little water that exists is stored.

Large areas of Provence lack water, though irrigation schemes have made much unproductive land fertile. Plants and animals which are not adapted to aridity do not survive. Even the non-naturalist can see how vegetation is dominated by dwarfed trees, as though to reach skyward would be injurious. There are conifers everywhere, their needles keeping summer respiration and subsequent water loss to a minimum. A gentle, sage-green colour paints the landscape all the year: there are holm and cork oaks; Aleppo, maritime and the aptly named umbrella pines; almonds and cypresses, and that quintessential symbol of the Mediterranean, the olive.

Where the forests have been thinned, a *maquis* — sandy scrub — undergrowth of tree-heather, strawberry tree, juniper, myrtle,

A mature Provençal vineyard backed by pine woods

broom, cistus, butcher's broom, mastic and turpentine trees, forms a nearly impenetrable mass of rough and prickly shrubs.

In wide clearings — and for thousands of years man has ruthlessly cut down forests for his many needs — rocks protrude, like ribs poking out of the carcass of the land. This is the *garrigue*, described by the writer Posidonius in the second century BC, who wrote, 'The country is wild and arid. The soil is so stony that you cannot plant anything without striking a rock.' In the thin soil of such clearings, grow the aromatic culinary herbs and low spiny shrubs such as kermes oak, gorse and ling. Here too, are the countless bulbs and tubers which flower so briefly yet profusely in the spring, then die back in the first parching weeks of summer to leave a tawny desert.

The feature that is common to these strange but attractive patterns of vegetation is that they have adapted so that they can retain moisture. The variety of ways which have been adopted to do this or, at least, to slow down the loss of moisture to the air is remarkable. Trees have thick and roughened bark. Leaves are usually small: sometimes they are reduced to mere thorns; sometimes they are curled inwards; they may be thick, leathery or shiny; or their undersides are covered with a down of pale hairs; and many exude protective oils. The long, scimitar-shaped leaves of the eucalyptus turn so as to keep only the narrow edges of their blades facing the sun. As with the eucalyptus, so with the grasshoppers. In Britain we are used to seeing them with their flanks tilted full into the sun's rays like basking blackbirds. In Provence they face the sun head-on to ensure a minimum of exposure.

The climate is sometimes intemperate, and never more so than when the master-wind, the *mistral*, hurls itself down the funnel of the Rhône Valley and imposes its will on western Provence. It is most violent in late winter and early spring when low atmospheric pressures over the Mediterranean Sea suck down air currents from the snow-covered Massif Central. A chill, insistent wind blows for a few days, a non-stop wind that can drop temperatures by 10°C (50°F).

To gauge the effect of that wind on the inhabitants of Provence, look at how the old farmhouses (or *mas*) were constructed to withstand it. They are squat and massive, the north side often blank, with windows that are covered with hefty shutters — these also serving to keep out the summer's heat — and heavy roofs weighted with rocks. These defences are good, but do not entirely succeed in making the interior cosy; the *mistral* whistles through every cranny. Notice too, that the farmers plant row upon row of stately cypresses or bamboo as windbreaks for the tender crops.

The winter *mistral* can be freezing and maddening — 'enough to pull the tail off a donkey' according to the people of Avignon and Marseille, who receive the fiercest lashings. However, the purity of light it brings draws distant hills, almost invisible at other times, into startling detail. From the Rhône Delta, the wind fans east. The hills of Maures and Esterel break its power, and the Maritime Alps exhaust it to impotence. This fact, coupled with the heat-storing and radiating qualities of the rocks of the Côte d'Azur, explains why Cannes, Nice, Monaco and Menton became pre-eminent as winter resorts.

The *mistral* can blow in summer too; in 1989 it blew hard for several days, fanning fires that had started all too easily among the parched, tinder-dry forests of the coastal belt. When the smoke eventually cleared, there were still pockets of fire among the blackened stumps that had been forests, and the smell of wood smoke hung over the area for days. However, that is exceptional, and should not be allowed to deter the visitor.

This weather pattern occurs because Provence, to put it rather dramatically, is the most northerly perimeter of the Sahara Desert. Without the Mediterranean, that almost tideless and strongly salted inland sea, Provence would be literally Saharan. The summer that the visitor treasures ·is created by the hot air of tropical Sahara expanding northwards. As it does so, it reduces from its norm of 6 months without rain in Algeria to 3 months in Provence. This tropical air and the more polar air from the Alps have their 'dogfights' and that is what produces the occasional, but violent, downpours of summer. Sometimes, hot gusts from Africa, the *sirocco*, carry clouds of sand-particles, and the whole landscape is turned to an intense yellow or purple according to how the sun's rays are refracted. In winter, the Saharan air retreats and cold continental air presses into Provence, its effect being reduced by the warmth of the sea.

History

There are traces of men having lived in the area for millennia. This is no great surprise as the land bridge from Europe to Africa, over what is now the Straits of Gibraltar, survived until relatively recent times. However, the first impact that man had on the landscape was in Neolithic, New Stone Age, times, with the building of long barrow burial mounds. Skeletons have been unearthed which precede these mounds — some dated to 30,000BC, uncovered in the coastal Rochers Rouges outside Menton, were adorned with shell and fishbone necklaces and bracelets indicating a hunting, fishing, gathering culture. However, the burial mounds are the first tangible reminder to the layman.

In its original form, the barrow was a series of upright stones supporting a capstone and so forming a chamber. The dead would be laid within the chamber and then the whole structure would be earthed over to form a mound. Sometimes the mound still exists but usually it has eroded away to leave the stones of the chambers, gaunt and enigmatic. These curious objects attracted myth and legend, they have been considered the work of supermen or magicians. In Britain such chambers are normally called cromlechs, though the word dolmen is also used, and it is this latter word that is used in France. One such dolmen, and a superb one, is the Fairy's Stone, close to the town of Draguignan. It is not the only example, as sites exist all over Provence, though cave-paintings, which occur frequently in western France, are conspicuous by their absence.

The terrain of southern Provence was too rough and the climate too warm to support the great mammals — bison, mammoth, woolly elephant, reindeer — which were hunted and immortalised in paint by the earlier (Upper Palaeolithic) cave-artists in Dordogne. Ibex, red deer and rabbits were the staple meats of Provence, hardly heroic subjects to inspire masterpieces in cave-sanctuaries.

Quite suddenly, hunting gave way to a pastoral life, an event that coincides with the first domestication of wild animals in western Europe, which took place in south-west Provence. This precocious Neolithic revolution started a pastoral tradition which has been at the root of Provençal culture ever since, though industrialism has tried here, as elsewhere, to supplant it. Even in the last 20 years, the tradition was expressed by the *transhumance*; a slow, ritualised, month's trek on foot by thousands of sheep and their escorts. They left the lowland pastures as late spring began to shrivel the grass, wound their way to the lower Alps and returned as the first snows fell in October. Changes in the law then put an end to the tradition and the flocks were carried by train. Now the few animals that are still moved are moved by lorry.

On the stony plateaux around Bonnieux and Gordes there are beehive huts known as *bories* which, though mostly of relatively recent construction, are examples of how the earliest farmers built the first free-standing stone buildings. They were the work of the early semi-nomadic shepherds, perhaps driven to the plateau by other farmers who had settled on the richer, lower ground.

In the Val des Merveilles above Tende, there are tens of thousands of rock carvings, the earliest of which are thought to be evidence of Bronze Age shepherds who came each summer to these inhospitable highland valleys. The meaning of the petroglyphs, if meaning in our sense of the word there ever was, remains a mystery. All these early semi-nomadic shepherds, along with traders in skins and salt, trod out the first recognisable tracks which became the waymarks for Roman engineers who arrived later to construct their stone-slabbed highways.

Until the coming of the Romans, Provence north of the Durance was occupied by Celtic tribes, while south of it there were the Ligurians. The earlier quotation from Posidonius, giving the historian's views on the country of the Ligurians, continues with his observations of the Ligurians themselves. 'Work is an ungrateful toil, and daily hardships are such that life is truly difficult for these people

French artist selling paintings; a popular sight in Provence

whose bodies, as a result, are skinny and shrivelled. It sometimes happens that a woman gives birth in the fields, covers the young one with leaves, and then returns to her work so that a day will not be lost.' An unforgiving landscape indeed, and one in which the compensation of superb light might have been lost on the toilers.

The Ligurians built the first *oppida*, defensive positions of drystone walls at vantage points. Their residual heaps of stones can still be found on some hilltops, the one at Chastelard-de-Lardiers in the Lure Mountains was also a major religious sanctuary. Examples of the strange, yet strangly beautiful, Celto-Ligurian art can be found in many of the area's museums.

Traders from the Eastern Mediterranean had been sailing along the Provençal coast from at least 1,000BC, but it was not until 600BC that Phoenician navigators founded a Greek colony on the site of Marseille, which they called *Massalia*. They traded with the natives, introduced the vine and the olive, founded trading posts to both the east and the west along the coast, and peacefully penetrated the Rhône Valley. The Greek foundations of *Massalia* have now been laid bare and other Greek buildings can be seen at the open-air site of

Glanum outside St Rémy-de-Provence. Most astonishingly, the Greek defensive wall at St Blaise is still in mint condition.

As Marseille expanded, its commercial power clashed with the interests of the Carthaginians and the Etruscans, so it was natural for the town to side with the Romans when the Punic Wars broke out. The Celts allied themselves with Carthage and, well-bribed by Hannibal, gave him and his elephants passage along the Rhône and into the Alps for his attack on Rome in 218BC. When Rome acquired provinces in Spain, Marseille assisted by keeping open the land route through Provence and subscribing a fleet which hastened the Carthaginian defeat at sea.

In 181BC, Antibes and Nice, both outposts of Marseille, came under threat from pirates but Rome came to the rescue. As time went by, Marseille found itself relying more and more on Rome's military might, so by 125BC, when Rome had largely subjugated the lands between the Alps and the Pyrenees, Marseille became Roman. Garrisons were installed and a huge *Provincia Romana* was created, of which today's Provence is only a fragment.

At about this time, the strategic highways were built, of which traces can still be seen. *Via Aurelia* was the main artery between Rome and Spain, following the Italian coast to Nice and Fréjus, then going inland through Le Luc, Aix, Salon and Nîmes, essentially the same route that the RN7 takes now. The demi-god Hercules was supposed to have walked this way on his return from the Garden of the Hesperides, and Monaco was named after him, *Portus Herculis Monoeci*. *Via Domitia* descended the mountains by way of Embrun, Sisteron and Apt to join *Via Aurelia*, while *Via Agrippa* led north from Arles to Avignon, Orange and St Paul-Tros-Châteaux. Numerous branch roads were then constructed that gave an effective network of communications.

As southern France became Romanised, there were tribal disputes, revolts against bureaucracy, taxation and commercial exploitation, but Julius Caesar was to govern the region for 7 years with skill and authority. With the decline in the power of Marseille — hastened by its mistaken support of Pompey in his struggle with Caesar — Arles gained supremacy.

Provence can be said to have prospered under Roman rule, particularly during the reign of Augustus when agriculture, stock-breeding and trade expanded. At this time, Arles became the granary of Rome. Goods were transported across the sea by the powerful guilds of boatmen (called *utriculariae* because they kept their cargoes afloat with inflated animal bladders) based in the Rhône Delta.

Natives could become Roman citizens, and Roman law was tolerant of alien religions as long as Rome's absolute authority was not questioned. Christians, who first appeared in Marseille in AD95, did not acknowledge this authority and suffered persecution until Christianity was made the official religion by Constantine the Great, early in the fourth century. He settled in Arles, which was by then the second city of the Empire and known as 'the little Rome of the Gauls'. The Romans gave the whole of France south of the River Loire the Low Latin occitan tongue of which Provençal is a derivative, a language used by all classes, and the medium in which the troubadours of the Middle Ages expressed their formalised love-songs.

Attracted by the wealth of Arles, the Visigoths began the first of many sieges of the city and Marseille in AD413. They were unsuccessful but they heralded the disintegration of the Western Roman Empire, a disintegration which lead to Provence coming under the rule of the Franks in AD536, though they left it as a semi-autonomous state.

When the Arabs crossed the Pyrenees they were not halted until Charles Martel defeated them at Poitiers in AD732. To stop them crossing the Rhône, he invaded Provence and the region called on the Arabs for help. After 7 long and bloody years, Martel was victorious, returning a sacked and massacred Provence to the firm administration of the Frankish Empire. The eighth century was one of the most tragic in Provençal history. Saracen raids were continuous, not only from the sea but from their settlements near Hyères and St Tropez, until their final defeat in AD972.

Long periods of anarchical feuding, depopulation and pestilence ensured the economic and moral decline of Provence. However, early in the thirteenth century, the wise rule of Raymon-Berenger V unified and modernised the country and gave it a sense of identity.

In 1246, a combination of intrigue and marriage gave Provence to Charles of Anjou who became Charles I of Provence and King of Sicily, an act of inheritance which the port of Marseille turned to great profit. This was the period of the great religious pilgrimages. St Louis set off on the Seventh Crusade from Aigues-Mortes in 1248, which saw the building of splendid Romanesque churches such as St Trophime at Arles and that at St Gilles, as well as many rural churches and chapels. The art of the troubadours flourished at the

Courts of Love, of which Les Baux was one of the most famous.

In 1229, the territory of Comtat Venaissin — which approximated to present-day Vaucluse, though it excluded Avignon, Orange and some other bits of land — was bought for 80,000 florins by the Pope and so became detached from the rest of Provence. In the following century, the Popes acquired more territories, including Valreas, now a little enclave of Vaucluse surrounded by Drôme. These enclaves remained the possession of the Holy See until 1791. As a result of these purchases, this corner of Provence, hitherto unimportant in the wider affairs of Europe, held centre stage. In 1309, a French Pope, Clement V, fled Rome, settled at Avignon, and installed the Holy See in what was to become the massive fortified Palace of the Popes. Five

Windsurfing

Popes ruled from there until 1377 when the Papal Court returned to Rome. The Comtat Venaissin was then administered by papal legates for more than 400 years.

In this phase of pomp and power, Avignon attracted the political, financial, intellectual and artistic elite of Europe. While the rest of Provence suffered incursions from Gascons, Spaniards, English, and the freebooters of Du Gueselin — all part of the devastating effects of The Hundred Years War — the presence of the Popes ensured a measure of protection to the papal territories.

In the fifteenth century, an economic and artistic upsurge came under the impetus of René d'Anjou, a poet and artist with neither political nor military gifts who is remembered as Good King René. After his death in 1480, Provence (excluding the Comtat Venaissin and Monaco) entered into formal union with the crown of France, royal power being exercised through the Parliament of Aix. Official transactions now had to be conducted in French, not Latin, to the resentment of many Provençaux who felt they were being deprived of their cultural heritage and identity by this centralisation. Resentment simmered until it found creative expression in the Provençal Renaissance of the nineteenth century under the leadership of the poet, Frédéric Mistral.

In the mid-sixteenth century, the Luberon Hills saw massacres and the total destruction of villages. The victims were the Vaudois, a fundamentalist heretical sect akin to the Albigensians in Languedoc who had been dealt with most cruelly early in the thirteeenth century. All Protestant settlements in Provence provoked equal hosility with the Catholics, the two sides becoming embroiled in the Wars of Religion between 1560 and 1598, even though the Edict of Nantes (revoked in 1685) was supposed to give freedom of worship and conscience. In fact, not until the Edict of Toleration in 1787, were protestant minorities freed from the fear of persecution.

With the opening of the eighteenth century, it looked as though stability and prosperity would return. Instead of this, Provence found itself devastated by the worst of many visitations of the plague. In 1720, a ship from the Levant brought it to Marseille. The main towns were decimated; 90,000 people died in two years. The authorities of the papal estates put up a wall, 100km (62 miles) long, with frequent sentry boxes, in the hope of confining the plague to the Provençal side, and traces of the wall can still be found near Pouraque, south of Venasque. St Sebastian transfixed by arrows, a common pictorial theme in churches and chapels, symbolically represented the dreaded plague.

Yet prosperity came in the wake of distress. Merchants from Marseille and Aix built their handsome *hôtels* or town mansions, country seats, new churches and public buildings, and Aix became a centre of elegance and learning. Even the Seven Years' War (1756-63) had an unforeseen benevolent consequence. Nice and its *Comté* belonged to the Dukes of Savoy and the King of Sardinia, allies with Britain in maritime rivalry with France. British families lived in Nice and Tobias Smollett, learning of the delights of its climate, visited Nice for his health in 1763-5 and wrote his influential (and still very readable) *Travels*. Publication marked the beginning of the British association with the Côte d'Azur. A century later, Lord Brougham 'discovered' Cannes, while Dr Henry Bennet did the same for Menton.

A gradual convergence of social and economic unrest throughout France precipitated the French Revolution in 1789. These included flagrant inequalities; selfish and absentee landlords; despotism; corruption; mal-administration and unfair taxation; high grain prices, particularly in Marseille and Toulon, as well as a grain failure after a cold winter. In 1788, the Parliament of Aix had protested against the privileges and perquisites enjoyed by the nobility and clergy. Passions were inflamed in Provence by Count Mirabeau, a powerful orator, through his *Address to the Provençal Nation*. Violence was widespread, the Parliament of Aix held its last meeting and with that ended the constitution of Provence.

In 1789, the National Assembly in Paris abolished the Aix Parliament by decree, the administration of the province being effected from then onwards by three newly created *départements* — Bouches-du-Rhône, Var and Basses-Alpes. Two years later, during which time there was virtual civil war in the region, the Comtat Venaissin was given up by the Popes and became the fourth *département*, Vaucluse. Nice and Monaco temporarily joined the new *département* of Alpes-Maritimes.

In 1792, a contingent of volunteers marched from Marseille to Paris in support of the revolutionary cause. At a farewell banquet in their honour, someone sang a revolutionary song, the battle song of the Army of the Rhine and actually composed by Rouget de Lisle, a young sapper officer, in Strasbourg. It was a hit with the 500 volunteers and they sang it frequently during their long march to Paris. By the time they had reached the capital, the song, a rousing one, had become a nationwide symbol of the new era. Today it is known as the *Marsellaise*.

Broadly speaking, the revolution was espoused by the urban working classes in Provence, who were known as 'The Reds'. Conservative rural communities tended to have monarchical sympathies and were called 'The Whites'. When the king was executed in 1793 there was widespread revulsion against the Revolution, and Toulon even opened its port to the young Republic's enemies, the Anglo-Spanish fleet. The Convention in Paris sent an army to recapture Avignon and Marseille where 'The Whites' briefly dominated. After weeks of siege, Toulon was also recaptured, with a young officer, one Captain Napoleon Bonaparte, distinguishing himself.

For all the great social and legal reforms introduced by Napoleon, his relations with Provence were not happy. Royalists felt affronted when he proclaimed himself Emperor and commercial interests suffered as a result of the Allied blockade his campaigns brought about. On the way to his Elban exile, the Provençaux threatened his life. When he landed at Golfe-Juan in 1815, at the start of the 'Hundred Days', the first part of his journey towards Paris along stony tracks — which approximate to the proudly named Route Napoleon (RN85) — was that of a fugitive, abused and cheated. It was not until he reached Gap that he heard his first cheers.

With the collapse of Napoleon's empire, royalists in Provence started a brief reign of 'White Terror' by assassinating Bonapartists in Marseille and Avignon. From these events, and for 50 years afterwards, Parisians convinced themselves that the Provençaux were brutal, reactionary fanatics. The restoration of the Bourbon monarchy in 1814 led to the July Revolution of 1830, and the next king from the House of Orleans gave birth to the greater upheaval of 1848. Neither regime sensed the mood of the people and the growing ideas of socialism. The next king, Napoleon III, nephew of Bonaparte, was popular for a while in most of France but not in Provence.

Only after the ill-judged Franco-Prussian war of 1870-1, when a new republic was established, did the government reflect the long-held egalitarian and democratic traditions, and the new-found patriotism of Provence.

New industrial technologies — metallurgical and chemical among others — came to Provence. Bridges were thrown across the Rhône and the Durance; bauxite was first mined at Les Baux; railways, canal systems and marshland drainage were extended; and steam navigation favoured the growth of Marseilles. Agriculture, still the mainstay of Provençal life, suffered mixed fortunes. Wheat, sheep and olives remained static staples but the silkworm cottage industry was destroyed by disease. Vineyards were ruined by phylloxera and their slow recovery was largely due to Pasteur's discoveries; the madder dye industry was quickly supplanted by German chemicals. Rural depopulation gathered pace as youth was drawn to the coast and to industry, and the Basses-Alpes became one of the poorest *départements* of France.

World War I left the territory of Provence untouched but bled its manhood and bequeathed stagnation. World War II saw the Italians occupy the Côte d'Azur and the French fleet scuttling itself in Toulon. After 1942, the Germans occupied the whole of the Midi which was to know deprivations, deportation, the Maquis (resistance movement), Allied air attacks, destruction by the retreating

Celebrities of Provençal History

Folquet 1160-1231 (Marseille).
Most original of the troubadours.

Louis Bréa 1443-1520 (Nice).
Leader of the Nice school of Primitive painters.

Michel de Nostradamus 1503-66 (St Rémy-de-Provence).
Doctor, astrologer, author of the famous predictions, *Centuries*.

Adam de Craponne 1519-76 (Salon-de-Provence).
First major canal engineer in Provence.

Bellaud de Bellaudière 1532-88 (Grasse).
Influential poet.

Fabri de Peiresc 1580-1677 (Belgentir).
Celebrated universal scholar.

Pierre Gassendi 1592-1655 (Champtercier).
Philosopher, priest and polymath.

Nicholas Saboly 1614-75 (Monteux).
Poet, author of still popular *Noëls*.

Pierre Puget 1622-94 (Marseille).
Powerful Baroque sculptor, architect, painter.

J. Pitton de Tournefort 1656-1708 (Aix).
Early scientific botanist.

Luc de Clapiers, Marquis de Vauvenargues 1715-47 (Aix).
Influential moralist respected by Voltaire.

Bailli de Suffren 1726-88 (St Cannat).
Vice-admiral, campaigned against British in West Indies.

J.H. Fragonard 1732-1806 (Grasse).
Famed for fashionably erotic paintings.

André Masséna 1758-1817 (Nice).
Marshall of France, Wellington's opponent in Peninsula War.

Adolphe Thiers 1797-1877 (Marseille).
Statesman, historian, first President of Third Republic, 1871.

Guiseppe Garibaldi 1807-82 (Nice).
Italian general and patriot.

Honoré Daumier 1808-79 (Marseille).
Painter and political caricaturist.

Frédéric Mistral 1830-1914 (Maillane).
Poet, leader of Provençal literary revival.

Paul Cézanne 1839-1906 (Aix).
Neo-Impressionist profoundly influencing European art.

Emile Zola 1840-1902 (Aix).
Novelist, boyhood friend of Cézanne.

Auguste Escoffier 1847-1935 (Villeneuve-Loubet).
Chef, inventor of *pêche Melba* at Carlton Hotel, London.

Albert Calmette 1863-1933 (Nice).
Inventor of anti-tuberculosis vaccine.

Edmond Rostand 1868-1918 (Marseille).
Dramatist, poet, author of *Cyrano de Bergerac*.

Raimu (Jules Muraire) 1883-1946 (Toulon).
Great Provençal screen character actor.

Edouard Daladier 1884-1970 (Carpentras).
Radical politician, prime minister 1938-40.

Fernand Benoit 1892-1969 (Avignon).
Distinguished archaeologist.

Darius Milhaud 1892-1972 (Marseille).
Composer, member of 'Les Six'.

Jean Giono 1895-1970 (Manosque).
Major novelist using regional landscapes as backgrounds.

Marcel Pagnol 1895-1974 (Aubagne).
Film-maker and writer.

Fernadel (Fernand Constandin) 1903-71 (Marseille).
Comic screen actor depicting Vieux Port Marseillais.

German divisions, airborne and seaborne landings, liberation and recriminatory vendettas.

The Algerian War brought large numbers of French refugees to Provence who have been absorbed into the social, commercial and political life of the province. A whole town, Carnoux, was built for them. At different periods, influxes of Italians, Spaniards and Algerians have supplied the unskilled and semi-skilled labour on roads, building sites and in vineyards.

Provence, whose existence as a political reality was erased by the Revolution, has been reborn officially, though its geography and political intentions are different. In 1956, the central government created a series of economic regions in France. Provence was resurrected as Provence-Côte d'Azur-Corse: the five *départements* this book covers, plus Corsica and Hautes-Alpes; the latter thought to be an error of judgement for traditionalists.

Great changes have been wrought in 30 years. Now only a small percentage of the population works on the land, but agricultural productivity has been vastly increased. Industry has tended to concentrate along the Rhone Valley. It includes petro-chemicals, electronics, hydro-electrics, iron, steel, aluminium, cement, nuclear fission for civil and military purposes, food production and tourism.

The tourist may not be interested in this face of Provence but it is a face of prosperity which has put the region in the forefront, and no longer in the backwater, of European affairs.

Accommodation

Tourist hotels are classified officially by the government in 'star' categories which range from 'four-star L' — the fabled 'palace' hotels of the Côte d'Azur, and the elegant and often beautiful 'Relais et Châteaux' — through three intermediate grades, to 'one-star', which is of moderate, but quite adequate, comfort. These are objective ratings based on facilities in relation to the number of bedrooms; they are not in themselves recommendations of quality.

The one- and two-star hotels are reasonable as to both price and comfort. They may not offer the chintzy, armchair comfort frequently expected of hotels in Britain, but traditionally the French have been less interested in comfort than the British, though things are changing. These one- and two-star hotels make up most of the largest hotel-chain, the *Federation Nationale des Logis et Auberges de France* or *Logis de France* for short. This is a loose and fundamentally independent association of nearly 5,000 hotels. All of them undertake to provide a good standard of welcome, comfort, cleanliness and food at reasonable, inclusive prices. They are small and medium-sized (many have less than twelve bedrooms) family hotels in rural areas and small towns. *Auberges* are small and simpler than *logis* and so tend to be cheaper. It is worth remembering that in France there is no sacrifice of individuality as a result of belonging to a chain.

To give an impression of what an authentic Provençal hotel is like means piecing together a composite picture because they are all so very different. Perhaps the shell of the hotel is an eighteenth-century town house; grave and restrained to look at from the outside. The interior retains the old, high-ceilinged beams. The bedroom furniture is polished walnut with ornately moulded baroque panels. On the bed is a cover of strong yellow, green or red, dotted with contrasting motifs of such charm as to make you want to go out and buy one at once. With luck, the bed-linen will be rough, white and lavender-sweetened. Copper pots hang on the restaurant walls and each table has a blaze of welcoming colour from the tablecloth and is finished off with polished glasses. The floor is surfaced with hexagonal terracotta tiles, smelling of beeswax.

The annual handbook of these useful hotels is free to callers at the French Government Tourist Offices (see Useful Addresses in the Further Information section at the back of the book).

Many other more modest, non-tourist hotels exist in most towns and villages, as do furnished rooms and flats to let. Properly equipped country houses, villas, cottages and farms (or self-contained parts of them) can be rented as holiday homes (*gîtes rurales*). Well-equipped camp and caravan sites, sometimes in very lovely settings, can be found almost everywhere.

The months of July and August are the hot, high season when it is unwise not to have booked holiday accommodation in advance. Both earlier and later in the season, the hotels in popular centres, whether inland or by the sea, tend to be fully booked. This is particularly so in September when the stored warmth of late summer attracts many visitors.

Food and Drink

Traditional Provençal food is distinctive, being based on olive oil, herbs and garlic. Garlic is milder in the south of France than it is to the north and, when properly cooked in Provençal dishes, tends to enhance the flavour of the dish rather than leaving an unpleasant smell or taste. Those who do not like garlic may have a little difficulty with the local fare in which 'the truffle of Provence', otherwise known as the 'Friend of Man' or the 'Divine Condiment', features prominently.

Restaurants, like hotels, run the whole gamut from the magnificent to the simple. Some of the most prestigious restaurants in the world can be found in this area. Gastronomes come from far and wide to l'Oustaù de Baumanière at Les Baux; to La Bonne Auberge at Antibes; Le Moulin de Mougins at Notre Dame-de-Vie, outside Mougins; and to l'Oasis at La Napoule, to name only those to whom experts have given the highest accolades. A meal at any of them is an experience, but it is best to go prepared neither to quibble nor blanch at the cost.

Most visitors, looking for a more modest yet still memorable experience, turn to the annual *Michelin Red Guide*'s maps of restaurants which provide 'good food at moderate prices'. Over the years many have found these recommendations reliable, though an even better source of information can be the place where one is staying. Fall into conversation with a French family familiar with the local area, and good advice as to where the food is choice and the price is right will usually be forthcoming.

Substantial and inexpensive meals are provided by *Les Relais Routiers*, which are mostly on main roads. Orginally, these catered for lorry-drivers, now passing motorists patronise them as well. However, do not expect opulence as well as nourishment; at some of these roadside cafés the surroundings are stark.

The menu which is displayed outside the door of your chosen restaurant will include a fixed-price tourist menu, usually a basic, inexpensive three-course meal. A second *table d'hôte* will have more choice. A third, a *menu gastronomique*, including regional specialities, will also be shown. All the dishes appear on an *à la carte* list. It is almost invariably cheaper to choose the *table d'hôte*.

Before leaving for France, it might be best to consult one of the excellent books that are now available in English on regional French cooking so as to be alert to local Provençal specialities, of which only some can be mentioned here.

Near the coast, fish and seafood dishes naturally take pride of place. It is a well-known saying of the region that while fish live in the sea they die in olive oil. The classic fish dish is *bouillabaisse*. Experts

Palm trees, like these at Hyéres, are a common sight along the Mediterranean coast

disagree as to its vital ingredients, but basically it is a stew of a variety of Mediterranean fish, garlic and saffron. It must be ordered the day before and should be consumed with gusto and ritual by a party of four or more. Like some other great Provençal dishes, it is not for the budget-or calorie-conscious traveller.

The second great dish is *bourride*. Again, it is a stew, made with grey mullet, sea-bass, whiting and other white fish, topped with *aïoli*, an unctuous mayonnaise of garlic and olive oil known as 'the butter of Provence' — though the great Mistral himself referred to the mix as 'insipid jam' ! *Aïoli* transorms plates of plain vegetables or hard-boiled eggs into a feast.

Every restaurant serves *soupe de poisson*. It can be something mediocre out of a tin or packet, but at its best it is a stock of various fish, pungent and peppery, served with toasted cubes of bread, cheese and a rust-coloured sauce of garlic, hot peppers and saffron called *rouille*, which also means rust in French.

Brandade de morue is pounded, dried salt cod, made creamy with olive oil and milk; if it is on the menu at all it is likely to be on a Friday. Other sea fish which are seen on the slabs at market or in restaurants are John Dorey (*daurade*), sea-bass (*loup de mer*) and red mullet (*rouget*).

Nice, on account of its long political association with Italy — which lasted until 1860 — has a distinctive, Italianate cuisine. Look out for *soupe au pistou*, a vegetable soup thickened with a *pommade* of pounded basil, garlic and olive oil. For a substantial picnic, buy a *pan bagnat*, French bread with olive oil, spread with chopped anchovies, tomatoes, onions and peppers. An alternative is *tourte aux blettes*, an open-crust pastry covered with leaves of *chard* (rather like spinach). Another alternative is the local vegetable flan called *tian*. It is also worth trying *anchoïade*, an open sandwich, eaten hot or cold, with anchovy paste and oil, garlic and vinegar. Two dishes with Niçois names are known everywhere: *pissaladière* (akin to the Italian pizza), and *salade niçoise*.

The Camargue supplies the cattle for *boeuf en daube*, stew in red wine and aromatic herbs, as well as for *boeuf gardianne*. Rice-growing (the area now produces the bulk of French rice) gives a local risotto dish, *riz de Carmargue*, made with mussels and other sea-foods. Eels are bred in vast numbers in the Carmargue, a local dish has them stewed in wine and served with tomatoes and potatoes.

From the herb-covered hills comes succulent lamb, the small grey snails called *cantareu* in Provençal, rabbit, thrush and blackbird pâtés and, but no longer frequently, wild boar.

A splendid variety of early vegetables makes salads and *crudités* — raw vegetables which when attractively dressed and presented are a much-appreciated first course since the quantity of cooked vegetables with the main course is sometimes small. Tomatoes, cabbages, marrows, lettuce, dandelions, aubergines, pumpkin, artichokes, asparagus and pimentoes stuffed or combined in a variety of ways ought to avoid any complaints about repetitious meals.

The fresh fruits of Provence are famous. There are olives, figs, cherries, peaches, apricots, grapes and melons, as well as the ubiquitous golden and red delicious apples. Try the thirst-quenching *pastèque à la provençale* — chilled water-melon filled with either a fine red or rosé Provençal wine. Fritters made with flowers such as mimosa or marrow make agreeable sweet courses.

Cheese boards may be loaded with a variety of French cheeses, but those from Provence will be few, though the disc-shaped *Banon* goat cheese should be among them. Its flavour is delicate yet distinct, and no wonder, for it is first wrapped in the leaves of the herb savory, then dipped in *eau-de-vie* before receiving its final wrapping of vine or chestnut leaves and being tied with straw. Allied to *Banon* is *poivre d'âne* or ass's pepper (*pebré d'assé* in Provençal), its peppery flavour is imparted by finely ground savory leaves on the outside. Look out too for the particularly strong ewe's milk cheese, *cachat*, usually only found in season, between May and November.

For the sweet tooth, the delicately almond-flavoured *calisson d'Aix* biscuits are a temptation, as are the crystallised fruits of Apt, Spanish chestnut purée and *marron glacé* from Collobrières. There are also candied flowers and figs from Grasse and Nice; caramel sweets called *berlingots* from Carpentras, with a more fragile flavour than our boiled sweets; and the famous nougat of Montélimar, whose ingredients are the high quality regional honey and almonds. Nougat is also made in smaller quantities at Draguignan, Sault and Sisteron.

Finally, there are the wines. For the most part, wines produced in the broad coastal belt of southern Provence have no great merit beyond, perhaps, their high alcohol content. These are the Côtes de Provence, Coteaux d'Aix and Coteaux du Var. Quantity rather than quality is the rule, but the reds go well enough with the robust meat dishes of Provence, and the whites and rosés adequately accompany fish.

Exceptions are the strong red and white wines of Bandol; the very dry Cassis white; Palette from near Aix produces red, white and rosé, of which the red from Château Simone is most highly regarded. Château Vignelaure, its neat vineyards curving up at a bend in the D561 between Rians and Jouques, produces a respectable red; Bellet, behind Nice, also makes red, white and rosé wines in small quantities — it is a chic drink.

More interesting wines are found further afield. Stray into Gard to taste Tavel, the best dry rosé of all, at Tavel itself. Its near neighbour, Lirac, also produces a distinguished rosé. Near Aigues-Mortes is the 'wine of the sands', Listel *gris-de-gris* rosé. Also in Gard — if one dare mention it in the same breath — some 16km (10 miles) south west of Nîmes, is the Perrier factory. The famous mineral water rises as a spring from a subterranean lake and is bottled under pressure. The plant can be visited most weekdays of the year. There was a time when the drinking of bottled water was widely believed to be yet another French eccentricity, but no longer.

Cross to the north bank of the Durance and you are in Vaucluse, the southern part of Côtes du Rhône country. Châteauneuf-du-Pape is the only classic wine of Provence, of which a little white is also produced. Gigondas is a good red from the slopes a few kilometres north-west of Châteauneuf. When Côtes du Rhône labels are hyphenated with one of a dozen communes in Vaucluse, a bold, smooth wine is promised. Visan is a faintly sparkling rosé which gives a brief, champagne-like lift. Coteaux du Tricastin, Côtes du Luberon and Côtes du Ventoux have been exported for a number of years now, during which time their quality has improved.

A sparkling wine is made in Drôme by the *méthode champenoise*. This is Clairette de Die, which comes both *brut* and *demi-sec*. One of the lightest fortified sweet wines is Beaumes-de-Venise, drunk either as an aperitif or as a dessert, as is its close neighbour, Rasteau.

The most popular of aperitifs — indeed the 'national drink' of Provence — is the aniseed-flavoured *pastis*, clear until water is added and tasting innocuous to begin with. Beware, the kick comes a little later. The shelf of most bars will display a bewildering variety of *pastis* bottles, and it takes constant practice for the taste-buds to distinguish them all. The indigenous variety is Ricard, a name associated all over Provence, not only with this drink but with Paul Ricard's leisure and sports centres as well. Recently, a non-alcoholic Ricard *pastis*, thick and sweet, has come on to the market. The other locally made aperitif is the quinine-based St Raphaël; the red is full and sweet, the white is drier and less fruity. Something of a rarity is a yellow, punget, herb-flavoured liqueur called Sénancole, originally developed to a secret formula — as these liqueurs always are — by the monks of the abbey of Sénanque, not far from the village of Gordes in Vaucluse.

Wine-tasting and comparing wine-notes can be one of the delights of a Provençal holiday, but the truth has to be told — wine prices in restaurants are sometimes as high as they are back home. A local wine is not necessarily cheap for being local. Some restauranteurs still include a carafe of wine in the price of the meal. In the Michelin guide this is indicated by the letters 'bc' (*boisson compris*) following the price of the meal. Others provide an acceptably priced carafe or jug (*pichet*) of *vin de table* or *vin du patron*.

Wine in groceries or supermarkets is still cheap, as it is at wine co-

Oranges grow prolifically in Provence

operatives, the *caves co-operatives* or *vinicoles*, which are dotted about the wine-growing districts. A small *bonbonne*, a glass demi-john encased in whicker, holds 10 litres, the more pratical *cubitaine*, the now familiar wine-box, is sold in various capacities from 10 litres to 33 litres. Wines which have been enjoyed on holiday can be bought in this way and stowed in the boot of the car. Even after duty has been paid at British customs, the purchase is worthwhile, all the more so if the quality of the wine is good because the tax is always the same.

1
THE RHONE VALLEY
TO AVIGNON

The traditional highway from the north into Provence is the valley of the River Rhône. Until the railways came, the produce of the region was loaded on to great barges at Avignon and hauled by teams of horses to Lyon and beyond. Visitors came south by boats which had to shoot the twenty-five arches of the still-standing medieval bridge at Pont St Esprit. A swift current demanded considerable skill and sobriety of the pilot, as well as steady nerves of his passengers. Most people now travel in rather more haste, taking the Autoroute du Soleil (A7), a journey that calls for equally steady nerves. Those with rather more time to spare can follow either of the Rhône's banks, the west bank's N86 getting the motorist as rapidly into Provence as does the N7 on the east bank.

A more rural route climbs out of Vienne and follows the edge of the Dauphiné foothills through Romans-sur-Isère, Crest, Nyons, Carpentras and so to Cavaillon. As far as Nyons this is the D538.

Nyons is in Drôme, yet is good preparation for Provence proper. French families stay there in both summer and winter, as the rounded, shrub-dotted hills shelter the resort from the *mistral*. In summer, the cooling *pontias* breeze blows down the Aygues Valley, a river whose name is sometimes written as Eygues or Aigues — all of these variants mean water.

Arcaded streets on the northern side of the town lead to the Quartier des Forts, built in the Middle Ages. The beautiful, covered Rue de Grands Forts leads to an old gateway, once part of the town's protective castle, but it is best just to wander at will through the narrow streets. When you are ready to leave, take the narrow road known as the Promenade des Anglais north-west out of Nyons to complete a circular trip that offers the best view of both the town and the valley. Those interested in the olive oil industry, and anyone arriving in Provence with even half an idea to try the local cuisine, can pursue that interest in the town. Nyons is a local centre for oil-making and one of the several oil mills in the town will probably be offering trips when you arrive. Call at the local Tourist Information Office for exact details.

West of Nyons is **Valréas**, chief town of the Vauclusian enclave that is surrounded by the Drôme *département*. The enclave was formed when Charles VII banned the selling of further land in the area to the Papacy. Typical of so many towns (or *bourgs*) of Provence, Valréas stands on a hill. Its circular boulevards, overhung with plane trees, keep the feel of the old part of the town intact, and the fifteenth-century Château du Simiane holds centre stage.

Grignan, 9km ($5^1/_2$ miles) to the north-west, is a place of literary pilgrimage for admirers of the Marquise de Sévigné, whose letters in the seventeenth century about court life in Paris and the Provençal countryside are still read. The letters were written to her daughter who was married to the Count of Grignan, a man the Marquise described as being 'very ugly, but one of the most honest men in the kingdom'. It is debatable whether the Count viewed this as being a compliment. The Marquise wrote her letters at the castle, which can be visited. It is an elegant, and beautifully decorated, Renaissance mansion that offers a superb view over Mont Ventoux. The Marquise loved it; it was, she wrote, 'fine and magnificent' and offered shelter from the *mistral* that 'cuts one to the quick'.

The D538 south of Nyons enters Vaucluse at **Vaison-la-Romaine**. A hundred years ago, Baedeker did not mention the place, for the fame of Vaison began only with the excavation of Roman *Vasio* in 1907. A patrician city, it was founded as a Roman town(there had been a Ligurian settlement) in the fifth century and retained its position until the Franks destroyed it 400 years later. The Roman town, excavated as the Quartier du Puymin, includes a fine villa, the House of Messii, which shows how well the senior officers of the Empire lived. Pompey's Portico is an elegant public promenade, while the Nyphaeum, the town's water-source fountain, gives a good impression of why the Romans are considered a civilised race. The site museum houses the best of the excavated finds.

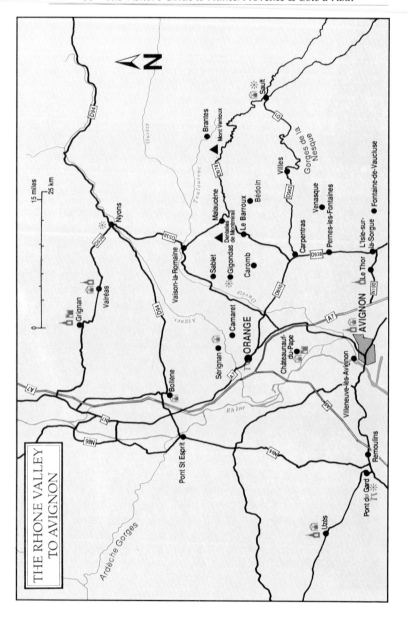

THE RHONE VALLEY TO AVIGNON

Vaison-la-Romaine

Medieval and Roman Vaison are surrounded by the modern town on the right bank of the River Ouvèze. The one-time cathedral of Notre Dame de Nazareth, dating from the twelfth and thirteenth centuries, gives a good idea of the simple strength of Provençal Romanesque architecture. It stands on the site of a sixth-century church, parts of which are preserved in the structure of the later building. To reach the Upper Town, which has a maze of old streets and houses, occasional fountains and a seventeenth-century chapel, cross the single-span Roman bridge over the Ouvèze. A castle of the Counts of Toulouse, the feudal owners of the town, crowns the hill. Sadly, it is ruinous, and is not open to the public.

The prime excursion from Vaison is to the top of 'The Giant of Provence' — Mont Ventoux 1,909m (6,260ft). Be sure to choose a clear day because the summit of the mountain — rounded, smoothed and blasted white by the weather — often wears a thick halo of cloud. The direct route is by Malaucène, its main streets massively guarded by plane trees. Clement V, the first of the Avignon popes, had the church built early in the fourteenth century, and Malaucène (the name means 'bad sands', on which it had been built) was his summer residence. The church is on the site of one founded by Charlemagne. The D974 passes a delightful twelfth-century chapel — one of hundreds all over Provence — and then the source of the Grozeau Stream, harnessed by the Romans through a now vanished aqueduct.

It is 21km (13 miles) to the top of Ventoux, first through forest, then pasture and finally over bare, stony slopes. If the day is clear, it is likely to be windy. Ventoux means 'The Windy One', and the peak's high point is called Col des Tempêtes. About the summit are a hotel, Ste Croix chapel, observatory, Air Force radar station, television masts and a plaque commemorating the climb undertaken by the poet Petrarch and his brother on 9 May, 1336. For its time, that was an audacious ascent and, since they came to see the views, they can also claim to be the area's first tourists.

The views are tremendous. From the viewing-table, a panorama carries the eye from the sea beyond Marseille to the Pelvoux Massif in the north-east. Given a clear day, Mont Canigou, a 2,800m (9,200ft) peak in the Eastern Pyrenees can be seen. Dawn and dusk provide the most breathtaking moments, as Petrarch found. For the best descent, go down to Chalet-Reynard and swing right through St Estève to **Bédoin**, a large village of ochre-coloured houses and little

Places of Interest Around Mont Ventoux

Valréas
Château du Simiane
Fine, fifteenth-century house.

Grignan
The Castle
Superb castle that overshadows the town. Beautifully furnished and hung with tapestries. The views from it are also exceptional. Not to be missed.

Vaison-la-Romaine
Quartier du Puymin
The Quartier is the ruin of the Roman town. It includes the ruins of a theatre and many houses, both fine villas and simple town houses. The small site museum (Musée Théo Desplans) holds the best of the site finds.

Caromb
Museum of Old Tools
An interesting collection of old tools and farm implements.

Aulan
The Castle
Much restored castle in good position above the valley.

Rocher du Cire
(The Rock of Wax)
Near Sault
Famous honey-bee site.

squares. It is from here that time trials were started which aimed at discovering the abilities of the new-fangled motor cars by driving them up the hill. Just before World War I, the record stood at just under 18 minutes. Today it is closer to 9 minutes, an average speed of close on 90mph. From Bédoin, a narrow, interesting, road leads to **Caromb**, where there is an equally interesting museum of old tools.

About 3km (1³/₄ miles) out of Bédoin, set back a little from the D19, is the Chapel of Ste Madeleine, one of the most enchanting of rural chapels. The simple, square building is eleventh-century, and is clearly derived from the Roman basilica. Bereft of ornament, it is gently severe; a sloping roof holding a square belfry, domed by a stone-tiled skull-cap, in place. A tiny slit aperture is at first floor level, a small rounded double aperture above, and highest of all, a proportionately larger double orifice. Three rounded apses, each crowned by Provençal tiles, cling like upside-down swallows' nests to the apsidal wall.

While the views from the top of Mont Ventoux are spectacular,

Vineyards below Mont Ventoux

Mont Ventoux

*Colourful fountain,
Malaucène*

*The popular French
game of* boules

there are even more satisfactory ways of savouring its majesty. From Vaison make for Entrechaux and turn right just before Mollans-sur-Ouvèze. An east-west road above the poplar-lined Toulourenc Valley now runs for about 20km ($12^1/_2$ miles) along the northern flank, allowing the traveller to keep Mont Ventoux in sight all the way. Steep slopes rise sheer to the top, buttressed by huge pyramids of grey limestone and yellow sandstone which seem to cement the whole mountain into place.

Turn up the hill to see the precariously balanced village of **Brantes** which commands an extended view of the bare, flat ridge of Ventoux. A very fine walk from the village crosses the Toulourenc Stream and climbs Ventoux, following the marked GR9 track all the way, but it is only for the fit and well-prepared. In June, the locals around Brantes gather lime blossoms which are dried and made into *tisane* herbal drinks.

Continue eastwards to reach Reilhanette. Beyond here a left turn reaches Montbrun-les-Bains from where a road leads off to visit the *château* at **Aulan**, a carefully restored castle in a magnificent position. Alternatively, go right to **Sault** whose belvedere looks on to the sunbaked, southern face of Ventoux. In July, great acres of lavender perfume the town.

From Sault it is 45km (28 miles) by the D942 to Carpentras. A considerable length of the route is taken up by the Gorges of the Nesque. From the first signposted belvedere, the traveller can see the (Rocher du Cire) Rock of Wax where generations of wild bees have nested, coating the rock with wax. Frédéric Mistral, in his epic poem *Calendau* wrote of the Rocher du Cire, and the lines are quoted on the stele at the viewpoint.

At the end of the deeply incised gorge, the landscape opens out on to the Plain of Comtat Venaissin. At Villes-sur-Auzon another excursion can be made up the Combe de l'Hermitage which rejoins the D942 near Sault, a narrow, winding but attractive route.

On the eastern outskirts of **Mazan**, there is a cemetery along whose retaining walls are ranged sixty-two Gallo-Roman sarcophagi, taken from the Carpentras to Sault roadside. The sacophagi at Arles are more famous, but Mazan's can be inspected in tranquillity. Also in the Mazan cemetery is the half-buried chapel of Notre Dame de Pareloup (Our Lady Protectress against Wolves), first built in the twelfth century to exorcise demons in the guise of wolves which devoured buried corpses. At the time when the chapel was built, real wolves did prowl freely in these parts during cold winters.

Nearer to Carpentras, on the right, the traveller passes the handsome aqueduct with forty-eight arches. It is 729m (2,400ft) long and was built between 1720 and 1729 to supply the town's water. **Carpentras** is a lively town, ringed by boulevards, and lying in a fertile market-gardening plain. The town has always been important, having been the capital of the Memini, a local tribe of Gauls. Later, under the Popes of Avignon, it was the capital of Comtat Venaissin. Today, the town, sometimes called 'The Crucible of Mont Ventoux' for the way the mountain watches over it, is the local market centre. Those interested in the history of the town should visit its history museum which is housed in the old chapel of the Grey Penitents.

Most of the interesting sights are in the narrow streets of the Old Town, so sightseeing is best done on foot, leaving the car either near Place de Verdun or in Boulevard Maréchal Leclerc. Friday mornings are market days and there is a both a general market and a flea market. Between November and late March there is also a truffle market, for truffles are something of which Vaucluse is justly proud.

The only vestige of the ramparts put up by the Popes in Avignon in the fourteenth century is the Port d'Orange, a 27m (90ft) high fortified and restored tower near where Boulevard Leclerc and Boulevard du Nord meet. An eye-catching building in Place Aristide Briand is the elegant eighteenth-century hospital, the Hôtel-Dieu, whose upper balustrades are surmounted by carved oriflammes. Inside is a graceful monumental stairway; the eighteenth-century pharmacy displays local and Italian faïence-ware behind painted cupboards.

The one-time Gothic cathedral of St Siffrein is entered by the south door. He is the patron saint of Carpentras who appears in no orthodox hagiography but may have been a sixth-century monk, Siffred or Siegfried, who came to evangelise the area. The south door is the Jews' Door by which Jews, recently converted to Christianity, went to worship.

Inside are figures by the sculptor Jacques Bernus (1650-1728) from Mazan, the greatest Provençal sculptor after Pierre Puget. There are also paintings by two artists whose works hang in innumerable churches and museums in Provence; Nicolas Mignard (1606-68), a Provençal by adoption, and Pierre Parrocel (1664-1739), one of a large family of Parrocel painters.

Next to St Siffrein is the seventeenth-century Palais de Justice or

Entrechaux

Law Courts whose court rooms are decorated with striking friezes.
Tucked behind, is the Roman Municipal Arch, erected in the first
century AD during the reign of the Emperor Nero. It marked the
entrance to the Gallo-Roman town, originally called *Carpentoracte*
and changed to *Forum Neronis*. Although not well preserved, its bas-
reliefs of two prisoners are distinct; they commemorate the victories
of Augustus in Germany and the East.

A little to the north-east and reached by Rue d'Inguimbert, is the
oldest synagogue in France, although it has been much reconstructed. The first building was erected in 1367 when the Popes at
Avignon were heavily dependent on Jewish financiers and gave
Jews sanctuary in Comtat Venaissin after they had been expelled
from France and the rest of Provence. Consequently, the town, like
Cavaillon, had a flourishing Jewish ghetto. Baths for ritual purifica-
tion, called in Provençal the *cabussadou* ('head first'), are in the
basement. Ovens for baking unleavened bread can be seen. Carved
woodwork, panellings, wrought ironwork, candlesticks and other
liturgical objects impart an air of delicate elegance.

For the non-specialist, the Comtadin Museum in Boulevard
Albin-Durand is enjoyable. Objects that were in daily use many
years ago make it an agreeable bygones collection. Of particular

interest are the bells used for the age-old sheep-drives, the *transhumance*, because Carpentras was the centre where generations of bell-makers from the Simon family worked. Bells of different shapes and tones for sheep, rams, goats, donkeys and horses were made to harmonise musically as in a carillon, for the sheep-drive was conducted in a recognised order of procedure, almost as a religious ritual. So great was the Simons' reputation, that no other bells but theirs were sold in the market stalls throughout Provence.

Above the Comtadin Museum is the Duplessis Museum of paintings by local artists. Elsewhere, the visitor should find the Hôtel Armand-de-Château-Vieux, a well-restored eighteenth-century town house.

The return to Vaison from Carpentras gives intriguing glimpses of the Dentelles de Montmirail which calls for a separate excursion. This is a small range of dramatic, naked rocks, elegantly eroded into a lacework that is ideal for rock-climbing. They rise to a little over 730m (2,400ft) but look much higher, and are virtually encircled by the roads between Vaison, Malaucène, Beaumes-de-Venise, and Sablet.

Leave Vaison by the D938 and, just before Malaucène, turn right and follow a scenic road upwards past the Cirque de St Amand. There is a backward look along this view to Mont Ventoux's western end which, while not having the dramatic appeal of the view from the north, is a fine sight. The road now continues through Suzette, Lafare and

Street scene, Carpentras

Places of Interest in Carpentras

History Museum
The history of the town in the old chapel of the Grey Penitents.

Comtadin-Duplessis Museum
Items dating from the time of the Revolution, when the town was capital of the local Comtat Venaissin, are housed in the Comtadin Museum; the Duplessis holds a collection of local artists' work.

Sobirats Museum
The eighteenth-century Hôtel Armand-de-Château-Vieux, restored to its former glory.

Synagogue
The oldest in France, originally built in the fifteenth century but much rebuilt and restored . It was once the centre of a ghetto, relics of which are on view.

the wine-village of Beaumes-de-Venise. A beautiful run at any time, this journey is particularly so in early summer when the evening sun slants behind the Dentelles and sets the scented yellow masses of Spanish broom ablaze.

From Beaumes-de-Venise the D81, and then the D7, turn into the road which runs on the west side of the Dentelles. On the right, a grass track leads to the rural chapel of Notre Dame d'Aubune whose tall, square belfry is ornamented with three fluted pilasters and carved decorations on each face, an unusual, much admired design. Some believe that the chapel dates from the twelfth century, but others believe that it is much older, perhaps dating from the ninth century. Either way, it is one of the most attractive buildings in this area of Provence.

Folk-legend has it that Charles Martel, having defeated the Saracens outside Poitiers in AD732, fought them again during their retreat in the vicinity of the Dentelles. The Tour Sarrazine (Saracens' Tower) is said to be a ruined, eighth-century signal tower. It lies up the valley from the hamlet of Montmirail, above the spring which once provided curative waters for a long-forgotten spa. The Saracens' Cemetery stands on a little plateau just above Notre Dame d'Aubune, marked by the ruins of the chapel of St Hilaire that most agree dates from the seventh century. There may be no historical evidence for these names. It is just as likely that 'Saracen' refers to gypsies for, since the fifteenth century, the Provençaux, seeing a physical resemblance, have called gypsies *sarrasins*.

Places of Interest in the Ardèche Gorge

Auriolles
Mas de la Vignasse
A silkworm farm, once the home of the Daudet family, of whom Alphonse is one of the foremost French authors of the nineteenth century. The farm is now partly a museum to the work of Alphonse and partly a museum dealing with the traditions of the area.

The Madeleine Cave
Show cave formed by a stream that has long since dried up.

Marzal Aven
Excellent show cave with fine formations. Site also includes a small museum (Musée du Monde Souterrain) on the history of caves and caving, and a prehistoric zoo with dinosaur models.

Orgnac Aven
One of the finest show caves in Europe. A visit involves the descending and ascending of nearly 800 steps, but the huge chambers and formations make up for it.

Boat trips down the Gorge from Vallon-Pont-d'Arc

On the D23 is **Gigondas**, second only to Châteauneuf-du-Pape as a red wine of quality. The road continues past another delightful rural chapel of St Come and St Damien whose external apse-roofs are covered with fish-tail tiles while the main roof is weighted with massive blocks to hold off the *mistral*. Higher still is Hôtel Les Florets, a centre for horse-riding, walking and rock-climbing.

After Sablet on its hillock, it is worth making a small detour uphill to **Séguret**, snuggling under a sheer wall of rock, for a stroll about its alleys, washhouse, old gateways and views over orchards and vines to the plain. A track leads back to Vaison.

The excursions from Vaison are far from exhausted. Many other villages are dotted about, each with its distinctive character, thick-walled houses, shady little squares and arches, and moss-covered fountain. Of all the sounds on a hot summer's day, the most refreshing to the spirit (as well as hands and face) is the village fountain, that paradox of prodigally flowing water in a parched country. Mollans-sur-Ouvèze, Entrechaux, Roaix, Rasteau, Buisson are but some of the places which provide something fresh for camera and memory.

To the south, the next town is Orange with its Roman monuments. Before we reach that town, we cross the A7, straying from our area for just a while, in order to visit the Ardèche Gorge. Though

*Vineyards below the
Dentelles de
Montmirail*

A fountain in Séguret

hardly Provençal, it would be a very strong-willed visitor indeed who came as far as Orange and did not go that way.

Though the whole of the Ardèche Valley is worth exploring, it is the lower section, between Pont St Esprit and Vallon-Pont-d'Arc, that holds the main interest. There the river has carved a narrow way through a limestone plateau, producing spectacular scenery and gouging out a number of excellent caves that have now been opened up for the visitor. The best of these is the Orgnac Aven which lies out of the Gorge on the limestone Plateau d'Orgnac. The cave is huge — the Upper Chamber itself is over 250m (820ft) long, 125m (410ft) wide and nearly 40m (130ft) high in places — and has a number of fascinating features. There has been a tendency to give these fanciful names, but that tendency is less than elsewhere; both the Chaos Chamber and the Red Chamber certainly live up to their names.

In the Gorge itself, the best cave is that of St Madeleine. However, Marzal Aven, a little to the north of the main Gorge, is better and includes a museum of underground exploration and a prehistoric zoo with all sorts of dinosaurs, which are life size but made out of plastic.

Throughout the Gorge there are fine viewpoints. The visitor will find his or her own, but everyone should follow the High Corniche in the central region of the Gorge where there is a succession of excellent viewpoints. The alternative is to take a boat down the Gorge, which gives the low level view. It is possible to borrow boats and canoes for the journey, but it is a long one, and not for the inexperienced. It is better to join a trip in a tourist boat which will not only guarantee a dry trip, but will also get you back from its end. Finally, in fact just outside the Gorge, to the north, there is a fine museum of the area's traditions in the old silk mill at Auriolles.

Orange, from where Provence was left for a quick trip up the Ardèche, was a Celtic capital, *Arausio*. It was later colonised by veterans of the Roman Second Legion who built the theatre, the triumphal arch, temples, baths and other public buildings the Romans regarded as essential in their major cities. The present name dates from a much later period when the town was the property of the House of Orange. The Princes of Orange held it for 400 years until the French attacked and took it in 1689. Today it is more peaceful, even more so since the A7 autoroute has removed the bulk of the traffic that used to use the N7.

Before exploring, there is a good general view of the town, the

Rhône and the nearby mountains, from the top of Colline St Eutrope by the Montée des Princes d'Orange-Nassau. At its foot is the Roman theatre whose circular tiers of seats were set into the hillside. The huge façade of red sandstone, 36m (120ft) high and 103m (340ft) long, was said by Louis·XIV to be 'the finest wall in my kingdom'. In its heyday, this magnificent stage backdrop in three tiers was decorated with seventy-six columns, friezes, niches and statues. A great awning was held aloft by poles whose supports are still visible. The statues have all vanished except the one of Augustus, 3.5m ($11^1/_2$ft) tall, discovered in fragments and lovingly pieced together. Today the Emperor even has his baton. The statue was placed high in the central niche, a Gaul grovelling for mercy at the Emperor's feet; the Romans were always a little tactless in their reminders to the local populace as to who their overlords were.

Vandals, time and wind may have eroded the wall but the acoustics are still excellent. All the intricate ornamentation of the original wall and the sophisticated scene-shifting machinery are carefully explained if you take a guided tour. An international music festival is held in the theatre during the last two weeks of July.

Close to the theatre are the excavations of a large Roman gymnasium (the only one known in Gaul), 400m (1,300ft) long by 80m (260ft) wide, with baths, athletics track and temples. On the raised platform at one end, gladiatorial contests were held.

In the Municipal Museum opposite the theatre are items which have been removed during excavations. Perhaps the most interesting one is a cadastral plan engraved in AD77. On a huge marble slab are recorded the configuration of the region, the boundaries of the properties of the Roman veterans and the Gaulish inhabitants (who had the poorest land). Names of owners, bondsmen, tax rates (6per cent surcharge on arrears), show how efficient Roman bureaucracy was.

From the museum it is about 700m (2,300ft) to the triumphal arch. It stands now in the middle of a roundabout at the centre of the busy N7, at the north-east end of Orange. It is a rather inconvenient site for today's visitor but it has to be remembered that the route now taken by the N7 was once followed by Via Agrippa to Lyon. Military and naval (the latter is unusual for the Romans) motifs are carved in rich profusion over the whole edifice to make it one of the masterpieces of the Roman Empire. Carvings of naked and hairy Gauls are again in evidence, further powerful advertisements of Roman mastery.

Places of Interest In and Near Orange

Orange
The Roman Theatre
The best preserved and the most beautiful Roman theatre still in existence. It was built at the time of Christ, measures over 90m (300ft) across and 36m (120ft) high, and is still used as a theatre. Not to be missed.

Town Museum
Has some Roman relics which include a local survey carried out in AD66, together with more recent historical items.

Other Roman remains in Orange include a gymnasium and a triumphal arch.

Sérignan-du-Comtat
Natural History Museum
L'Harmas.
In honour of J.H.Fabre, with a local natural history collection.

Pont du Gard
Tremendously impressive Roman aqueduct. Almost complete and beautifully situated. Not to be missed.

Uzès
The Gide Museum
Small museum of local crafts and traditions and memorabilia of Charles and André Gide, the former a famous local economics professor, the latter (his son) the Nobel Prize-winning author.

Ducal Palace
Fine medieval castle dominating the town.

Crypt
Rock cut cell with relief carvings.

Châteauneuf-du-Pape
Musée du Père Anselme
Fine exhibition of old wine-pressing equipment and the tools of the coopering trade.

As an antidote to all that Roman architecture, the visitor should see the ex-cathedral of Notre-Dame. This large Romanesque church was built in the twelfth century, but needed considerable rebuilding after it was damaged in the Wars of Religion.

From Orange, an essential excursion for naturalists is to the village of **Sérignan-du-Comtat**. Go 3km (1³/₄ miles) along the N7 past the Roman arch, turn right on to the D976 and cross the vine-filled plain. On the outskirts of Sérignan, on the right, is a high wall behind which the entomolgist Jean-Henri Fabre (1823-1915) lived and worked between 1879 and his death. The 'Homer of the Insects' is universally remembered by the translation of his important obser-vations in the *Souvenirs Entomolgiques* which give a lucid insight into

The Roman Theatre, Orange

Orange, seen from the Roman Theatre

The Pont du Gard

An orchard in blossom at Remoulins, near Pont du Gard

the complex lives of the insects of Vaucluse, in a style both intimate and elegant. Fellow-scientists tended to dismiss him because of his refusal to accept Darwin's theory of evolution by natural selection. However, the most recent views about the theory may yet go some way to rehabilitating Fabre, showing him to be not quite the arch-reactionary he was held to be in his lifetime.

Fabre's house and garden are now a museum run by the Natural History Museum in Paris. His laboratory, collections, primitive research equipment, and child's writing desk are all on view. Fabre is buried in the cemetery outside Sérignan, and his statue stands in the village square.

With the fine Roman monuments of Orange in mind, it is sensible to visit another splendid Roman construction in the vicinity, the Pont du Gard. The D976 leaves Orange and almost immediately goes above the Autoroute du Soleil and runs more or less parallel to the other autoroute, La Languedocienne, which branches off at Orange. Keep right at Roquemaure and on through Remoulins to the **Pont du Gard**, 38km (24 miles) from Orange.

Although the rule imposed by the Romans was imperious, stern and sometimes brutal, the sight of this great work goes some way towards accepting Rome as a civilising influence. Six lower arches span the wooded banks of the River Gardon. Above them are eleven wider, lighter arches by the side of which runs the roadway. Uppermost are thirty-five small arches, 275m (900ft) long, which carried the water-duct 2,000 years ago from the source of the Eure near Uzès to the Roman town of *Nemausus* (Nîmes) 50km (160 miles) away. Four hundred litres of water a day were channelled over the Pont du Gard for every inhabitant of *Nemausus*, more than is considered necessary today. For 400 years, the conduit was regularly maintained before it fell into neglect and lime deposits choked the channel. In the nineteenth century, Napoleon III had the aqueduct restored.

Near the aqueduct there is a large car park from which waymarked paths wind there way upstream for the best views. The aqueduct can also be crossed on foot, but it needs a head for heights as there is little in the way of a safety rail.

The Pont du Gard is a feast for the eyes; with its setting, its bold dimensions, and the warm colour of the rough, dressed drystone blocks. Its vitality and beauty derives from the fact that the arches are deliberately, though only slightly, irregular in span.

Uzès, where the water for Nîmes started its journey, is a fine town, virtually a living museum of seventeenth- and eighteenth-century architecture. The town became rich through its interests in the silk trade and there is a superb street of fine houses around every corner. The Ducal Palace overshadows everything, an excellent castle with sections dating from between the eleventh and the seven-

A view down the River Gardon from the Pont du Gard

teenth centuries. Opposite its north-east corner is the Crypt, an early Christian cell hacked out of the rock and with a carved relief of John the Baptist. The town also houses a small museum devoted to the Gide family whose most famous son is André, the Nobel prize-winning writer.

The distance from Roman Orange to medieval Avignon is less than 30km (18 miles). Take the D68 which reaches a village in 10km (6miles) whose name is familiar to every wine-lover — **Châteauneuf-du-Pape**. Rows of green vines rise out of a sea of large pebbles once rolled by the Rhône. They act as a furnace which reflects the sun's heat onto the ripening grapes that produce the well-known red wine. Up to thirteen varieties of grape may be used in making the wine. As might be expected, there is a museum to the wine trade in the town.

Above the village are the imposing ruins of a fourteenth-century castle built by Pope John XXII as his summer residence. It has been plundered down the years, the last assault was by German troops who blew up most of the huge keep in 1944.

Avignon has a long and enviable history. It was inhabited,

*Street café,
Avignon*

*Local artists selling
their paintings,
Avignon*

The Palace of the Popes, Avignon

though obviously not as a city, in the Bronze and Iron Ages, and has a Celtic history too. It grew prosperous due to its position at the confluence of the Rhône and Durance Rivers, but made the mistake of choosing the wrong side in the Albigensian Wars. The wrathful French king, who was victorious, dismantled its defensive walls. At a later stage of the Wars the city was taken by the Holy Roman Empire and it was as a safe haven of the Empire that it saw the transfer of the Pope from Rome in the early fourteenth century. This was the period in which the city's greatest architectural treasures were built. Despite the return of the Papacy to Rome, the city's future was assured, and it thrived, even after 1791 when it finally passed back to France.

Today Avignon is a large town of 93,000 inhabitants, the great majority of them living outside the intact medieval ramparts — the medieval town wall is complete, all 5km (3 miles) of it, together with its thirty-nine defensive towers. If outer Avignon is bustling and banal, the Old Town's narrow streets enclose the sense of history.

The chief place of interest is the Palace of the Popes.

Built mainly by Benedict XII and Clement VI during the years from 1334 to 1352, the Palace is actually more fortress-like, a design that mirrored the Pope's insecurities. The Palace is huge, extending over about $2^1/_2$ acres, and externally is a marvel of grey stone, all high, filled arches and soaring walls. Internally it is equally grand; the Grand Courtyard is spacious, and leading from it is a myriad of interesting rooms. The Robe Room is hung with fine tapestries, while the Papal Bedroom is painted with birds and vines. More impressive murals are found in the Stag Room, which also has a superb wooden ceiling. The Great Hall on the lower floor is breathtaking for its sheer size alone. It is unfurnished, but that seems merely to add to the beauty.

The Grand Courtyard is also the venue of an international drama festival during the last three weeks of July. Its great prestige draws enthusiasts from all over the world to see productions which some consider too avant-garde and elitist.

Within the Palace Square is the Petit Palais, originally a cardinal's palace, then a bishop's palace and now a fine museum with an excellent collection of early paintings. Elsewhere in the town there are several other good museums, including one to the history of printing built around the collection of Théodore Aubanel, a friend of Frédéric Mistral.

Places of Interest in Avignon

The Palace of the Popes
A huge white stone maze of a building built during the resident papacies in the early fourteenth century. Internally the palace is a disappointment, being almost bare of furnishings, but it is still, rightly, a major draw. Not to be missed.

Pont St Bénézet
A bridge that needs no introduction. It is, in fact, now only half a bridge, but is still a fine sight.

St Nicholas' Chapel
Standing about halfway along what remains of the famous bridge, the chapel is part Romanesque and part Gothic.

Musée Petit Palais
Originally a bishop's palace, the Petit Palais now houses an excellent gallery of very early paintings, including work from the thirteenth century, and later, medieval work, chiefly from Italy and the Avignon area.

History Museum
A museum of Avignon's history, housed in a seventeenth-century Jesuit college.

Requien Museum
An interesting collection on the botany, geology and natural history of the area.

Calvet Museum
Chiefly the donation of François Calvet, a late eighteenth-century Avignon doctor, the museum comprises paintings and sculptures, together with coins and ceramics.

The Chapel of the Grey Penitents
A fine, sixteenth-century chapel.

Louis Vouland Museum
Chiefly showing eighteenth-century French furniture and local pottery.

Théodore Aubanel Museum
A very interesting museum of printing processes built around the collection of Théodore Aubanel, a friend of Mistral and a man who did much to preserve the Provençal language.

Town Museum
Chiefly showing items from the nearby charterhouse, including fine paintings and furniture.

A stroll through almost any part of old Avignon within the ramparts reveals the architectural styles of 200 and 300 years ago in the façades of mansions (*hôtels*) of wealthy merchants and the nobility. Two of the most picturesque streets are Rue Banasterie (Weavers' Row), and Rue des Teinturiers (Dyers' Row) where the River Sorgue flows gently past inert, ancient mill wheels. The latter street, in the

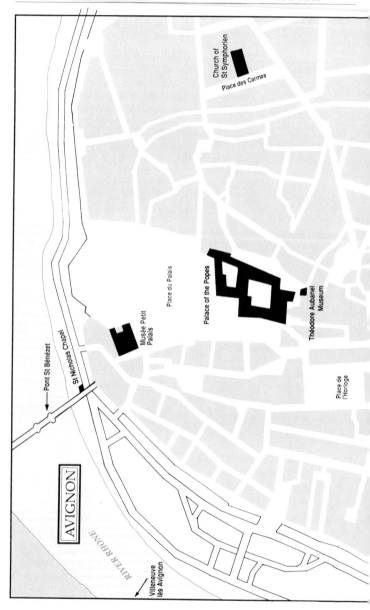

AVIGNON

RIVER RHONE

Villeneuve lès Avignon

Pont St Bénézet

St Nicholas Chapel

Musée Petit Palais

Place du Palais

Palace of the Popes

Théodore Aubanel Museum

Place de l'Horloge

Church of St Symphorien

Place des Carmes

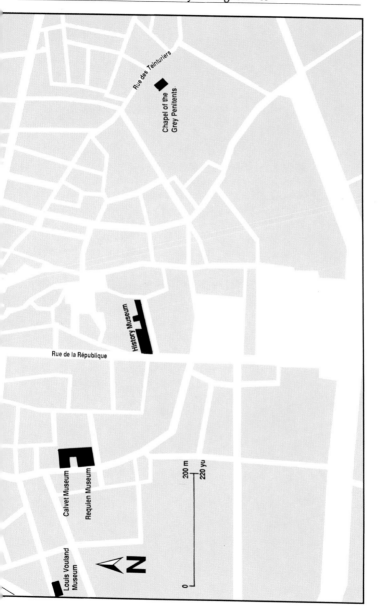

Rue des Teinturiers

Chapel of the
Grey Penitents

History Museum

Rue de la République

Calvet Museum

Requien Museum

Louis Vouland
Museum

N

0   200 m
     220 yd

south-east corner of the Old Town, is widely believed to be the finest that Avignon has to offer, and should not be missed. Numerous churches and chapels of different periods are scattered about the old town, one of the best of these being the chapel of the Grey Penitents, restored to its sixteenth-century glory.

For many though, the chief place of interest will be the bridge, immortalised in song. It, or rather what is left of it, stands beyond the town wall to the north-west. The dancing in the famous song actually took place on an island *under* the bridge, not on it, but that makes little difference to the visitor who comes to relive a childhood memory. Today's visitor will readily see that the bridge was too narrow for dancing. It was built in the late twelfth century for carriages. The legend is that a local shepherd boy claimed to have been told to build it in a vision and proved the story to a sceptical townsfolk by miraculously picking up a huge stone to start the work. The church promptly gave money for the bridge's completion. Over the years, floods have reduced the bridge to half its length. The chapel of St Nicholas on one pier is all that remains of medieval fortifications.

If there is a temptation to sentimentalise Avignon's past while gazing at its ancient remains, the fulminations of one who served at the papal court — Petrarch — will restore the balance. He left to posterity his view that Avignon was a living hell, a sink of vice with neither faith, nor charity, nor religion; the city was odious, pestilential when there was no *mistral*, insufferable when it blew.

Across the Rhône from Avignon is **Villeneuve-lès-Avignon** (*lès* here meaning 'near'), once connected to Avignon by the shepherd boy's bridge. Belonging to the Kingdom of France, it was fortified by the French kings with the Fort de St André and Tour de Philippe le Bel (the Fair) to keep frontier watch on Avignon which was then part of the Holy Roman Empire. When the Popes came from Rome to Avignon, the cardinals chose the rising ground of Villeneuve to build their summer palaces, but most of these were destroyed at the time of the Revolution.

Villeneuve is a quieter place to stay than Avignon. Be sure to stand at the top of the Tour de Philippe le Bel as the sun begins to set; it throws Avignon and the palaces into a warm relief and illuminates the distant hump of Mont Ventoux. Be sure, too, to visit the nearby charterhouse of Val-de-Bénédiction, a fourteenth-century monastic house that is now a cultural centre hosting many events.

Finally, go east from Avignon to the village of Le Thor which has

Places of Interest Near Avignon

Villeneuve-lès-Avignon
Tour de Philippe le Bel
Interesting old tower with excellent view of Avignon.

The Charterhouse of Val-de-Bénédiction
Built in the late fourteenth century and soon after the most important monastic house in France, this is now a cultural centre with an annual programme of events. The fine buildings can also be visited. The church holds the tomb of Pope Innocent VI.

Fort de St André
Fourteenth-century fort that once defended the town of St André. At present the fort and the buildings within it — a twelfth-century monastery and a Romanesque chapel — are being stabilised, so only the gardens are open.

Thouzon Cave
Near Le Thor
An impressive show cave.

a fine thirteenth-century church and, nearby, the Thouzon Cave, a fine show cave. East again is L'Isle-sur-la-Sorgue, where the River Sorgue divides into five branches, each of which once drove a mill wheel. Today the mills are gone, but one waterwheel still turns in the village's public gardens, a moss-covered reminder of the past.

The Pont St Bénézet, Avignon

Place du Palais, Avignon

2

UPPER PROVENCE
AND THE DURANCE VALLEY

From the direction of Grenoble, two routes make for the heart of Provence. One is the N75 which goes over the Col de la Croix Haute 1,176m (3,860ft) in the Devoluy Range to Serres. The other, more easterly, road is the N85 which traverses the Col Bayard 1,246m (4,090ft) in the Campsaur Range, and leads to Gap. They converge just north of Sisteron.

Sisteron is a theatrical gateway into Provence. The harsh Dauphiné Mountains are to the north, while to the south the valley opens on to richer, warmer land. At the town, the Durance has barged its narrow way through buckled, striated mountains. This weathering process was aided by the last Ice Age because the glaciers of the Alps never reached further than Sisteron, though their melting debris, tons of sharp angular rocks, helped carve the gorge. The town is cleverly set where the Durance joins a lesser stream, the Buech, and is built into the rocks on the west side of the gorge facing the towering Rocher de la Baum. This is a vast natural defence to approaches from the east, its town-side face composed, it seems, of candles of rock, so intense has been the geological folding in the area. Today the town is bypassed by the road, the main route on into Provence being taken under the Rocher by tunnel. This has left the town more peaceful than it used to be, giving the visitor time and space to breathe.

The strategic importance of the site was not lost on the Romans who fortified it, called it *Segustero* and ran the *Via Domitia* past it. Such was the site's importance, however, that very little remains of that 'first' town, later settlers having laid waste the early work while building their own defences. In the thirteenth century, it was still considered 'a grandiose portal dividing Provence and Dauphiné', though at that time it was also the place that sealed the fate of Provence forever. Here, in a Franciscan monastery that had been built near the town, the Count of Provence, Berengar V, signed his will. He left Provence to one of his daughters who later married Charles of Anjou, taking her proud possession with her and so making the region a part of France.

As late as 1944, the strategic importance of the town was re-emphasised when it suffered from Allied air attacks which destroyed some of the medieval quarters. Thankfully, they have been reconstructed.

Near the Place de la République (where cars can be parked) are the town hall, church, and the four remaining fifteenth-century towers whose ramparts have all but disappeared. The Museum of Old Sisteron is also close by, its archaeological items were discovered during reconstruction work after the bombing raids.

The full name of the one-time cathedral is Notre Dame-des-Pommiers, a strange looking name, and one that has nothing to do with apples, but is a corruption of *pomerium*, an area which must be left free. Its architecture reflects Sisteron's geographical position; both Lombard and Alpine influences show in the octagonal tower and its external gallery. The perfect alignment of the masonry is characteristically Provençal.

A warren of narrow streets, stepped and vaulted (*andrônes*), and linking tiny squares, make up the old quarters. Where the main street enters a tunnel there is a bust of Paul Arène (1843-96), a Sisteron writer of lightness and charm who, under a pseudonym, wrote the famous *Lettres de Mon Moulin* with Alphonse Daudet in 1866.

The Citadel of massive ancient fortifications, started in the eleventh century and added to later, stands supreme above the town. A curtain wall on a narrow ridge and supported by high arches leads to the Citadel which is reached by a steep climb, with a panorama at the top whose items are identified by a viewing table. Both Citadel and rock are floodlit on summer evenings, when broadcasts in French explain Sisteron's history. In the guardroom at the entrance, there is a museum of local wartime resistance. It is an appropriate place as the Citadel was itself badly damaged by the Allied raids.

Sisteron is a good starting place for excursions into the scenically interesting local countryside. Pride of place must go to a visit to the

Places of Interest in Sisteron and Digne

Sisteron

The Citadel (Sisteron Castle)
Little survives of the earliest eleventh-century fortifications, and later, sixteenth-century work, was badly damaged by Allied bombing in 1944.
What remains is interesting and the parkland and views are excellent.

Sisteron Museum
Small museum with ancient and medieval finds from around the town.

Digne

Town Museum
Collection of archaeological remains, paintings, shells and stuffed animals.

World War II Museum
Memorabilia.

Alexandra David-Néel Foundation
Collection of Tibetan and Himalyan memorabilia of Alexandra David who married explorer Philippe Néel.

Geology Centre
Exhibitions on local geology.

Vançon Valley, to the north-east of the town. This is a drive that some might call interesting, others choosing a more colourful adjective. It all depends on how you find the hairpins of the D3 that soon leaves the D951 and heads east and sharply upwards. Soon you reach the Pierre Ecrite Gorge, steep sided, narrow and with a strange Roman inscription carved in one of its rocky walls that implies, most improbably, that there was once a city in the valley. Beyond the Gorge, the valley continues in fine style, the road being easier, but never easy. Look out for the eleventh-century pilgrimage chapel standing beneath the Rocher du Dromon.

To the west there is a fine drive along the D946 that follows the valley of the River Jabron back towards its source in the Lure Mountains. It is possible to cross the range, going all the way to Séderon, and on to Mont Ventoux.

These are only two of the numerous excursions to both the east and west of the Durance. As a rule, the eastern ones are more Alpine in character because they penetrate valleys whose peaks are over 2,000m (6,560ft), while the valleys to the west run into lower peaks and are more open and Mediterranean in aspect.

If, instead of entering Provence on the route to Sisteron, the traveller has left the side of Lac de Serre-Poncon and taken the D900, then a pleasant drive brings him to **Digne**, a popular stopping place, ✻

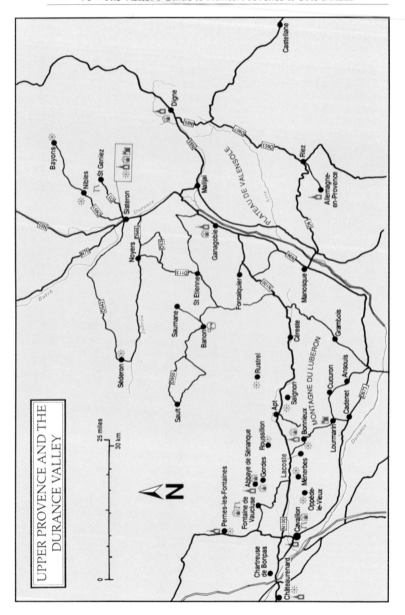

UPPER PROVENCE AND THE DURANCE VALLEY

Lavender — an important crop in Provence

well-supplied with hotels and a spa for the treatment of rheumatism. Digne does not quite have the feel of a Provençal town, its mountainous setting of steep and sombre crags making it seem more Alpine. Yet, for all that, it is a centre for the growing of fruit and flowers, and especially of lavender. Each year, in September, there is a lavender fair.

Digne is, in fact, the capital of a vast area where lavender is grown. Several types grow in Provence. True (or common) lavender is the plant from which the finest essence is distilled. Aspic, which flowers in late August, is not cultivated but hybridises with true lavender to give *lavandin* which yields great quantities of inferior essence. Lastly, French lavender, found mainly on silica soils like those of the Maures Mountains, has deep purple flowers but is of no commercial value.

Boulevard Gassendi, in Ville-Haute, is the main artery of activity and interest. On each side of it are car parks. At one end is the Grande Fontaine, its Doric structure buried under tufa and moss. At the centre of the Boulevard is the Place Charles de Gaulle and a statue of Pierre Gassendi (1592-1655), philosopher and polymath, born at nearby Champtercier. Gassendi is little known to the layman, though one of his debating partners, René Descartes, has become famous, if only for his proclamation 'I think, therefore I am'.

The old part of the town lies to one side of Boulevard Gasssendi. The Municipal Museum, housed in a one-time hospice, provides a visual survey of Digne's prehistory and the Gallo-Roman period. Paintings by local artists are augmented by better-known painters such as Natoire and Ziem. A natural history collection includes specimens of unusual local moths.

Notre Dame-du-Bourg, once a cathedral, stands at the northern outskirts, and the Lombard and Alpine influences that were apparent at Sisteron are seen again. This majestic building has a particularly fine rose window, but now the church is only used for funerals, and the caretaker has to be found at the cemetery if you want to get in. This is not the grandest way to spend your holiday, so perhaps you should settle for a look at the outside and a walk around the old town. A visit to the geology centre is worthwhile for its fascinating collection of local samples, though a visit to the World War II Museum will make you wonder whether it might have been better situated somewhere other than in Paradise Place.

Also in the town, and a true must for all readers of the works of early explorers, is the collection of the work of Alexandra David-Néel, the famous explorer. The collection includes items from the Himalayas, including Tibet, and is priceless for what it has to say about the local cultures before the massed armies of climbers and trekkers got to them.

Places other than Sisteron or Digne suggest themselves as centres for short stays. Manosque and Forcalquier have a town atmosphere; Valensole and St Etienne are villages where the countryside comes to the doorstep. Gréoux-les-Bains, although primarily a spa where arthritis and lesions are treated, has pleasant hotels.

As a peaceful excursion centre with modest but agreeable hotel facilities, **St Etienne** (St Etienne-les-Orgues on some maps) is to be preferred. From Sisteron an attractive secondary road, D951, passing the villages of Mallefougasse and Cruis, reaches St Etienne at the foot of the southern slope of Montagne de Lure. In medieval times, the village was famous for the 'country remedies' that its locals made from herbs that grew—and still do—on the flanks of the Lure. These remedies were sold far and wide; while some may indeed have been useful in treating the ills they were taken for, the practice has an aura of the American West quack doctor about it.

The Lure Range is the natural extension of Mont Ventoux, separated from it by the depression at Sault. It, too, is a limestone mass riddled with underground caves (*dolines*) into which streams vanish abruptly. Walkers will love the Lure — although it is only slightly lower than Mont Ventoux, it is a friendlier range with its easier, angled slopes. The summit of the range, known as the Signal de Lure and standing at 1,826m (5,990ft), is reached by GR6 which goes from Sisteron to Tarascon. This is a magnificent walk, but there is no need to complete it to reach the top nor, in fact, to do too much walking at all. A road gets the less intrepid walker to within about 30 minutes of the top. This road, the D113, leaves St Etienne's open valley and climbs through up oaks and conifers. At the roadside oratories of St Joseph, a path descends to the right to the Lure Hermitage, originally founded in AD500 by St Donat, but now a small Romanesque chapel surrounded by old lime trees.

The road goes no higher than 1,700m (5,580ft) and from its high point a steep climb reaches the Signal de Lure. Some dwarf juniper, beech and gorse are scattered near the barren summit. Saxifrages, fritillaries and Mont Cenis violets appear as soon as the snows melt and later the orchids appear. Butterflies are quite plentiful with about 70 per cent of them being either Alpine or central European and Asiatic species. After climbing the last few metres, visitors can treat themselves to a little refreshment at the summit hut and are treated, in turn, to the best panorama that this area of Provence has to offer. The view is dominated by Mont Ventoux, but also includes Mont Viso and Mont Pelvoux as well as a good section of the coast.

Those who have visited the summit and feel invigorated, can try the brusque, zigzag descent which goes into the Jabron Valley. However, this section of road is closed between mid-November and the end of May.

Of motoring excursions out of St Etienne, two attractive roads go to Forcalquier, while a longer westward journey aims for **Banon**, 2km (1^1/$_4$ miles) near which is one of the deepest caves in France. The Gouffre du Caladaire, some 480m (1,575ft) deep, is reached on foot. Close to it is the romantically abandoned village of Montsalier-le-Vieux.

By turning right 9km (5^1/$_2$ miles) out of St Etienne, in the direction of Banon, the traveller can take the D12 which leads to tiny **Lardiers**. On a nearby hilltop are the remains of an important Gallo-Roman shrine, the oppidum of Chastelard-de-Lardiers. A double wall enclosed some 20 acres which surrounded a sanctuary. Vast deposits of gold, silver and bronze rings and 50,000 tiny clay lamps — all votive offerings to Mercury, patron of travellers — have been excavated.

The road from Lardiers continues northward to Saumane and then swings back to Banon. **Simiane-la-Rotonde**, about 10km (6 miles) to the south-west, is a real fairytale village when viewed from a distance, but one that has been the centre of some historical controversy. The problem is the rotunda that tops off this superbly concentric, rising village. It could be a mausoleum, a defensive structure or even a chapel. Some say the lords of Simiane built the rotunda in imitation of the castles erected by Crusaders in the Holy Land; others think it is a likeness to the circular kitchens of medieval abbeys. To see for yourself, enquire for the key in the village. You will find a curious, lantern-like hexagonal tower that certainly dates from the twelfth century, is built into the remains of a castle, and furnished with a cone-like roof. Inside, the rotunda is irregularly twelve-sided, formed by twelve blind arcades. Below is a crypt, while above there is an ornamented chamber. Stairs built in the thick walls give access to upper terraces of this strange building. One thing is certain; aesthetically, the rotunda is in just the right place, whatever its original purpose.

A stay at **Forcalquier** (*Furnus calcarius* in Latin or *Fourcalquier* in Provençal, each name deriving from the Middle Ages when local limekilns kept the men in work) usually begins with a visit to the impressive but darkly brooding church of Notre Dame, begun in 1196. In front is a fifteenth-century fountain surmounted by an octagonal pinnacle with a plaque commemorating the marriage in 1235 between Eleanore of Provence and Henry III of England. By then, the town was the capital of the local area of Haute-Provence, and a very powerful town it was, a seat of Counts and famous for its court where Provençal troubadours kept the revellers happy. One Count whose court was especially famous for its revelry was Raymond Berengar who had four daughters, each of whom married a king. It was said that, on one occassion, all four kings were in the town·together.

On markets days, the square in front of Notre Dame is thronged with stalls. Nearby is an excellent restored Franciscan monastery, founded in 1236. The community was one of the earliest Franciscan houses in France, though the building is older, having been built as a mansion. A visit to the monastery is well-worthwhile, especially for a walk in a restored section of the cloisters. Another walk, this time through the town's old quarters where there was once a Jewish community and a synagogue, leads to the citadel which has terraces with fine views.

Forcalquier's cemetery, about 1km ($^1/_2$ mile) north of the town, is sufficiently unusual for a French cemetery for it to have become a tourist attraction in its own right. The terraces are lined by tall and ancient yews which are neatly clipped and shaped into arched niches and topiaries. It also contains small, cylindrical, drystone buildings with pointed roofs called *cabanons.*

A vineyard sign near Manosque

In all directions from Forcalquier there are charming villages ; St Maime, Dauphin (a good example of a perched village) Limans and Sigonces.

To the north-east, the priory of Ganagobie is reached by a winding road from the N96 that follows the right bank of the Durance. The priory stands on the tree-filled plateau, where there are holm oaks and pine, together with broom and wild lavender, as well as a balcony view of the valley. Originally this plateau was the site of a Ligurian settlement on top of which a town was built in the early Middle Ages. The Benedictine Monastery was founded in

AD980, rebuilt in the twelfth century but partially destroyed in 1792. Today it is an interesting site with a unique triple-arched doorway decorated with oriental-looking carvings. A Christ in Majesty decorates the lintel of this striking doorway.

The site guide will show visitors the profane, twelfth-century mosaics and a Virgin in the nave painted by Adolphe Monticelli (1824-86) who spent his orphaned childhood at Ganagobie. Although this is not one of his better paintings, it is a reminder that this highly original artist, whose jewel-like brushwork fired Van Gogh with admiration, was partly responsible for the Dutchman coming to Provence for two momentous years.

Manosque, 23km(14 miles) south of Forcalquier, and set above the sluggish coils of the Durance, has a population of 19,500, and offers a range of hotels within and around the town. It has grown rapidly as the marketing centre for early vegetables, fruit and truffles, and as the hometown for workers at the Cadarache nuclear power station downstream where the Verdon joins the Durance.

Two fourteenth-century fortified gateways, Porte Saunerie and Porte Soubeyran, mark the bounds of the old town. Porte Saunerie is the gate by which the French king François I entered the town on a day when it earned the title 'Modest Manosque', a title that it still bears, though more now in disparagement than in respect. The king was presented with the keys to the city by a local girl renowned for her beauty. At the time this seemed a good idea, but the king was more than a little taken with the girl and became adamant that *droite de seigneur* should be added to his gifts. The city's mayor, the girl's father, was appalled by the idea. Not even for a king would his daughter suffer such a fate as to lose her virtue outside of marriage. He promptly threw acid into her face to cruelly mutilate it. The king was horrified when he saw her and lost all interest. The mayor was presumably satisfied, but history does not record how the girl felt about it.

Elsewhere in the town, be sure to see the handsome wrought iron belfry which surmounts the square tower of St Sauveur church. Such eighteenth-century campaniles are common in Provence and are poetically spoken of as 'God's sheep bells'.

North-eastwards, Manosque rises to the Mont d'Or, the place where the novelist Jean Giono (1895-1970) lived for most of his life. Incidentally, he claimed that François I never visited the town and that the story of the mayor's daughter was an evil gibe. Many of his

St Sauveur church, Manosque

novels used his native landscape as being representative of elemental forces. Readers of these books will conjure vivid images from the names that recur in them: Vachères, Banon, Le Revest-du-Bion, Ste Tulle and Manosque itself. Giono is buried in Manosque's cemetery.

From the town, cross the Durance Canal and River by the D907 and take the D6 which rises through wooded country to the open plateau of undulating hills covered by bristling rows of lavender and almond trees around Valensole. Distant peaks jut coyly beyond the rim of the plateau, and the Luberon Range, across the Durance, is a luminous blue in this limpid light.

When the Burgundians invaded this part of Provence, **Riez** was *Reia Apollinaris* — an important administrative centre in the Roman Empire. It was *Julia Augusta Reia Apollinaris* in full, but that was too long even for the Romans. Arriving from Valensole, you will see, on the right, four columns of grey granite with Corinthian capitals and

Wayside shrine on the road to Manosque

Colourful tiles on a roof in Riez

Riez church

an architrave of white marble, the remains of a first-century Roman temple, presumably dedicated to Apollo. The nearest quarry of grey granite was at Pennafort near Callas in Var, 117km (73 miles) away.

Another uncommon relic is the baptistry at the edge of Riez on the road to Allemagne-en-Provence (named after *Alemona*, a fertility goddess). Experts disagree about when it was erected, though most favour the fourth century. Outside it is square with a later dome; it is octagonal inside with four apsidal chapels let into the thickness of the walls. A ruined baptismal font is surrounded by eight Corinthian columns of grey granite (as at the temple), again surmounted by marble capitals. A collection of sarcophagi, a taurobolic altar, slabs with inscriptions, carved masks and fragments of pillar can be seen through the iron grille.

There are some charming places in Riez and a sundial of 1806 in Place St Antione bears a reflective message, 'The most serene moment is marked by a shadow'. The natural history museum in the

Places of Interest In and Near Forcalquier and Manosque

Forcalquier
Convent of Cordeliers
One of the oldest Fransiscan houses in Provence, dating from the thirteenth century, though the building itself is older. There are frequent exhibitions and concerts in the summer months.

Sauvan
Château
An elegant eighteenth-century *château*.

The Haute-Provence Observatory
Visits to the observatory itself are possible, but even if only the site is visited, the journey is worthwhile for the views.

Ganagobie Priory
A Benedictine priory dating from the tenth century but substantially rebuilt in the twelfth century.

The church doorway is one of the finest examples of the period in France. There are also fine cloisters and a magnificent view up the Durance Valley.

Riez
Natural History Museum
Small museum in the town hall — built in the fifteenth century as the bishop's palace — with collections of fossils and minerals. Includes a remarkable, and remarkably well-preserved, 35 million-year-old fossil bird.

Allemagne-en-Provence
Château of Castellane
Perhaps the most beautiful *château* in Haute-Provence. This superbly situated, early sixteenth-century building seems too romantic for the south, it is more like those in the Loire Valley.

town has an extraordinary fossil bird.

Allegmane-en-Provence is worth a visit, especially if you are intending to continue to the more austere corner of Provence mentioned below, to see its Renaissance *château*, looking like a refugee from another part of France.

North of Riez lies an empty corner of Provence where the Asse Valley cuts the Plateau de Valensole in two. One or two farm roads meander across this more severe part of the plateau. To savour this isolation, take the D953 past Puimoisson, then the D8 northwards from Bras d'Asse through the Ravin des Cardaires to reach the River Bléone opposite Malijai on the *Route Napoléon*. Continue on the D4 for 5km (3 miles) until a long alignment of conglomerate rocks

appear. They are the Rochers des Mées (from the Latin *metae*, milestones), or more popularly, the Pénitents Blancs, because the line of high rocks, detached from the hill-formation behind them by erosion, looks like a procession of cowled figures.

West of Manosque is the Montagne du Luberon, like other Provençal ranges pointing east-west and gently concave in the middle. It is a regional park, having been created to preserve the area's natural assets.

A much more intimate mountain than either Ventoux or Lure, Luberon is 65km (40 miles) long, divided into Grand Luberon east of the Combe de Lourmarin with Bonnieux at the col, and Petit Luberon to the west. Once a walker's preserve, a road along the crest of Grand Luberon has more recently opened out its expansive vistas to the motorist.

There is an almost secret atmosphere here. Dozens of varied villages repay a visit; no two are alike in character and architecture, though many have shared the suffering of sixteenth-century massacres. Members of the Vaudois sect, who were followers of the twelfth-century fundamentalist Petrus Valdo, seeking to escape persecution in Piedmont, settled in the Luberon in the fourteenth century. The Popes at Avignon declared the Vaudois to be heretics and the repression of their 10,000 homes took place in 1545 with fanatical inhumanity. Some of the villages were never allowed to be rebuilt, their names extirpated from maps and records. Old Mérindol, the religious centre of the Vaudois, is still just a heap of stones.

From Forcalquier to Cavaillon is a distance of 73km (45 miles), almost all of it on the N100. It is a quick run but there are a number of tempting diversions to the north of the road, that is on the opposite side of the road to the Luberon.

Near **Mane** — a delightful, terraced village, looking as though it has been piled up by a child — is the empty twelfth-century Notre Dame-de-Salagon priory with its simple portal and carved capitals depicting the Baptism of Christ. Once an important monastic house, what remains stands almost forlorn in a field. Further along the road is the elegant eighteenth-century Château de Sauvan.

A turning leads to the Haute-Provence Observatory which can be visited on certain days in summer. The days are variable, so it is best to ask at the Tourist Office in Forcalquier. The Observatory site offers a wonderful view of the ocean of holm oaks close to the town, while the building itself is of interest to both the amatuer astronomer and the layman alike. Not far from the Observatory site is St Michel-l'Observatoire, which sounds as though it should be part of the Observatory, but is not. It is, rather, the remnants of a once-fortified town, still displaying a few bits of defensive wall and a group of medieval houses. Another road leads to the fine perched village of **Reillanne**.

To the west is **Céreste**, enclosed in its walls, while a valley road leads to Carluc priory, an early Christian necropolis cut from rock.

Apt is next, a village that demands more time. The name was Celto-Ligurian, *Hath*, before the Romans changed it to *Apta Julia*. Today, the town is known for its crystallised fruits.

Two archaic crypts, one above the other, are the curiosity in the church of St Anne. The upper was hollowed out in the eleventh century but an even earlier altar rests on a Gallo-Roman monumental pillar or *cippus*. Six small, thirteenth-century ossuarial sarcophagi fit neatly into niches.

In the lower crypt, the relics of Ste Anne, mother of the Virgin Mary, were supposed to have come to light in AD776 after having been brought from Palestine. This was the year Charlemagne came to consecrate, so it is said, the earlier church on the site. The original church was erected in the fifth century using the foundations of a Roman temple. Archaeologists have unearthed fourth-century Christian sarcophagi in the vicinity, so where St Anne's stands was one of the earliest organised Christian communities in the whole of Gaul. This may also have been the first church in the Occident to venerate the Virgin's mother.

Not surprisingly, Apt became a place of pilgrimage. Anne of Austria came here in 1623, prayed to be made fertile — a prayer that came true, though it took 15 years for her wish to be realised — and bequeathed valuable reliquaries which are in the treasury and St Anne's chapel.

Close to the church, in Rue de l'Amphitheatre, is the Archaeological Museum with local Roman items that include a fragment of the arena and some pottery. The town now also houses the Luberon Museum which has items on the local national park, its history, geology and wildlife.

The best preserved Roman bridge in France, Pont Julien, is reached by going west from Apt along the N100. After 8km (5 miles), turn left on to the Bonnieux road which almost immediately crosses the humpback bridge over the River Coulon. It was built in the first century AD to carry the *Via Domitia* across what must then have been

Places of Interest In and Near Apt

Apt
Archaeological Museum
A small collection of local archaeological finds in a fine eighteenth-century house.

The Church of St Anne
The town cathedral until the Revolution. Superb Romanesque crypt and wrought iron bell-tower.

Luberon Museum
A recently opened museum with exhibits on the local natural park, its geology and history.

Bonnieux
Bakery Museum
Museum in an old bakery.

Lourmarin
The Château of Lourmarin
A combination of an old building, from the late fifteenth century, and a 'new' castle from the mid-sixteenth century. The wood and stone arcaded courtyard is exquisite.

Silvacaine Abbey
Cistercian abbey built in 1144, but abandoned in the fourteenth century. Now partially restored and including some impressive thirteenth-century work.

Cucuron
Marc Deydier Museum
A museum of the local area of the Luberon.

Ansouis
Château Sabran
A pleasant building (half-castle, half-mansion) and very nicely decorated. Good views from the grounds.

The Extraordinary Museum of Georges Mazoyer
An interesting but not particularly 'extraordinary' collection of shells, fish and Provençal furniture.

Grand Luberon
Mourre Nègre
The highest point of the range, needing a walk to reach, but offering tremendous views.

Lacoste
The Château of Lacoste
Impressive eleventh-century fortified mansion.

St Hilaire Abbey
Near Lacoste
Twelfth-century monastery of which little but the chapel remains.

a turbulent stream, for the pillars of the three powerful arches have openings which allowed floodwater to flow more freely and relieved stress on the structure.

Take the Pont Julien road (D108) north to **Roussillon**, surrounded by now-abandoned quarry pits of various ochre colours, the most startling one being an intense red-brown. All these shades appear on the façades of the houses. At the village's end, pause to look at the curious needles of rock — the Fairies' Needles — that rise from the hillside. More quarries of grey, green and pink marl occur near Gargas, east of Roussillon; these are still worked.

Even more spectacular are the iron-oxide quarries near Rustrel, about 19km (12 miles) east — reached via St Saturnin-d'Apt — on the edge of the Plateau de Vaucluse. Rustrel Colorado, as the quarries are known, can be visited on foot after leaving the car near the Doa Stream. Columns of red ochre, capped with clay like giant mushrooms, are bizarre features in the landscape.

By turning the opposite way near Pont Julien, **Bonnieux** is reached; a village with a very interesting bakery museum. South again, **Lourmarin** has a fifteenth-century *château* with one of the prettiest courtyards you could hope to see. In one room there is a fireplace protected by caryatids. In the cemetery are the graves of Albert Camus, a French winner of the Nobel Prize for Literature, and of Henri Bosco, a less well-known Provençal novelist and poet. South from the village is the Abbey of Silvacaine. The abbey's name is from the Latin *Silva Cannorum* (forest of reeds) because this area is drained swamp. Externally, the abbey is plain Romanesque, but inside, the roof is a wonder of the stonemason's art, with high-soaring ribs supporting stone vaulting, the ribs themselves supported on elegantly twisted columns.

Moving eastwards from Lourmarin, the traveller passes through a series of delightful villages. There is **Cucuron**, with an interesting museum devoted to the history and culture of the Luberon, and **Ansouis**, with a fine fortified *château* and a museum that claims to be 'extraordinary' but is hardly earth-shattering. The village itself is rather more interesting; a pretty place, well-situated on the Luberon.

Go east again, rounding an edge of Le Grand Luberon — so called to distinguish it from its little brother to the west of Bonnieux — to reach the twelfth-century priory of Carluc at the end of a short, peaceful valley. Next comes Castellet, a hillside hamlet, and Auribeau where a road leads off up towards the high Lubéron. From the road's end, the motorist can turn walker and follow GR92 to the summit of Mourre Nègre, at 1,126m (3,400ft) the highest point of the Luberon. The walk will take about 1 hour, but the view makes the effort worthwhile, with the Durance Valley, the Lure and Mont Ventoux, as well as part of the coast, being visible.

Had the visitor gone west from Bonnieux, in the shadow of Le Petit Luberon, he or she would have reached **Lacoste** where there is an interesting abbey and yet another fine *château*. West again is **Ménerbes**, a very ancient place, seemingly glued to the hillside, and **Oppède-le-Vieux**, romantically set on a high rock. **Maubec**, the next village, has the remains of a medieval castle.

Back on the main N100, the next town is **Cavaillon**, which is on the right bank of the Durance in the flatlands at the foot of the Petit Luberon. It is a thriving commercial centre for the early season fruit and vegetable market, and its name is associated with fragrant, pink melons. At least five places are worth making for in Cavaillon.

The thirteenth-century former cathedral of St Veran is a good example of the Provençal style. A pentagonal external apse is dominated by an octagonal tower. All the side chapels contain paintings and carvings in wood and stone.

Walk along the Grand Rue from the church to enter the Archaeological Museum which has a display of prehistoric finds, a reconstruction of Cavaillon's Roman arch, and a room showing 500 Greek, Gaulish and Roman coins found on Colline St Jacques above the town.

At Rue Chabran there is a beautifully preserved eighteenth-century synagogue. What were known as the four Holy Communities of Avignon, Carpentras, l'Isle-sur-la-Sorgue and Cavaillon, ensured the protection of Jews from early in the fourteenth century until the French Revolution. Consequently, the Comtat Venaissin came to be known as 'the Jewish paradise', under the direct authority of the Popes and administered by elected chiefs called *baylons*. Below the synagogue, in the part reserved for making unleaven bread, is a small Judeo-Comtadin museum.

The first-century Roman arch in Place du Clos, was moved stone by stone in 1880 from the wall of St Veran church in which it had been embedded. Unlike arches commemorating victories, this one, though richly decorated, is conspicuously — one might even say pleasantly — lacking in military motifs.

From Place du Clos, a 15-minute walk up a stepped path takes the visitor to the top of the abrupt rock of Colline St Jacques. Neolithic and Ligurian tribes inhabited the site on which the seventeenth-century chapel of St Jacques now stands. Then it became a powerful Celtic *oppidum*. Later, the Greeks of *Massalia* (Marseille) set up a trading post for their goods, which were carried up the Durance by

The village of Gordes

boatmen who were the forerunners of the powerful guilds formed under Roman rule. In about 42BC, the Romans founded *Cabellio* in the plain below.

Close to Cavaillon is **Gordes**, a medieval village of some importance, which seems to clamber up the hillside. Gordes was overtaken by events and declined in the 1920s, only to make a recovery under the impulsion of the artist, André Lhote. It was severely damaged when war came this way in 1944, but its fortunes were revived, again because of artists, when peace came. Today Gordes flourishes and attracts many visitors.

Its *château* enjoys a lofty perch and is, like many others in Provence, a mixture of medieval and Renaissance, with finely proportioned rooms, decorations and stairway as well as an exuberant chimney-piece. It contains the striking Vasarely Museum. Here, the

The mill and an example of stained glass at the Duran Museum, near Gordes

versatile, Hungarian-born artist Vasarely, who restored the *château*, and did much to restore the town's fortunes, is remembered by some 1,000 of his own works. Geometric, undulating designs of pure colour express his notion of continuous move-ment. Also on show are some of his earlier figura-tive works.

Take the D15 south of the town to join the D2 and follow it to a left turn on to the D103, and left off this on to the D148 (this sounds complicated, but it is not, the whole journey only being about 4km [2^1/$_2$ miles]). Here there is a fine, stained-glass museum set up to honour the work of Frédérique Duran, but also illustrating the history of stained-glass window production. The museum is in a modern building that stands next to a sixteenth-century olive mill. On the road to the museum, near to the point where the D15 joins the D2, is a village of *bories*, which can be reached by parking the car and walking up a marked path for about 15 minutes or so. *Bories* are traditional Provençal peasant hovels. This site is a good one, with the restored, drystone, beehive-shaped huts grouped around an old bread oven, and is part of a museum of local traditions.

In the opposite direction from the *bories* and the stained-glass, north along the D177, is Sénanque abbey, the last of the 'Three Sisters of Provence' another of which, Silvacaine, has already been visited. The abbey buildings are interesting — note the Romanesque, barrel-vaulted ceiling — as is the permanent exhibition on the life of the Tuareg people of the Sahara, an exhibition with the somewhat grandiose title, the 'Desert of Man'.

West of Gordes is **Fontaine-de-Vaucluse**, which is reached by taking the D15, the Cavaillon road, turning right after 6km (4 miles) to Cabrières-d'Avignon, then taking the D100 and D100A to the village.

The 'fountain' of the name is the resurgent River Sorgue which appears as a lake at the cavernous foot of a huge semi-circular crag. *Son et lumière* shows are given here on summer evenings, looked over by the ruined castle of the bishops of Cavaillon. What looks like a placid lake and stream turns into a foaming torrent when the heavy rains of winter and spring have seeped into the fissured limestone rocks of Mont Ventoux, Lure and Luberon. The underground streams come to the surface through this powerful siphon. The remains of the Roman aqueduct which carried the waters of the Sorgue to Arles are visible by the roadside of the D24 near the village of Galas.

In Fontaine-de-Vaucluse itself, there is the Norbert Casteret Speleological Museum. This contains material relating to Casteret's 30 years of exploration to solve the mystery of the subterranean passages beneath the emerald green waters of the Sorgue.

The column in the square honours the Italian poet Petrarch who retired to this spot from Avignon between 1327 and 1353. Here he wrote many of the poems which speak of his unrequited love for Laura of Avignon, and his attachment to the solitude (as it then was) of Fontaine-de-Vaucluse — his *Vallis Clausa*, the Closed Valley. A small Petrarch Museum stands on what is thought to be the site of his house. It has been extensively renovated so it is worth asking for

Places of Interest in the Western Durance Valley

Cavaillon
Archaeological Museum
Housed in an old hospital and including local finds together with a collection of seventeenth-century remedies and medical equipment.

Synagogue
Finely decorated with Louis XV panels and wrought iron.

Chartreuse of Bonpas
Near Cavaillon
Formal gardens of thirteenth-century charterhouse and excellent chapel.

Gordes
Vasarely Museum
Museum devoted to the work of the artist Vasarely, housed in the fine twelfth-century castle.

Bories Village
Near Gordes
A restored village of old hovels grouped around a traditional bread oven.

Duran Stained-Glass Window Museum
Near Gordes
A museum on the history of stained-glass window-making and a collection of the work of Frédérique Duran.

Sénanque Abbey
Near Gordes
Founded by the Cistercians in the twelfth century, but abandoned at the time of the Revolution. Currently being restored.

Fontaine-de-Vaucluse
Norbert Casteret Speleological Museum
A collection of stalactites and stalagmites by Casteret, a speleologist. Interesting, but probably looked better in the original caves.

Vallis Clausa Craft Centre
Display of local craft work.

Museum of Rationing
The history of rationing during the wars of 1870-71, 1914-18 and 1939-45.

Pernes-les-Fontaines
Tour Ferrande
The last remnant of a thirteenth-century castle. Interesting frescos and a good view of the town and area from the top.

Châteaurenard
Griffon Tower
The tower is virtually all that remains of a medieval castle. From the top there is a fine view over the Durance Valley.

Fontaine-de-Vaucluse

Pernes-les-Fontaines

opening times at the local Tourist Office (☎ 90.203222).

Over the centuries, men of letters have come here in pilgrimage out of respect for a major innovative poet and his romantic attachment to Laura. He has been called the first modern man, the one who took the step away from medievalism's fearful submission to divine authority and towards the individualistic Renaissance assertion of man as the measurer of values.

On a more mundane level, the village is also the site of a craft centre that takes the Latin name to advertise its display of local crafts. Here, too, is an extraordinary museum devoted to the history of rationing in France during the last three European wars.

North-west from the village is **Pernes-les-Fontaines**; a village grouped around an ancient clock tower, but with another tower — Tour Ferrande in Rue Gambetta — that is thirteenth-century and contains some quite beautiful frescos dating from the last quarter of that century.

Finally, we return to Cavaillon and go west from that town to the Chartreuse of **Bonpas**. A beautiful little chapel is almost all that remains of a thirteenth-century monastery. The village name is interesting. Originally it was *malus passus* as it represented a possible but difficult crossing of the Durance. When the first monks arrived, they built a bridge and the name was changed to Bonpas.

At nearby **Châteaurenard**, the remains of the hilltop castle are still impressive, and a climb to the top of the remaining tower offers a fine view of the Durance Valley.

3

ARLES AND THE CAMARGUE

A rles, 38km (24 miles) south of Avignon, is a rightly popular centre, perhaps the most Provençal of all the region's towns. It is full of reminders of its illustrious past, reminders that cover the centuries, from the Arena of the early Roman Empire to the blazing yellow cornfields of Vincent van Gogh's paintings.

The town has a Celtic-Ligurian past, though it is with the Greeks that the first positive records arrive. Then it had two names, *Theline*, (the Provider) which was replaced by *Arelate*, (the town in the marsh). Both are apt, as the land around the town is remarkably fertile, while to the south there are the swamps of the Camargue, swamps that seeped closer to the town 2,000 years ago. Its position on the Roman roads to Gaul meant that it was important when the Romans finally subdued the area, and it soon rivalled the nearby Phoenician port of *Massalia* (Marseille). The rivalry grew when Arles took the side of Julius Caesar in his feud with Pompey, and when Ceasar emerged victorious, it is possible to imagine that the noise of the cheering in his town was rivalled only by that of falling masonry as the defences of Pompey's town were dismantled.

Thereafter, Arles became increasingly important. Originally, when the town was the first Roman foundation in Gaul, it was known as 'the granary of Rome', a somewhat disparaging title which implies that it existed only to fill its master's bread basket, though an interesting flashback to the Greek name. Later, Arles gained a better title, 'the little Rome of the Gauls'.

By the fifth century, Arles had become so prosperous that 'all that the Orient, or unguent Arabia, luxuriant Assyria, fertile Africa and fecund Gaul produce is to be found there'. As soon as the Romans

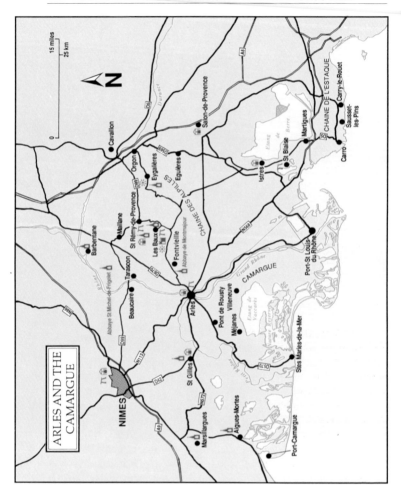

had retreated from this area of Gaul, pulling in their horns as the barbarian hordes poured in on Rome, this wealth brought others keen to replace the town's Roman masters. First came the Goths, then the Franks. Finally, in the early eighth century, the Saracens arrived. They did not stay long, freedom for the townsfolk of Arles being apparently heralded by the arrival of Charles Martel's army. Martel attacked the town, routing the Saracens at first but facing stiffer

A panorama of Arles and the River Rhône

opposition when they barricaded themselves in the Arena. Martel lost many men in taking that last defence and, when the dust had settled, he took out his anger and frustration by slaughtering the townsfolk. The poor people must have wondered whether they should really have been so enthusiastic when Martel arrived.

Today Arles is a museum city, proud of its Roman and medieval heritage. Savour its atmosphere on foot; a car is of no help in the narrow streets. Start in the tree-lined Boulevard des Lices, which is thoroughly modern, with thronged cafés and restaurants, and make for the Place de la République where there is a Roman obelisk of Egyptian stone. This was moved here from the chariot racecourse in a suburb of Trinquetaille.

On one side of the Place is the seventeenth-century *hôtel de ville*, on another is the west façade of St Trophime church. The west porch is a delight of Romanesque art. There are elaborate carvings in great rhythmical patterns and borrowed motifs from Syrian, Persian, Nordic and antique Roman sources. Illiterate pilgrims, on their way to St James of Compostela in Spain, received the carved messages of election and damnation as effectively as a television advertisement today. Those pilgrims retraced a route followed by St Trophime himself who, it is said, reached the city in the first century, arriving just as the townsfolk were preparing to sacrifice three youths to their pagan gods. The saint hurled himself at the crowd and pagan priests, shouting that the true ethic was to love, not slaughter, your fellow man. The priests fled and the city was converted to Christianity. In the first church that stood on the site, St Augustine was consecrated as the first Bishop of England.

The interior of the church of St Trophime is equally as fine and strong as the exterior. An unusually narrow nave lends exaggerated height to the vaults. Paintings, carvings in wood and ivory, Aubusson tapestries and sarcophagi adorn the church, giving it a rich, but not overly ornate feel. It is also possible to visit the cloisters of the one-time town cathedral — they are superb. Two of the four sides are twelfth-century and are pure Romanesque, while the other two sides were added two centuries later and are Gothic, not quite so pure in their form as there was some attempt to match the earlier work. The carvings, in particular, are quite exquisite.

Just north of Place de la République is the small and shady Place du Forum in which stands a statue of the poet Frédéric Mistral; the wrought ironwork surrounding it is in the form of a *ficheiroun*, or trident, traditionally used by the cowboys or *gardians* of the Camargue. Embedded in the angle of the wall of the venerable Hôtel Nord-Pinus are two Corinthian columns which once formed part of a temple adjoining the Roman forum.

The Place du Forum is a reminder of Vincent van Gogh's brief stay in Arles, between February 1888 and May 1889, when his painting reached full maturity. In that 15 month period, Van Gogh painted about 190 pictures, 100 of them local landscapes, together with 50 portraits and 40 still-lifes or interiors. It is an often-repeated irony, but no less true for being so, that he did not sell one painting, despite the fact that his work now changes hands for millions. Indeed, it was at Arles that the famed incident occured when one of his paintings was discovered boarding up a broken window.

The setting for Van Gogh's *Café Terrace at Night* is now a furniture shop and that for *The Yellow House* in Place Lamartine, which he shared with Paul Gauguin, was destroyed by bombs in 1944. However, the cemetery of the Alyscamps remains much as it was when he painted it. The famous drawbridge (the Pont de Langlois, erected by an earlier Dutchman) over the Marseille and Rhône Canal just south

Places of Interest In and Near Arles

Roman Remains
The remains include a fine Arena that is nearly 137m (450ft) long and could seat 25,000 people. The Roman theatre could hold 7,000 people but is less well-preserved. Constantine's Palace is a well-preserved Baths from the fourth century, while the Alyscamps is the remains of the Roman necropolis. The Arena, at least, should not be missed.

Church and cloisters of St Trophime
The church was once the city cathedral. Built first in the seventh century, it is now an eleventh-century Romanesque building with additions from later centuries. The cloisters, with their superb Gothic rib vaulting, are twelfth-century to the west and south, fourteenth-century to the east and north.

Museum of Pagan Art
Includes items from the town's pre-Christian Roman past.

Museum of Christian Art
Charts the development of Christianity in the Roman town and also includes a Christian sarcophagus from the fourth century, excavated from the Alyscamps.

Arlaten Museum
The museum of Arles was founded by Frédéric Mistral late in the nineteenth century and includes items from the town's Provençal history and examples of folk art and craft.

Réattu Museum
A museum dedicated to the work of eighteenth- and nineteenth-century Provençal artists as well as work by contemporary artists.

Espace Van Gogh
A new centre based in the six-teenth-century Hôtel Dieu du Saint Esprit. It will offer facilities to Van Gogh scholars in a fine library of material on the artist and will also house a library of books on Provence.

Montmajour Abbey
Near Arles
Superb remains of a tenth-century Benedictine monastery, including fine abbey building, church with Romanesque crypt and twelfth-century cloisters.

of Arles was sketched and painted by Vincent into immortality. This was pulled down in 1926, only to be reconstructed later. It no longer moves, as the original did, but is no less appealing for that. The Arlesian costumes he painted are no longer seen today, except on rather self-conscious folkloric days.

Unfortunately, there is no museum to Vincent van Gogh in Arles.

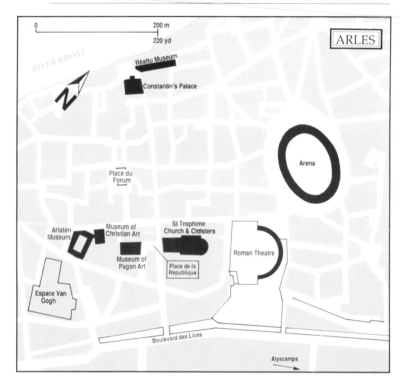

The Roman Arena, Arles

The Arena by night

Left — Pont 'Van Gogh', Arles

The problem now is that if the town, which is very conscious of the tourist value of the artist, were to erect one, they would have to sell all the inhabitants into slavery to afford to cover even one wall with paintings. The town does, however, have one building named after him, the Espace Van Gogh, which, when fully open, will have an extensive library of books on the most famous inhabitant. The building will also hold exhibitions.

After Van Gogh, the next biggest attraction for the visitor are the Roman remains. The Arena, or Amphitheatre, is the chief place of interest, and rightly so. It is truly impressive, a statement in stone of the Roman Empire's feelings about its own permanence. The Arena is about a twentieth of the size of those that survive, being 137m (450ft) along the long side of its oval, 107m (350ft) across the short side. When completed, it is estimated that it could have seated over 25,000 spectators who filed in to watch the full range of events and contests that the Roman citizen felt was his due. Below the walls of the Arena, the visitor can still see the caged areas where animals would have been kept before they went to the arena to kill or be killed.

Today it is bulls that are led to the Arena. Usually, the events here and at nearby Nîmes are Provençal, the nimble bulls of the Camargue being used. In this event, the bull has a rosette attached to its forehead and is put in the ring with several *rasetteurs*, each dressed in his uniform of white shirt and trousers, who try to remove the rosette while preserving life and limb. The bull is never harmed, though the same cannot be said of the *rasetteurs*, many of whom have been severely gored. The event raises ethical questions in the minds of all animal lovers, but at least in Provençal bullfighting there is no final killing. However, bullfights of the Spanish variety are also held both at Arles and Nîmes. These involve a larger, more dangerous bull that is killed at the end of the contest, either by the matador or by ring men.

The Arena was erected in the first century AD, though there was probably an earlier wooden one on the same site. That would have dated from around the first century BC, the same time that the Theatre was built. The Theatre, built when Augustus was emperor, was sumptiously decorated with statues and marble facings, and was designed to hold about 7,000 people. Sadly, it was badly damaged in medieval times and only some columns and seating now remain. Constantine's Palace, which is actually the public baths and occasionally is known as the Trouille Baths, is much later, dating from the fourth century, the time of Constantine the Great. The water to supply the baths was brought by aqueduct from Eygalières, 25km (15$^1/_2$ miles) away.

The last significant Roman site is The Alyscamps, the remains of a necropolis that actually survived its original users. At the end of the site is a large ruin that was once the church of St Honorat. Over a period of about 900 years — though chiefly in three periods, in the fourth, eighth and twelfth centuries — thousands of burials took place here. The site was later used as a convenient quarry but the best of the stone tombs can now be seen in the Museum of Christian Art. The Museum of Pagan Art holds the better objects from Arles' pre-Christian period.

Other museums include the Réattu which has a large collection of Fine Art, including tapestries, furniture, ceramics and paintings. There are also a large number of drawings by Picasso. Behind the museum, a really good walk along a bank of the Rhône is possible. The Arlaten Museum was created in 1896 by the traditionalist poet Mistral as 'the true museum of the living life and people of Arles', and enlarged with the money he won as Nobel Prize Laureate for Literature in 1904. He packed the thirty rooms with anything which recorded the culture of his beloved *pays d'Arles,* all the items being labelled in Provençal in his own hand. From herbs to costumes, poems to furniture, theatre programmes to life-size tableaux; here is yesteryear's Provence.

Finally, the visitor should take the N570 northwards, and turn off right along the D17 to visit the abbey of Montmajour, built on rising ground above what had been marshland drained by the monks. Founded in the tenth century, it fell into a long decline and is now being restored. The keep is a powerful and commanding presence, in sharp contrast with the demure twelfth-century cloister and the church, whose crypt is partly hewn out of the rock.

While at the site, do not miss the tiny burial chapel of Ste Croix in the form of a Greek cross in a field just below the abbey. It is a gem of Provençal Romanesque art and is surrounded by tombs cut out of the rock.

The Roman and medieval impressions gained in Arles can be extended by visiting St Gilles and Nîmes in Gard. **St Gilles,** 16km (10 miles) west of Arles on the N572, was also a stopping-place for pilgrims on their way to St James of Compostela. Three rounded

A typical back-street scene, Arles

Aigues-Mortes

doors fill the width of the west front of the abbey-church, and the
effect is even more impressive than the one at St Trophime. The
carvings surrounding them were completed in the late twelfth and
early thirteenth centuries and depict scenes from the life of Christ. St
Gilles' tomb is in the crypt which is an early example (eleventh-
century) of ogival vaulting.

A belfry contains a spiral staircase — Le Vis de St Gilles — whose
fifty steps are roofed with stone like a curving tunnel, an early
example of the stonemason's craft. It is said that stonemasons come
from far afield in order to view the staircase, so perfect is its
execution.

North-west from St Gilles, the D42 passes the Garons airfield and
enters Nîmes, but first it is worth going west once more to visit
Aigues-Mortes (the town of the dead waters). From a distance, the
town appears to rise out of the surrounding marshland — which
originally gave it its name — as though it were the painted backdrop
for a Disney cartoon. It was built almost from nothing as there was
only a very tiny fishing village here when Louis IX came in the mid-
thirteenth century. The king needed a Mediterranean port so that he

could take his army on a crusade but, as France was fragmented, he did not have one until he found a fishing village nestling among the dead waters of the Western Camargue. The king built his port, and that is what we see today; it is virtually untouched, its ramparts are still complete and, since the population is less now than it was then, the village is still confined within them.

To walk the ramparts — especially if it is a walk taken at dawn or dusk — is one of the delights of Provence. It takes about 1 hour to make the journey, the walk taking the visitor over several gates, particularly on the seaward side, and past many towers. One of these is the Wick Tower, where a lamp burned, not, as you might suppose, as a beacon to ships, but as a constant source of fire for the lighting of the powder in cannon.

The Burgundian Tower has a much less attractive reason for its name. In the Hundred Years War, the Burgundians held the town and sided with the English in the fight for the French crown. In 1418, the Gascons laid siege to Aigues-Mortes, eventually gaining secret access one night and slaughtering the garrison to a man. Needing a quick solution to the problem of a pile of dead Burgundians and not wanting to pollute the near-stagnant waters around the town, the Gascons threw the corpses into this tower, pouring salt in on top of them to preserve them for the moment when they could arrange a more discreet burial.

Near the town's Old Port is the Constance Tower, separated from the main ramparts by a bridged moat. This massive structure, almost 55m (180ft) high, has been used as a prison on several occasions. A climb up the steps to the tower's top is rewarded by a fine view over the town.

North of Aigues-Mortes, the traveller is on the road to Nîmes, but before reaching that town he or she should stop off at Teillan Castle, near Marsillargues. This fine Renaissance *château* is actually a converted monastery. The outbuildings include a pigeon loft with over 1,500 nest holes and a rotating nest ladder.

Nîmes is the old Gaulish tribal capital of *Nemausus* — named after a local god said to live in a spring near the first town site. The town was taken early by the Romans and was soon important because of its position on the road to Spain. In medieval times, Nîmes was always in the wrong place or on the wrong side at the crucial time and was looted and plundered on many occasions. On one occasion, when it was free of the ravages of war for a moment, the

Places of Interest In and Near Nîmes

Aigues-Mortes
Constance Tower
Part of the sixteenth-century defences of the town. Interesting for the evocation of life in a medieval castle, and also for the wonderful view of the town and surrounding area from the top.

Teillan Castle
Near Marsillargues
A building with an interesting history. Built originally as a fort, it was first transformed into a monastery and then, in the seventeenth century, into a mansion.

Nîmes
Amphitheatre
Although not one of the biggest of the seventy or so remaining Roman arenas, Nîmes is, by common consent, the best-preserved. More than 20,000 spectators could pack into this superbly decorated arena. Not to be missed.

Maison Carrée
An equally well-preserved first-century BC temple, probably the best-preserved of all remaining Roman temples. Not to be missed.

Temple of Diana
Less well-preserved temple standing in fine gardens near the remains of the Roman baths and theatre.

Magne Tower
A 30m (100ft) tower probably built as a monument rather than a watch tower.
The tower can be climbed; not surprisingly, there is a fine view from the top.

Castellum
The collecting basin for the water supply to the Roman town.

Porte d'Arles
The gateway to Roman Nîmes.

Archaeological and Natural History Museum
The archaeological section is chiefly African while the natural history section deals with the local wildlife.

Fine Arts Museum
A fine collection of seventeenth- and eighteenth-century French paintings, gathered around a huge mosaic.

Museum of Old Nîmes
Housed in the seventeenth-century Bishop's Palace, the museum has a good collection of old, locally made furniture.

town was hit by the plague instead. Real stability did not arrive until the late eighteenth century, which means that the seeker after the architecture of that period will find the town well-worth a visit.

It is, however, for the Roman remains that most visitors come.

Fontaine Pradier & Ste Perpéture church, Nîmes

Maison Carrée, Nîmes

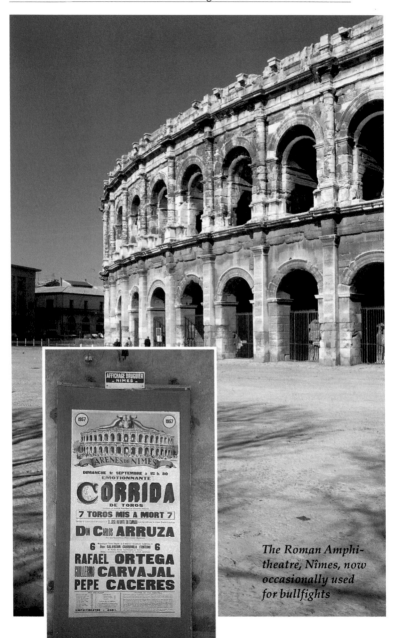

The Roman Amphi-theatre, Nîmes, now occasionally used for bullfights

The Arena (Amphitheatre) is smaller than that at Arles, but in a better state of preservation. Built in the first century AD, the Arena is 128m (420ft) long and 100m (330ft) across and could hold 20,000 people — it still does so for shows and bullfights. In medieval times, it served as a village, housing 2,000 people. As with Arles, the Arena bullfights are both Provençal and Spanish style.

Maison Carrée, the other really important Roman monument, stands a little away from the Arena. The name means 'Square House', which shows a certain lack of geometric awareness concerning what is now believed to be the finest surviving Roman temple, and was built in Hellenic style in the first century BC. It was probably dedicated to Jupiter, Juno and Minerva. The sanctum of the temple is walled and holds the town's antiquities museum. Here are the finest of the excavated pieces from the town, pride of place going to a head of Venus or, perhaps, to a bronze head of Apollo.

In the Fountain Gardens there are the ruins of a much less well-preserved temple of Diana, together with the remains of the town's baths. Close by, the Magne Tower is of first century AD construction and is believed to have been a monument rather than a watch tower. Elsewhere, the castellum was the collecting basin for the water brought by aqueduct from Pont du Gard. The start of the ten canals that distributed the water can be seen at this most interesting site, the only other example of which is at Pompeii. Finally, the Porte d'Arles is the old gateway through the town walls.

Those with enough time, can visit one of the town's non-Roman museums. The one for the Fine Arts has a collection from many schools and periods, while the Archaeological and Natural History Museum has some prehistoric items, an African collection and another collection on the local wildlife. The Museum of Old Nîmes is perhaps the best, with a collection of furniture and items on the history of bullfighting. The museum is housed in a fine seventeenth-century house that was once the Bishop's Palace.

East from Nîmes, and reachable by going north from Arles, are the twin towns of Beaucaire and Tarascon, staring at each other from opposite sides of the Rhône.

Tarascon's massive, fifteenth-century moated castle is an out-standing example of medieval fortification and is very well-preserved. After it was built, it defied the castle of Beaucaire on the opposite bank — independent Provence confronting the Kingdom of France. Elegant upper rooms served as the apartments of royalty and

Places of Interest
Around Beaucaire and Tarascon

Beaucaire
Beaucaire Castle
Little remains of the eleventh-century castle, but the Romanesque chapel is interesting, and the view from the top of the triangular tower is excellent.

Museum of Old Beaucaire
A small museum of the history of the town housed in part of an old monastery.

St Romaine Abbey
Near Beaucaire
Originally a monastery dating from the twelfth century, the building was transformed into a castle in the sixteenth century. It is still in the process of excavation.

Tarascon
The Castle of King René
Magnificent castle complete with moat in a superb position. Built in

the twelfth century and carefully restored early this century. The lord's apartments are excellent and include a sumptuous Great Hall.
The view from the castle walls is just as good.

St Michel-de-Frigolet Abbey
Near Tarascon
Beautifully positioned abbey remains.
The site museum has a collection of Provençal furniture.

Barbentane
The Château
A seventeenth-century *château* with a finely decorated interior.

Maillane
The Mistral Museum
A small museum to the famous Provençal writer in his house. There is a statue of the great man in the garden.

were used for banquets and for when the nobles were being entertained by strolling troubadours.

Close by is the restored twelfth-century church of Ste Marthe, which is said to contain her remains. Legend has it that the saint, coming from the Camargue, vanquished the *tarasque*, a monster which terrified the town and devoured its children. The saint pacified the monster by giving the sign of the Cross and, placing her girdle round its neck, led it to the Rhône, into which it vanished for ever. A festival, decreed by King René in 1496, has been kept alive on the last Sunday in June when a papier-mâché *tarasque* is paraded with much jollification — a symbol of Christianity's triumph over Paganism.

Beaucaire, on the far bank, has an equal amount to keep the visitor occupied. In contrast to Tarascon, the castle is disappointing, being largely ruinous, but its chapel is interesting and there are fine views from the upper ramparts. Many will find the museum of the old town fascinating for the light it throws on past centuries. The museum is housed in an old monastery. Another fine old monastery is that of St Romaine, an abbey of the twelfth century that lies a mile or so to the north-west of the town off the D986.

North of Tarascon, on the D35, is **Boulbon** which lies on the slopes of the Montagnette hills overlooking the Rhône and the Vallabrègues Dam. Boulbon is a pleasant old *bourg* whose focal point is its ruined castle. Each first of June they hold the Procession of the Bottles (*Fioles*) and blessing of the wine at the Chapel of St Marcellin, patron saint of wine.

Continuing northwards on the D81 and then bearing right, the visitor reaches the abbey of St Michel-de-Frigolet. This was named after the Provençal word for thyme, the building being set amid aromatic herbs of the *garrigue*, and it was immortalised in Alphonse Daudet's story, 'The Elixir of the Reverend Father Gaucher' from the *Lettres de Mon Moulin*.

North of the Abbey is **Barbentane** with a *château* whose interior is almost a museum devoted to the furniture periods of Louis XV and Louis XVI. There is also some fine porcelain and china. Alternatively, the traveller can turn east to reach Maillane where the great man of Provençal history, Frédéric Mistral, was born and lies buried. The house that he occupied for the last 40 years of his life is now a museum in his honour.

Southward now is **St Rémy-de-Provence**, a popular centre for its choice of hotels, its setting close to the Alpilles Hills, and the fruit and market-gardens which surround it.

The most famous of all astrologers, Michel de Nostradamus (1503-66) was born here, and the Musée Alpilles Pierre de Brun, in a handsome sixteenth-century mansion, has some souvenirs of the man who became physician to Charles IX, and was struck off for keeping his remedies secret. Turning to astrology, he wrote his highly obscurantist *Centuries*, quatrains of predictions which impressed Catherine de Medici. He became rich and famous.

A second museum in Hôtel de Sade, once the home of relatives of the notorious sadistic marquis, should be looked at after a visit to the archaeological site of *Glanum*, as many items from there are shown

Ruins at St Rémy-de-Provence

in the museum.

However, before going to *Glanum*, it is worth going to see two Roman monuments whose grace will delight the eye even of those not interested in antiquities. Less than 2km (1¹/₄ miles) south of St Rémy, on the right-hand side of the D5, they are unenclosed, surrounded by turf and trees. Their lightness and delicacy betray a Greek influence. One is the municipal arch of around 20BC, the oldest and smallest to survive in France. It stood at the entrance to the town of *Glanum* on the other side of the road, and the *Via Domitia* highway passed under it. The reliefs commemorate Julius Caesar's victories over the Gauls and Greeks of *Massalia* in 49BC, but there is a more mellow feature, too; a Gaul being granted his freedom. Next to the arch is a beautifully preserved little mausoleum in memory of Julius Caesar's two adopted sons.

In *Glanum*, excavations have revealed the presence of Neolithic, Ligurian and Gaulish peoples who settled here before Phoenician traders named the place *Glanon*, a name that Caesar later Romanised to *Glanum*. Houses with fine mosaics, a forum, baths, temples and a nymphaeum, can be seen in this extensive open-air museum where much remains to be uncovered. The state of preservation of the site owes much to the history of the city. After it was abandoned, but before there had been much time for pillage, the waterways to the site became blocked with debris, and silt from the hills was able to quickly build up, covering the site and hiding it from view.

On your return to St Rémy, turn in to the priory of St Paul de Mausole. Vincent van Gogh became a voluntary patient here in 1889-90 and continued, in periods of lucidity, to paint as expressively as before. Only his bust in the drive is a reminder of the event. Do not miss seeing the richly carved capitals of the twelfth-century cloisters.

The Chaîne des Alpilles, bare white limestone formations eroded into striking sculpted forms, dominate the otherwise flat, well-irrigated landscape to the south of St Rémy. They give an impression of height and grandeur, though nowhere do they reach 500m (1,640ft). A round tour of 80km (50 miles) reveals the loveliest parts; walkers can cross the chain on the GR6 pathway. This is one of the best walks in Provence, touching Eyguières, Aureille, Eygalières, the peak of La Caume, Les Baux-de-Provence and St Gabriel. If that is too far, then the walkers should limit themselves to following the GR either from Eygalières to Les Baux — a distance of about 27km (17 miles), taking about $7^1/_2$ hours — or from Les Baux to Tarascon — a distance of about 21km (13 miles) and taking around 6 hours. Each of these is a good day's outing by the time the bus has carried you back, but a day that does full justice to the fine, little hill range.

For most visitors, **Les Baux-de-Provence** is the main objective. This extraordinary village is hardly distinguishable from the spur of naked rock in which it is set. Prehistoric man has left traces of his safe *oppidum*, but little is known about his occupation. More is known of the Lords of Les Baux who, from the eleventh to the fifteenth centuries, were powerful far beyond the confines of Provence. They have a history that is filled for the most part with brigandage except for the thirteenth century, when Les Baux was famous for its 'Courts of Love' and the troubadours who performed there.

In the seventeenth century, the town embraced Protestantism; Louis XIII and Richelieu had the castle and ramparts destroyed. A once populous town then began to crumble into decay. Today, the rituals of the sixteenth-century Midnight Mass (*pastrage*) — symbolic of pastoral Provence — are kept movingly alive each Christmas Eve

Places of Interest In and Near St Rémy-de-Provence and Les Baux-de-Provence

St Rémy-de-Provence
Musée Alpilles
Housed in a huge sixteenth-century mansion built around a courtyard.
There is a fine collection of furniture, costumes and Provençal art and a library of material on Nostradamus, who was born in the house.

Archaeological Centre
A fifteenth-century house with items from the *Glanum* excavations.

Glanum
Near St Rémy-de-Provence
The remains of an extensive Roman settlement, built on the site of a Phoenician town. The excavated remains include the forum, temples, town houses, baths and some fortifications. Of enormous interest to anyone with an interest in Roman civilisation.

Les Baux-de-Provence
Museum of Modern Art
A museum that concentrates on the work of contemporary Provençal artists.

Louis Jou Foundation
Housed in the sixteenth-century Hôtel Brion, this is the donation of the gravurist Louis Jou which includes much of his own work, together with that of Durer, and other well-known artists.

La Cité Morte
Deserted, early medieval village seeming to grow out of the rock. The visitor can wander through 600-year-old chapels and houses. One fourteenth-century house, close to the entrance, houses the Musée Lapidaire, the site museum with the better of the excavated finds.
Not to be missed.

Cathedral of Images
Based in original bauxite mine caverns, suitably modified to allow projection, this 'gallery' uses nearly fifty large projectors to throw images of Egyptian temples, cave paintings and other rock structures on to the cavern walls.

Moulin de Daudet
Near Les Baux-de-Provence
A nineteenth-century mill, restored to its original form and housing a small museum devoted to the author Alphonse Daudet.

Barbegal
Roman Waterwheel
A waterwheel fed by cleverly positioned aqueducts. The mill race and grindstone slots are visible.

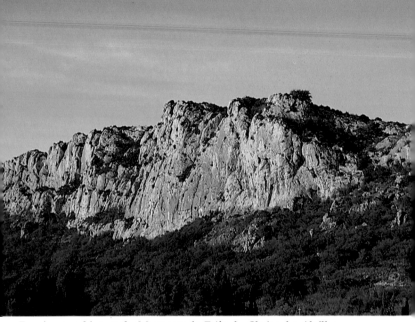

Evening sunshine on the Montagne du Défends, Chaîne des Alpilles

in the church of St Vincent which is packed for the occasion.

A suggested itinerary which combines an inhabited village of great charm and a deserted village of considerable interest would be as follows. Enter the village through the Porte Mage, cut in 1866, and pass the seventeenth-century town hall; next is Porte Eyguières, and then the Hôtel Brion which houses a collection of the art of the gravurist, Louis Jou. St Vincent Square offers a view over the Val d'Infer.

In the square are the Hôtel des Porcelets, housing a museum of modern art, and the chapel of the White Penitents. Next is the Hôtel de Manville, from the sixteenth century, and then a Protestant chapel of similar age. Now follow the Rue du Trencat which, like the bread ovens you pass, is hewn out of the rock, to reach the Hôtel de la Tour-de-Brau and the entrance to the old village. Here there is also a small museum of excavated items. Inside the old site there are several old chapels, a Saracen Tower, the Paravelle Tower which offers a fine view of the old castle, the castle ruins themselves and a stone pigeon loft. There is also a monument to the local poet, Charloun Rieu of Paradou, who wrote the words for Nöel at Midnight Mass.

*Les Baux-de-
Provence*

Bauxite, discovered here in 1822 as a vital mineral from which aluminium is extracted, perpetuates the names of Les Baux, although the major bauxite quarries are elsewhere in central Provence. The walls of one set of caverns have been used to display the life-size projected images of famous walls from the world — cave paintings, Egyptian wall paintings and so on.

An itinerary west of St Rémy is to follow the D99, turning off at St Etienne-du-Grés on to the D32. At the next crossroads, and set back on the hillside on the left, is the curious twelfth-century chapel of St Gabriel. The Auberge du Carrefour has the key. A mixture of antique Roman motifs, Romanesque, Oriental and Classical themes cover the façade. By contrast, the interior is severe and simple.

Now keep on the road signposted 'Fontvieille'. Outside the village is the **Moulin de Daudet**, a much-visited mill-museum ✳

because of its associations with Alphonse Daudet. The *Lettres de Mon Moulin* were not written here; Daudet did not write them entirely himself, and he hardly ever visited the mill. He was essentially a Parisian teller of elegantly turned tales borrowed from Provençal sources. Despite the truth, the mill still attracts the faithful.

Beyond the mill is a remarkable Roman ruin at **Barbegal**. A fourth-century water-mill was fed by ingenious aqueducts whose ruined arches can be seen nearby. Two parallel series of shutes worked sixteen water-mills which ground the local wheat for Arles and Rome. Slots which held the grindstones, and the course of the mill-race, are still visible.

An itinerary east of St Rémy allows a delightful part of the Alpilles to be discovered. Take the D5 south and, for a panoramic view, turn left after 4km (2$^1/_2$ miles) and go to the top of La Caume 387m (1,270ft) where a short walk reveals a view of the flatlands of Crau, the Camargue, lagoons, and the distant sea.

Continue on the D5 almost as far as Maussane where a left turn enters the peaceful valleys of the buckled, eroded flanks of the Alpilles. Follow the route through Le Destet, Mas-de-Montfort and Aureille to Eyguières, with its fountains. Turn left on to the Orgon road (D569), and left again where the Castelas de Roquemartine ruins overlook the road. Return to Mas-de-Montfort, and turn right to Eygalières. It is worth exploring here before continuing east to the twelfth-century chapel of St Sixte, which is on a slope bare except for some cypresses and is another of those unforgettable rural chapels. This area is Virgilian Provence.

To the south now is **Salon-de-Provence**, the olive oil capital of Provence. In the sixteenth century, the town was home to Adam de Craponne, a famous civil engineer, and Nostradamus, a much more famous astrologer. There is a museum to the latter man in what was his house. Elsewhere in the town, the beautiful, if somewhat angular, Château de l'Empéri is well-worth visiting. It stands on top of the Puech Rock and dominates the town. Inside is one of the finest military museums in France, with a collection of more than 10,000 pieces covering the history of the French Army from the Middle Ages through to World War I. Students of the campaigns of Napoleon will be especially interested in the museum.

Also in the town is the Salon and Crau Museum with a series of collections on Provençal furniture and wildlife, and some fine local landscape paintings.

Places of Interest In and Near Salon-de-Provence and Martigues

Salon-de-Provence
Château de l'Empéri
A huge castle on the Puech Rock above the town. Built in stages from the tenth century, the castle now houses one of France's foremost military museums with more than 10,000 items covering the history of the French army from medieval times to 1918. There is also a small collection of paintings.

Salon and Crau Museum
Small collections of local furniture and paintings in a nineteenth-century house.

Maison de Nostradamus
A museum of memorabilia of the famous astrologer in his house.

Martigues
Ziem Museum
Ferrières
A gallery chiefly showing the work of Felix Ziem, a local landscape artist, but including work by other artists of the same period (early nineteenth and twentieth centuries).

Istres
Museum of old Istres
Small museum of items on local history and folklore.

St Blaise
Les Fouilles
An archaeological site covering many centuries of occupation of a naturally defended position. The remains on show include a Greek defensive wall and part of a fifth-century church.

Lançon
Viewpoint on the north side of the Etang de Berre, on the D21. Includes a panorama dial.

For all the encroaching industrialisation, **Martigues** (to the south of Salon) is still a name to conjure with from the days when artists such as Augustus John fell in love with the little fishing port. Today, the town — where the poet Roy Campbell also briefly made his home — still has some old houses lining the canals. In Ferrières, in the northern part of the town beside the Etang de Berre, is the Ziem Museum with a collection of paintings by the local landscape artist.

Martigues is 53km (33 miles) from St Rémy, across the bleak and stony Grande Crau. Beyond **Istres** — where there is an interesting museum on local folklore — and left off the main road, is ramparted St Mitre-les-Remparts, while **St Blaise**, a few kilometres in the opposite direction, is a site that was inhabited in the seventh century

Château de l'Empéri, Salon-de-Provence

Mural of Nostradamus, Salon-de-Provence

BC. A near-perfect Greek wall is the chief sight. Further south of Martigues are small fishing villages turned seaside resorts — Carro, Sausset-les-Pins, Carry-le-Rouet — all in inlets at the foot of the arid Estaque Range.

South of Arles, the Rhône bifurcates and makes a triangular delta bounded on the east by the Grand Rhône and the Petit Rhône to the west. Some 40km (25 miles) separates the two estuaries which empty into the Golfe du Lion. In this triangle is the Camargue.

The Camargue is a strange place. Flat, featureless, windswept, mosquito-ridden, flooded or dried out, its luminous melancholy is captivating. Shallow, brackish lagoons, salt marshes and salt-tolerating plants, sand spits, coastal dunes, stunted tamarisks, small black bulls, and white horses; all these make southern Camargue a unique experience.

Coming from the direction of Arles, a quick impression can be gained by taking the D36, which follows the Grand Rhône

Ponies in the Camargue

for a while. Turn right for Villeneuve, go right again to skirt the north shore of the Nature Reserve of Etang de Vaccarès and pass rice paddies, vines and other crops in the desalinated area. Next turn left on the D570 at Albaron, close to which, in the farmhouse (*mas*) at the Pont de Rousty, there is a museum to the area, its history and natural history. The road then heads towards Stes Maries-de-la-Mer.

Single-storeyed thatched cottages, the dwellings of the cowboys (*gardians*) can be seen. They are blank on their north walls to keep out the *mistral* and are scattered about on the approaches to the only town of any size in the Camargue. Stes Maries is dominated by its fortress-church whose crypt contains the image of the black Sarah, patron saint of gipsies.

Huge and colourful gipsy celebrations take place every 24-5 May,

Places of Interest in the Camargue

Mas du Pont du Rousty
Museum of the Camargue
The geological, natural and human history of the area, housed in an old sheepfold.

Ginès
Camargue Information Centre
The central information office for the Camargue.

Pont de Gau
Ornithological Park
Near the Information Centre
Includes information on species that can be seen locally.

Boumain
Waxworks
Small exhibition of waxwork tableaux of eighteenth-century Camargue life. Curious, but informative in its way.

Stes Maries-de-la-Mer
Baroncelli Museum
Built around the library of the Marquess Baroncelli, but also including items from life in the Camargue.

and again over the weekend nearest 22 October. The folklore and wildlife of the Camargue are explained in the Baroncelli Museum. At nearby **Boumain**, wax tableaux recreate the way of life in ancient Camargue. Also near Stes Maries, at Ginès, is the Camargue Information Centre, from which there is a superb view across the Etang de Vaccarès, the heart of the Camargue. Here too, is a site where the local birdlife is identified.

For a longer stay in the Camargue, numerous ranch-hotels offer guided riding holidays. There are also landrover tours, and boat trips along the Petit Rhône. At **Méjanes** there is a holiday centre with a scenic railway, riding, mock bullfights in the arena, the branding of young bulls (*ferrade*) and equestrian shows.

At Pont de Rousty, off the D570 Albaron to Arles road, and near the Camargue Museum, it is possible to follow a path into the marshes. Once the Camargue covered 185,000 acres and was mainly a home to wildlife, man's intrusion being confined to the *gardians*, the European cowboys who herded little black bulls from white horses. However, during World War II, when France was starving, much of the northern part of the Camargue was drained for rice production.

Today, the much-reduced real Camargue is a nature reserve. It only admits accredited naturalists, but provides glimpses of birds, notably flamingoes (the only place in Europe where they breed regularly). These can be seen by following the road which skirts the eastern side of Etang de Vaccarès, turns right at Le Paradis and leads to the causeway of the Phare de la Gacholle (lighthouse).

Well over 300 species of birds have been recorded in the Camargue area; little wonder that ornithologists come from all over the world. For amateur and professional alike, the sight of massed flamingoes alighting, taking off, or standing on their raised nests, is the supreme delight. The appetite is whetted by the mention of a few other characteristic birds: herons, egrets, storks, vultures, eagles, plovers, avocets, stilts, owls, bee-eaters and rollers. Add to those visual joys the exquisite beauty of the nests of penduline tits and the mating call of hoopoes, and anyone with even a passing interest in birds will feel well-rewarded.

4
CENTRAL PROVENCE

Youthful vitality, as befits a university town; a character all its own; elegance inherited from its eighteenth-century past; these constitute some of the elements of **Aix-en-Provence**. In addition to these qualities, the town is full of shops, hotels and restaurants. It is a very attractive provincial city which has much to see, an undisputed magnet.

Some people do not like staying in large towns — Aix has a population of 114,000 — but there are also pleasant and quieter places in the vicinity, all with very acceptable hotels. These include Célony, Eguilles, Roquefavour, Beaureceuil and Vauvenargues. Yet a few days in the centre of Aix is a less tiring way of absorbing what it has to offer.

The Old City, surrounded by boulevards which radiate exits in all directions, exudes its seventeenth- and eighteenth-century personality. Aix really is very different from Avignon and Arles. It is best to begin an exploration with that aorta of Aix, the Cours Mirabeau, named after the scandalous and outstanding orator of the French Revolution, who ably represented Aix in the Paris parliament. The Cours runs east and west and, having been planted with with four rows of plane trees in 1830, it provides shade all summer long. Of its three fountains, the one at the eastern end is a statue of the fifteenth-century ruler of Provence, 'Good' King René (King of Sicily only, in Provence he was 'just' a Duke). He was a scholar and patron of the arts and husbandry.

The Good King was also a friend of the countryside and an amiable host, altogether a man out of his time. The statue has him holding a bunch of muscat grapes, which he introduced (along with

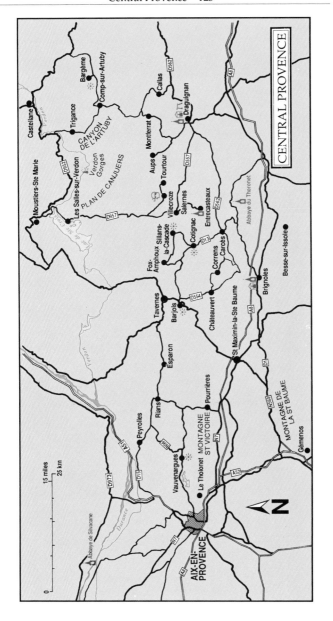

silkworms) into Provence. He may have been a politically incompetent ruler, but is viewed with affection in retrospect. As the visitor will notice, his name is used frequently by hotels, shops, cafés and little businesses.

In the centre of Cours Mirabeau is the moss-covered Fontaine Chaude, coming from the same hot springs tapped by the Romans when they founded *Aquae Sextiae Saluviorum* in 122BC. The water, mildly radioactive as well as containing a brew of minerals, reaches the surface at 36°C (97°F).

On the north side of the Cours are cafés, restaurants, bookshops and shops selling that speciality of Aix; *calissons*, delicate almond biscuits. On the south side are some seventeenth-century mansions (*hôtels*) whose handsome doors, caryatids and wrought ironwork characterise much of the old town. Beyond Cours Mirabeau, to the north as far as the cathedral, is Vieil Aix, the oldest part of the town. Some of the streets are pedestrian thoroughfares, lined with smart shops selling antiques or Provençal handicrafts.

To obtain the flavour of Vieil Aix follow Rue Doumer from Cours Mirabeau. Turn right into Rue Espariat; at No6, the Hôtel Boyer d'Eguilles contains the Natural History Museum with important collections of fish and plants. Of more than passing interest is a unique display of dinosaurs' eggs, found embedded in Montagne Ste Victoire. Thousands of these eggs were unearthed. There are various theories as to why they remained unhatched. It may have been a sudden cooling of the subtropical climate which caused the local dinosaurs to become extinct, millions of years ago.

Rue Espariat leads into one of many little squares dotted about Vieil Aix. This is Place d'Albertas, which is cobbled and has a fountain and terraced houses whose arches support the balconies of the upper windows. Turn right and go across Place St Honoré and Place de Verdun, passing the Palais de Justice. This dates, in part, from the late eighteenth century but with later, post-Revolution, additions in a simpler style. Place des Prècheurs is then reached, where a food market is held on Tuesday, Thursday and Saturday mornings.

In the square, the front of Ste Marie-Madeleine church is of little interest, but the interior has a masterly eighteenth-century marble 'Virgin' by the Avignonnais J.P. Chastel, and a fifteenth-century triptych of the 'Annunciation', full of mysterious symbols, perhaps painted by Jean Chapus. The church also contains works by such well-known artists as J.B. and Carle van Loo, Nicolas Mignard,

Places of Interest In and Around Aix-en-Provence

Méjanes Library and St John Perse Collection
Housed in the Hôtel de Ville, a fine mid-eighteenth-century building. The library has over 300,000 books and 1,600 manuscripts, and includes a Book of Hours of King René. The collection of work of the modern poet, St John Perse, was added in 1976.

Musée du Vieil Aix
Housed in a seventeenth-century *hôtel,* the museum has exhibits on Vieil Aix and a collection of old marionettes.

Tapestry Museum
The Archbishop's Palace Collection of eighteenth-century Beauvais tapestries in a mid-seventeenth-century palace.

Paul Arbaud Museum
Housed in the superb eighteenth-century Hôtel de Villeneuve d'Ansouis, includes pottery and paintings, together with the Library of Provence.

Museum of Fine Art and Archaeology (Granet Museum)
Chiefly the donation of François Granet and including Greek and Roman items as well as an excellent collection of paintings, with works by Rembrandt, Rubens, Cézanne and Pissaro. Not to be missed.

Cézanne's Studio
Reconstruction of Cézanne's studio as it looked at the time of his death in 1906.

Natural History Museum
This is housed in a seventeenth century mansion that is certainly worth visiting for its interior work. The museum includes collections of minerals, fossils and shells.

Pavillon de Vendôme
An interesting seventeenth-century house that looks surprisingly English, set in formal gardens.

Vasarely Foundation
Near Aix
Amazing building looking as much like futuristic dice as a gallery and holding the work of the Hungaro-French artist Victor Vasarely, an artist of the geometric school.

Entremont
Near Aix
Site of the capital city of the Celtic-Ligurian tribe of Saluvians who were the first people to have a town at Aix. Remains include both fortifications and houses.

Croix de Provence
Montagne Ste Victoire
Excellent viewpoint, though not the easiest to reach.

Vauvenargues
Château
Picasso lived here for the last years of his life, and is buried in the park. The *château* is not open to the public.

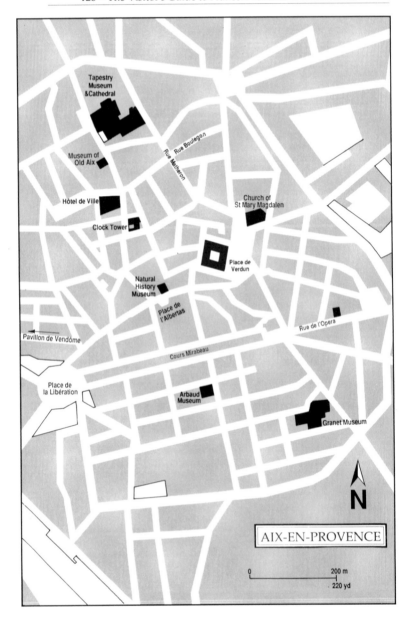

Tapestry
Museum
&Cathedral

Museum of
Old Aix

Rue Boulegon

Rue Matheron

Hôtel de Ville

Church of
St Mary Magdalen

Clock Tower

Place de
Verdun

Natural
History
Museum

Place de
l'Albertas

Rue de l'Opera

Pavillon de Vendôme

Cours Mirabeau

Place de
la Libération

Arbaud
Museum

Granet Museum

N

AIX-EN-PROVENCE

0   200 m

220 yd

Enjoying the winter sunshine, Cours Mirabeau, Aix

Michel Serre, and there is a 'Martyrdom of St Paul' attributed to Rubens.

If, instead of going ahead at Place d'Albertas, a left turn is taken, it will lead to Place Richelieu where a flower and vegetable market has been held for centuries. It is said that, at one time, poverty forced King René to sit at a stall and sell the produce of his own royal gardens. The former Corn Market, now a sub-post office, was strikingly decorated by Chastel, the Rhône and Durance Rivers being symbolised in the work by the mythological figure of Cybele.

Adjoining this is Place de l'Hôtel-de-Ville. Next to the town hall is a Flamboyant clock-tower of 1520. The lower, modern statues upon this — added in 1925 — represent Day and Night, while above there are wooden statuettes of the four seasons, each one visible for its 3 months. Higher still, there is an astronomical clock of 1661. The whole is capped by a Provençal bell-cage.

The much rebuilt Hôtel-de-Ville contains the Méjanes Library (founded in 1787) of 300,000 books and manuscripts, an indispensable source of reference for scholars. Also in the building is the Fondation St John Perse, a recent collection of memorabilia of this modern symbolist poet who won the Nobel Prize for Literature in 1960.

Turn right into Rue Gaston de Saporta — named after a nineteenth-century naturalist — which was once the Roman *Via Aurelia*. It is a street of elegant mansions and smart shops. Pierre Puget (1620-94) — Provence's greatest sculptor whose Baroque style was disliked by Louis XIV — is thought to have sculpted the façade of No17, which houses the Musée du Vieil Aix. It is full of things which illuminate the arts and crafts of the past: faïences from Moustiers; documents relating to Mirabeau; old prints of Aix; nativity cribs (*santons*); old costumes and furniture; paintings on velvet. A few paintings by J.A. Constantin (1756-1844) are interesting because he, even before John Constable, was painting from nature, a revolutionary practice.

Still further north is Place des Martyres-de-la-Résistance where the former Archbishop's Palace contains the Tapestry Museum, noted for eighteen Beauvais tapestries of the seventeenth and eighteenth centuries that include the *Life of Don Quixote*. During Aix's prestigious International Music Festival from mid-July to mid-August, the Palace courtyard serves as an open-air theatre. In the nearby Place de l'Université, there is a bust of Fabri de Peiresc (1580-

1637), a Provençal universal savant.

Beyond the bust is the cathedral of St Saveur, within which are
some of the oldest remains in Aix. The fifth-century baptistry, with
a full immersion pool, is supported by eight Roman columns and
covered by a sixteenth-century cupola. Part of the church began as
the nave of a twelfth-century church and the cloisters are also of this
period. Later, that building was incorporated into the Gothic structure, a large part of which is in the sixteenth-century style known as
Flamboyant Gothic.

Once in the church, the visitor should find the sacristan and ask
him to allow access to that section of the nave where the splendid
triptych, *The Burning Bush* is kept. Painted by Nicolas Froment of
Uzès in 1476, it shows King René kneeling on the left; portly, double-
chinned and earthy compared to the religious figures in the panels.
The painting represents the Virginity of Mary, and the visitor can,
perhaps, recognise the castles of Beaucaire and Tarascon on the side
panels.

The visitor should also ask the sacristan to open the walnut
panels of the West Door on which the four prophets and twelve
sybils are carved, work carried out in the sixteenth century. The
south door leads to the Romanesque cloisters.

Although it lies just outside Vieil Aix, the Pavillon de Vendôme
— at 34 Rue Célony, close to the thermal baths — is a charming
seventeenth-century town house set in formal gardens. Built for the
Cardinal Duke of Vendôme, it was later acquired by the influential
Provençal painter, J.B. van Loo (1684-1745) who died here — there
were eleven artists in this family of Dutch origin. A handsome
double staircase, period furniture and paintings sustain the original
atmosphere.

Turn now to the south side of Cours Mirabeau, the once aristo-
cratic Mazarin Quarter, smaller than Vieil Aix, the façades of its *hôtels*
more restrained.

Rue du 4 Septembre leads to the Paul Arbaud Museum, where
there are pictures by locally important artists, together with sculptures, ceramics and old furniture. Further along the street is one of
Aix's most popular fountains, that of the Four Dolphins, built in 1667
and standing in a Place of the same name. In Rue Cardinale, which
crosses the Place at right angles to our approach, is Lycée Mignet, the
school attended by Paul Cézanne, Emile Zola and the musician
Darius Milhaud.

Night lights, Aix

Go right into Rue Cardinale, at the end of which is the church of St Jean-de-Malte, the chapel to the former Priory of the Knights of St John of Malta, and the first Gothic church in Provence. Its interior is delightful for the purity of its proportions and the audacity of the lovely choir window. Its 67m (220ft) high belfry was built on the nave so that at street-level it is a chapel.

Place d'Albertas, Aix

Almost next door is the former priory itself. In 1825 it was owned by the painter François Granet who willed it to the town of Aix, along with his collection. Since that time it has been known as the Granet Museum, despite its formal title of Musée des Beaux-Arts. Among the archaeological exhibits on the ground floor is a collection of Celto-Ligurian items removed from the *oppidum* of *Entremont* outside Aix. These are the oldest of all the pre-Roman sculptures discovered in France. There are primitive carvings of warriors' heads, death masks, a hand resting on a head whose eyes are closed and a bas-relief of a galloping horseman carrying a severed head on the neck of his mount.

PAUL CEZANNE AT AIX-EN-PROVENCE
28 Rue de l'Opera: born in 1839
Eglise de la Madeleine: baptised in 1839
Rue des Epinaux: primary school 1844-49
14 Rue Matheron: family house
Rue Cardinale: Collège Bourbon (now Lycée Mignet), school with Emile Zola 1852-58
Jas de Bouffan: estate acquired by father 1859. This is now the site of the Vasarely Foundation, in Avenue Marcel Pagnol, 4km (2¹/₂ miles) to the south-west of the town.
44 Cours Mirabeau: site of Café Clem where he met friends.
Château Noir: on the D17. His favourite workplace where he rented a room.
23 Rue Boulegon: rented room 1899. Died 1906
9 Avenue Paul Cézanne: studio 1902. Now a museum.

The museum has many galleries filled with paintings of numerous schools and periods, but take a close look at the work of the Provençal *petits maîtres* whose interpretations of the landscapes around Aix give a profounder understanding of the contradictory elements in the countryside of Provence. These artists include J.A. Constantin, the earliest; François Granet (see also Ingres' sumptuous portrait of him) Prosper Grésy; Paul Guigou, the finest Provençal landscape artist before Cézanne, who created jewel-like colours and great atmospheric depth; Emile Loubon, the pastoralist; and Auguste Chabaud, who was nearer our time.

Of Cézanne himself, there is virtually nothing. Aix awoke too late to his genius to have been able to afford anything of significance. The

✳ most intimate momento is his studio, preserved more or less as it was at the time of his death. It is at 9 Avenue Paul Cézanne — in his day known as Chemin des Lauves — north-west beyond Boulevard Jean Jaurès. He had it built in 1902, the workshop of a man who willed the landscape into the harmonious architectural planes and restrained colours which informed the paintings of his maturity and made him one of the most significant figures in the history of art.

🏛 The estate acquired by Cézanne's father in 1859 is now home to the Vasarely Foundation, a modern museum about 4km (2$^1/_2$ miles) to the south-west of the town. This large structure — looking like a thrown collection of dices, each with one large spot, rather than up to six small ones,— is 'an intellectual and cultural tool'. This study and information centre also houses a large collection of the work of Victor Vasarely, the Hungarian-born geometric modernist.

𝝅 On the opposite side of the town is *Entremont*, the excavated remains of the capital of the Saluvians, the local tribe crushed by the Romans in 123BC. The foundations of ramparts, towers and houses are all that can be seen. There are fine views from the site, especially of the Montagne Ste Victoire, Cézanne's inspiration.

To the west of Aix — follow the D64 for about 12km (7$^1/_2$ miles) — the visitor will find a visit to the modern Aqueduc de Roquefavour interesting, if only to see how the work of 1842 compares to that of Pont du Gard. The more recent aqueduct is the larger of the two. Still on the D64, the visitor can continue to **Ventabren** where there is a

🏰 ruined castle that offers fine views of the Chaîne de Vitrolles and the Etang de Berre.

If the visitor goes to the east instead, he or she can round Montagne Ste Victoire. The D10 is the best starting route; follow it as it heads east. At St Marc-Jaumegarde a turning to the right leads to the Barrage de Bimont (Bimont Dam), a new construction, beautifully set in a wooded valley.

Further east, leave the car at the farm of Les Cabassols and follow GR9 to the Croix de Provence 945m (3,100ft). This is not an easy walk, the path rising about 550m (1,800 feet) and the climb taking between 2$^1/_2$ and 3 hours, but it is well-worthwhile. The walker passes the priory of Ste Victoire, which has fifth-century origins but is basically a restored seventeenth-century building, and reaches the top about 20 minutes later. The first cross on the summit was erected in the sixteenth century, but the present one — nearly 18m (60ft) high — is the third. The view from the top is superb, extending to Mont

Ventoux and the Maures. On clear days, the Dauphiné can also be seen.

From the cross, the walk can be extended to almost any day-size length. To walk the ridge here is to understand the inspiration that Cézanne sought. It is an irony that the mountain's name derives from a victory the Romans gained at its foot over an invading Teuton horde. The Roman historians claimed that the barbarians lost 100,000 killed, with a further 100,000 captured.

Having considered the inspiration of Cézanne, we go further east to **Vauvenargues**, to see the *château* on a spur of the hill where Picasso spent his last years. The artist is buried in the parkland here, but the site is not open to the public. Beyond Vauvenargues, the road continues east. At the first chance, turn right to Pourrières, and go west there on the D57 and so back to Aix.

The traveller on the A8 Autoroute or the N7 reaches **St Maximin-la-Ste Baume** very soon after leaving Aix, as it is only 38km (24 miles) by these direct routes. The basilica in the town is the best example of Gothic architecture in Provence. Built on a sixth-century church, the basilica was started in 1295 as a resting-place, according to pious legend, for the remains of St Mary Magdalene (and later St Maximin). The building was worked on intermittently until the sixteenth century, but no belfry was ever built, nor was the west front completed. Destined to be demolished during the French Revolution — when the town was renamed Marathon — good fortune found Napoleon's youngest brother Lucien (who called himself Brutus) turning the church into a storage depot. By having the *Marseillaise* played regularly on the very organ in use today, he saved both the building and its contents.

Inside the austere and finely proportioned basilica, the famous organ, built in 1773, can be seen. Wooden panels — twenty-two in number — painted by the Venetian François Ronzen in the sixteenth century, include the earliest known view of the Palace of the Popes at Avignon. Choirstalls, screen, gilded statues and pulpit are all carved to a high standard. Organ concerts of French music are given every summer on the church's instrument, while the adjacent former Royal Monastery is a cultural centre which holds concerts each July.

La Ste Baume, with which the church of St Maximin is associated, is a mountain 23km (14 miles) to the south-west. The most venerable of Provençal legends insists that St Mary Magdalene lived in solitary retreat in a cave on La Ste Baume for the last 30 years of her life,

Market in St Maximin-la-Ste Baume

Doorway of the Basilica, St Maximin-la-Ste Baume

having spent 13 years with the Virgin Mary after Christ's crucifixion. Mary Magdelene, St Maximin, the Virgin's sister and Mary, the mother of James and John, were cast adrift from the Holy Land in an open boat with various other saints and the black servant, Sarah. They landed at Les-Stes-Maries-de-la-Mer, where they parted and set about evangelising Provence. Maximin went to Aix to become its first bishop. Mary Magdalene made her way to La Ste Baume.

From the fifth century onwards, pilgrims streamed to the sacred place, until the Saracen invasions interrupted them. In the eleventh century, the monks of Vézelay in Burgundy claimed to have acquired the saint's relics and pilgrims went to Vézelay for five centuries. St Mary Magdalene's remains were then discovered in the little Merovingian church at St Maximin. The basilica was erected, and the pilgrims returned.

On Ste Baume, the cave (Grotte de St Pilon) can be reached on foot either from the one-time Hôtellerie (hostel) or the Carrefour des Chênes, both on the D80. Midnight Mass is celebrated on July 22. From the cave, a short but steep climb reaches the summit of St Pilon, named after a column, long since gone, erected to commemorate the saint. Today a small chapel marks the top. A further legend has St Mary Magdalene being brought to this spot seven times each day by angels because it was the best place to listen to the music of Paradise. The panorama from the top is impressive.

Nowhere is the contrast between the plant life of north and south slopes (in Provençal *hubacs* and *adrets* respectively) illustrated more clearly than in the Ste Baume range. South-facing slopes confront the full glare of heat and drought for which Mediterranean plants are adapted to survive. On the north slopes, which are shaded and moist, there is an extensive and remarkable forest. Beech, yew, maple, lime and privet — found hardly anywhere else in Provence — flourish in this grove once sacred to the Ligurians, and perhaps felled by Caesar as timber for his fleet. Royal decrees in the past and modern ideas on forest ecology have preserved the forest, a relic of distant times when the climate of Provence was more like Britain's.

Take the winding descent of the D2. On the left is Parc de St Pons whose trees, springs, waterfall, Romanesque chapel and ruined abbey offer a romantic parkland in which to roam. At **Gémenos**, which has a large eighteenth-century *château*, turn right and, in about 2km (1¼ miles), right again to come to the chapel of St Jean-de Garguier. Its interest lies in the collection of some 200 ex-voto paintings completed between 1500 and 1914. They are religious works, executed by anonymous local artists or artisans on behalf of people wishing to give thanks for divine interventions: for the safe delivery of a child, recovery from severe illness, or for any miraculous escape from death. Ex-voti hang in many a Provençal church, but those at St Jean-de-Garguier compress 400 years of gratitude for survival.

An attractive route running through the length of central Provence is the road between Aix and Draguignan. At first, the N96 northwards from Aix and then east as far as Peyrolles can be congested, but the D561 soon branches right and runs peacefully through open, wooded countryside. It links the widely differing villages of Jouques, Rians, Esparron, Varages and Tavernes to reach **Barjols.** This village has the largest plane tree in Provence, 12.5m (41ft) round its base, as well as a huge, moss-green fungal growth of a fountain that is nearly the largest in the region, and an enormous market-square.

This is truly a village of superlatives. Look out for the Hôtel de Pontevés which has a fine Renaissance doorway. Each year, in January, the people of the village celebrate the day of their patron saint, St Marcel (whose remains were brought to Barjols in the Middle Ages) by parading a bust of the saint through the streets, the bust being followed by an ox that is led to the slaughterhouse. The ox is roasted on the following day while the villagers dance and sing, and, on the third day, the ox is eaten. It seems that the celebration is only religious in part, the arrival of the saint's remains having corresponded with an existing festivity that celebrated an earlier escape from a siege.

A deviation south from Barjols, along the D554, goes through Châteauvert and then follows the D45 along the Vallon Sourn, a narrow valley enclosing the River Argens, before the landscape opens out again at Correns, a quiet village that is relatively untouched by tourism.

After Barjols comes **Cotignac**; this is a picturesque village with a distinguished hotel that makes a day or two spent here a pleasant experience. An 80m (262ft) high brown cliff of tufa rock, riddled with one-time rock-shelters, rears behind the village.

From Cotignac, a number of other charming villages, set in these wide valleys where evergreen oaks dominate the woodlands, repay a visit. These include perched Fox-Amphoux and walled **Sillans-la-**

Cascade. Here there is a waterfall which is reached by a short walk — no more than 1 hour for the return journey — which is signposted from the south side of the village. It is a fine waterfall, with the water cascading nearly 46m (150ft), but it is best to go in late spring, early summer or when there has been rain, because in long, dry summers the falls are reduced to a tap-like trickle. Also near Sillans are the Bresque Streams, one of which goes over the falls, where trout-fishermen meet. At nearby **Salernes**, where tiles are made, there are thirteenth-century castle ruins.

Entrecasteaux is complete with a large *château* and gardens, a fortified Gothic church, a humpback bridge and medieval streets. The *château*, a disproportionately long and plain seventeenth-century building, is open to the public. It houses a collection of furniture and knick-knacks from around the time of its building, the best of which is some porcelain.

On higher ground is **Villecroze** and, 5km (3 miles) away, there is a waterfall and a once-fortified cave whose petrified columns and fifteenth-century windows can still be seen. **Tourtour**, set at 633m (2,080ft), has restored, honey-coloured stone houses, smart hotels and two elm trees planted in 1638 to mark the birth of the future Sun King, Louis XIV. Today it is a fashionable holiday centre with uninterrupted views over the Maures Mountains.

To the north is **Aups**, its name deriving from the Celto-Ligurian *alb* (hill pasture). The village basks in a wide valley and is backed by sheltering hills, whose honey has a local reputation. There is a small but interesting museum of modern art here, set in an old Ursuline convent.

Lorgues, to the south-east, is a *bourg* with 4,500 inhabitants. Surrounded by vineyards and olive groves, its plane-filled square lends impressive dignity. A marble fountain, eighteenth-century church, and fourteenth-century fortified gateways all make a visit worthwhile. About 2km (1^1/$_4$ miles) west of Lorgues, along the narrow D50, is a remarkable little chapel. This is the simple sixteenth-century Notre Dame de Benva (Bon Voyage), partly built into the rock. From its façade an arch spans the narrow path — once the main highway — and contemporary murals are clearly visible on the inner faces of the arch: Virgin and Child, St Joseph, and St Christopher with the infant Jesus on his shoulder as he plunges a tree trunk into a stream. More murals can be found inside the chapel, but the door is almost invariably locked.

Brignoles, a centre of bauxite-mining, marble-quarrying and wine production, is the next big town and justifies a visit to the Museum of Local History to see what is thought to be the oldest of all Gaulish Christian sarcophogi. Dating from the second or third centuries, its carved messages are beautifully preserved. It was retrieved from the tiny chapel of La Gayole, 10km (6 miles) west, on the estate of the St Julien farm.

To the south-west of the town is Celle Abbey, built in the

The town mural, Barjols

thirteenth century as a convent. It always attracted the daughters of noblemen, but it was said that by the Middle Ages the sisters could only be told apart from the other women of the area by their nun's habit and the fact that their lovers were of the better classes. Not surprisingly, this eventually caused a scandal and the house was closed on the orders of the local bishop. Part of the old convent has now be taken over as a hotel, but other parts — including the cloisters and chapterhouse — can be visited. The old Abbey church can also be seen because it was taken over as the parish church.

South-west from the Abbey, the visitor should go to Montagne de la Loube. Continue on the D405 and take the narrow, marked road to the right. Drive as far as possible and then take the obvious track towards the mast. The climb — which will take about 1 hour to complete — becomes increasingly steep, finishing with a scramble up rocks to the summit. From here there is a good panorama over the

local forests and northward to the hills of Haute-Provence.

After Brignoles, continue south of the N7 by the D554 and D15 for 21km (13 miles) to reach yet another intriguing village, **Besse-sur-Issole**. Just outside is one of the few natural lakes in Provence. Besse was the birthplace of Provence's eighteenth-century Robin Hood, Gaspard de Besse. He spent a life of romanticised brigandage before he was caught and sentenced by the judges of Aix to be broken at the wheel. His execution was a social event attended by high-born ladies

Places of Interest In and Around St Maximin and Brignoles

St Maximin-la-Ste Baume
The Royal Monastery
A monastery that took nearly two centuries to complete. The cloister is excellent, a mixture of decorated stone and shrubs.

Grotte de St Pilon
An interesting cave nestling at the foot of a huge cliff.
A path close to the cave rises to the Col du St Pilon from where there is one of the best views in Provence extending from the mountains near Mont Ventoux to the coast at La Ciotat.

Aups
Simon Segal Museum
Collection of modern art in the chapel of an old Ursuline convent.

Entrecasteaux Château
Plain, seventeenth-century *château* with collections of furniture and porcelain.

Villecroze Caves
Not too spectacular show caves that were inhabited during the sixteenth century. The interest lies in the 'civilising' of the caves with windows and rooms.

Brignoles
Museum of Local History
Set in an old, partly twelfth-century, mansion owned by the Counts of Provence. Exhibits include the Le Gayole tombstone, from the second or third century, inscribed with Pagan/Christian iconography.

Celle Abbey
A thirteenth-century Benedictine Convent. The convent's Romanesque church is now the parish church. It contains a fifteenth-century crucifix.

Thoronet Abbey
A beautiful twelfth-century Cistercian Abbey comprising a fine Provençal Romanesque church, simple, dignified cloisters on the north side of the church, and an early Gothic chapter-house.

who wept at the untimely death of so romantic a young man.

The third, and finest, Cistercian monastery of the 'Three Sisters of Provence' is the secluded abbey of Le Thoronet, 16km (10 miles) from Cotignac along the road through Carcès. It is set, like all Cistercian houses, in a wild hollow to express the order's humility. The restored twelfth-century buildings are both austere and harmonious. These consist of a church, cloister, wash-house, dormitory and chapterhouse, where simple carvings representing local flora are the only adornment.

Draguignan, a town with more than 26,000 inhabitants, is not normally thought of as a tourist centre but as a place where the knowledgeable come to buy quality food at sensible prices, which almost seems recommendation enough. In fact, the town has considerable merits. There are modest but entirely adequate hotels and restaurants, it makes a good excursion centre, and the Old Town is agreeable.

The town was a Roman settlement called *Antea*, the present name apparently deriving from the fifth century when the Christian bishop of Antibes arrived to convert the locals. They lived in fear of a dragon who it is said lived locally and was making life a misery over a wide area. The bishop fearlessly tackled the dragon and killed it. In honour of this, not only did the locals become Christians but they also changed the name of the town. It is interesting that the town was named after the dragon and not Hermentarius, the dragon-slayer. The dragon is featured in the town's coat-of-arms.

The town's heart is traffic-free and dominated by a seventeenth-century Tour d'Horloge. The tower was built in the seventeenth century and can be climbed for a fine view over both the town and the Maures Mountains. Near the clocktower, the streets and squares have evocative names: Place du Marché with its fountain; Rue des Marchands; Place aux Herbes, with a medieval gateway; Rue des Tanneurs and the old Porte Aiguière; and Rue de la Juiverie, with the façade of a thirteenth-century synagogue.

The Bibliographic Museum at 9 Rue de la République is housed in a seventeenth-century Ursuline convent which was later used as a summer palace of the bishops of Fréjus. It contains Gallo-Roman finds, coins, paintings, busts and natural history specimens, as well as some remarkable manuscripts in the large library. One is a fourteenth-century illuminated manuscript of the *Romance of the Rose*. Close by, in Rue de la Motte, is a local craft museum with exhibits on both crafts and the traditions of the Draguignan area. Elsewhere, take a stroll among the six rows of plane trees that line the handsome Allées d'Azémar. The walk is flanked by gardens and mansions, and passes a bust of Georges Clemenceau who represented Draguignan in Parliament for 25 years.

To the east of Draguignan, on the D59, is an Allied Military Cemetery, where some of the men who were parachuted or landed

Fairy's Stone, near Draguinan

Draguignan

Fairground attractions at Draguignan

Typical French outdoor café in Draguignan

Places of Interest
In and Around Draguignan

Bibliographic Museum
Housed in a seventeenth-century Ursuline convent. Collections include porcelain and furniture and a Fine Art collection including work by Hals and Rembrandt. Library includes a fifteenth-century illustrated manuscript and other rare volumes.

Museum of Local Art and Traditions
Established in a fine old house, this museum explores the history and traditions of the local area.

Tour d'Horloge (Clock Tower)
Built in 1663. Excellent view from the top to the Maures Mountains and the Nartuby Valley.

Allied Military Cemetery
Resting place for 861 Allied soldiers killed during the campaign of 1944. The simple chapel has two large mosaics.

Malmont Viewpoint
A good viewpoint for the Esterel and Maures Hills.

Pierre de la Fée
(*The Fairy's Stone*)
Neolithic cromlech. Three dressed stones, each about 2m (6$^1/_2$ft) high, support a table stone, 6m x 4.5m (20ft x 15ft) and weighing 40 tons.

St Roseline's Chapel
All that remains of the twelfth-century abbey of Celle-Roubaud. Only chapel open, not cloisters. Good artwork, including Renaissance rood screen and contemporary work, including large mosaic by Chagall.

in gliders near the area on 15 August 1944, are buried.

Less sombre is St Roseline's chapel, reached by following the N555 south-eastward out of the town and then going right along the D91. The chapel is the only part of an old abbey that is open to the public, and contains the body of the saint in a remarkable state of preservation considering its age — around 650 years. Elsewhere, the chapel is noteworthy for its Renaissance rood screen and a very good Baroque altarpiece.

North of the town — leave along Boulevard Joseph-Collomp — is the peak of Le Malmont, reachable by car and famous for its panorama over the Maures and Esterel Ranges, the Argens Valley and towards Toulon. If, instead of going north, the visitor goes north-west, along the D955, he or she soon reaches the Pierre de la Fée, (the Fairy's Stone). This is a superb Neolithic cromlech — or dolmen, as they are known in France — with a huge table stone supported delicately on three stone fingers, each about 2m (6ft) long. It is easy to see why such objects had an aura of the supernatural to later folk unaware of their significance and builders.

Beyond the Stone, the visitor should continue on the D955 which goes through the Gorges de Châteaudouble. This is a fine, verdant gorge, but is only a prelude to the main event further north.

Europe cannot match Arizona's Grand Canyon, but the Verdon Gorges which borrow the name, Grand Canyon du Verdon, are nonetheless spectacular. Over countless years, the Verdon River, a tributary of the Durance, has cut into the limestone plateau over which it flowed. The production of such deep, clean cut gorges is not well-understood, as it requires a process that is at once both very rapid and very corrosive. The best explanation proposes that the erosion occurred at times of a general local uplifting or, alternatively, when the sea level was falling so that the river's pressure head was vastly increased. It is thought that this, together with the natural rifting of limestone, would allow very rapid cutting. Whatever the process, the result is clear, with the river now hemmed in by narrow cliffs which plunge 700m (2,300 feet) amid wild scenery. The Verdon gets its name from its green jade waters which add to the beauty.

There are interesting villages close to the Gorge. **Castellane**, at one end of the Gorge's finest section, is a a market-town as well as tourist centre and is dominated by a cube of rock 180m (590ft) high. It has good hotel accommodation and is close to the inter-connected artificial lakes of Chaudanne, Castillon and St André-les-Alpes. **Moustiers-Ste Marie** is set at the other end of the Gorge's Grand Canyon, and is famous for its pottery — reputedly introduced to the town by an Italian monk in medieval times, but refined over many centuries by French artists and craftsmen. The town has many shops showing modern Moustiers-ware but equally fascinating is the Musée de la Faïence (Pottery Museum) where the history and development of the local work is shown through numerous examples. Closer to the Gorge's western end (near Moustiers) is **Aiguines** where there is a small but very good craft museum.

It is, however, the Gorge which visitors come to see. Both the northern and southern edges can be followed. The Corniche Sublime (the D71) follows the south side, a road hewn from the rock in 1947. Going east from Aiguines, the Corniche enters the Grand Canyon at Illoire, soon reaching the Cirque de Vaumale, a hollowed-out section

The Verdon Gorge near Castellane

Castellane

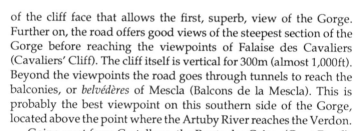

Places of Interest
In and Near the Verdon Gorge

Moustiers-Ste Marie
Musée de la Faïence
(Pottery Museum)
Showcases devoted to Moustiers master potters of the seventeenth and eighteenth centuries. Housed in the underground crypt of an old monastery, it also includes a collection of the tools of the trade.

Aiguines, Verdon Gorge
Craft Museum
Small but very good craft museum.

Best Viewpoints on the South Side of Gorge
Cirque de Vaumale

Falaise des Cavaliers

Balcons de la Mescla. Not to be missed.

Best Viewpoints on the North Side of the Gorge
Point Sublime. Not to be missed.

Trescaïre Belvédère

L'Escalès Belvédère. Not to be missed.

Tilleul Belvédère

Les Glacières Belvédère

L'Imbut Belvédère

Mayreste Belvédère

of the cliff face that allows the first, superb, view of the Gorge. Further on, the road offers good views of the steepest section of the Gorge before reaching the viewpoints of Falaise des Cavaliers (Cavaliers' Cliff). The cliff itself is vertical for 300m (almost 1,000ft). Beyond the viewpoints the road goes through tunnels to reach the balconies, or *belvédères* of Mescla (Balcons de la Mescla). This is probably the best viewpoint on this southern side of the Gorge, located above the point where the Artuby River reaches the Verdon.

Going west from Castellane, the Route des Crêtes (Crest Road), built in 1973, starts by offering a short walk to one of the finest viewpoints of the Gorge, the Point Sublime. Leave your car at the car park by the roadside inn and take the marked path for a walk of about 10 minutes to a stupendous view straight down to the point where the Baou River meets the Verdon. The Gorge here is 'only' 200m (650ft) deep. Back on the road, a succession of engineered viewpoints (*belvédères*) are passed, starting with Trescaïre and then reaching L'Escalès, by common consent the finest of all. From the viewpoint,

Moustiers-Ste Marie

the visitor is looking straight down the full height of the gorge to the footpath. If you are lucky, and have a head for heights, there will be a few ant-like people on the path to give scale to your view. After L'Escalès, there are fine viewpoints at Tilleul, Les Glacières, L'Imbut and Mayreste before the road exits the Gorge for Moustiers.

The Verdon Gorge was first explored by E. A. Martel, a founder of speleology in France in 1905, and a path through the Grand Canyon has been named in his honour, the Sentier Martel. This route links the Chalet de la Maline to Point Sublime, the walk taking a full, and hard, day. Walkers must be well-equipped. Boots with good ankle support are essential as there is a risk of a turned ankle on the uneven ground. Warm and waterproof clothing are also essential as there is no escape once the route has been started. Food must be carried, because there are no shops; the same applies for water, especially in summer when the Gorge is a sun trap and the river is too dangerous to attempt to reach. Head torches must be carried, the route uses tunnels through the rock in several places.

A good guide and a map — these are available from *Fédération Française de Randonnée Pédestre* and IGN (*Institut Geographique Na-*

Lac de Ste Croix, Verdon

tional) respectively — must be carried as some of the tunnels are not to be entered and it is important to know which ones. Finally, you **must** keep to the marked path, the river is part of a dam system and the opening of sluice gates upstream can cause very sudden rises in river level. If you are in an awkward position when this happens, it could be very unpleasant indeed, even fatal. However, do not be put off by all these precautions. The walk is straightforward enough for the experienced walker and offers a truly unforgettable experience.

Once you have walked the Gorge, you will want to get back to your starting point. There are no buses, so call a taxi on 92.744450 or 92.836538 from either the inn at Point Sublime or the chalet at Maline; the service is reliable.

5
WESTERN RIVIERA: MARSEILLE TO FREJUS

The French Riviera, the most renowned of all coasts, is the subject of this and the next chapter. Visions of sea and beaches spring to mind, so a few general comments about both will take brief precedence over discussions about town and countryside.

Cliffs, rocks, inlets, small bays, ribbons of sand, pebble beaches; all these help make up the coast's profile. There is no need to detail the facilities offered by each resort. On many public beaches there are areas (*plages aménagés*) where concessionnaires provide refreshments, hire beach equipment (sunshades, sunbeds, etc), sail-boards and pedalos, and where there may also be swimming and windsurfing instructors. Larger resorts have many ancillary recreational facilities, such as yachting and waterskiing, while there are subaqua and marine archaeological clubs for specialists.

A nearly landlocked sea produces an inter-tidal zone that can be measured in centimetres. The width of beach varies imperceptibly. Intense evaporation creates high salinity and a buoyancy for swimmers and physically handicapped people alike. The famous intense Mediterranean blue, which is a delight to the eye, indicates a low level of planktonic life. Pressure in this particularly deep sea creates a constant annual temperature of 13°C (55°F) and gives a thermostatic effect; the coast is warmed in winter and cooled in summer. As the following figures show, inshore water is slow to cool in autumn. However, the statistics are a little deceptive. The *mistral* can play havoc with surface temperatures, especially between Marseille and St Tropez. It may not blow for long in summer but the water is made chill and rough, particularly along west-facing beaches. As the water calms, the sun's heat quickly raises the water temperature about 3°C to make the difference between brave and comfortable swimming.

Average Sea Temperatures in °C and °F

	Marseille - Toulon		Toulon - Menton	
	°C	°F	°C	°F
May	15	59	16	61
Jun	20	68	19	66
Jul	19	66	21	70
Aug	21	70	23	73
Sep	17	63	23	73
Oct	18	64	19	66

For most of the year, French time is 1 hour ahead of British time. As sunset is earlier in the south, and the dusk is brief, the extra hour is an evening bonus in early summer and autumn.

Marseille is the major port of the Mediterranean—the oldest and second largest city in France. It is an expanding commercial, industrial and university city. Volatile, energetic, raw-humoured, chaotic at rush-hours; its Levantine origins seem never to be far from the surface. Its endearing character was affectionately portrayed by the popular and ebullient actor Fernandel (1903-71). Marseille is certainly stimulating, unless you are driving, when stimulating is a word far removed from the mind. A car is only an encumbrance; use the city and suburban buses, trolley-buses, taxis or the underground (*Métro*) service.

There is no shortage of hotels: impersonal, international hotels, a few elegant converted residences or adequate modest places, either in the centre of the city or along the Corniche Président Kennedy. There is an equally wide range of restaurants; some have a Michelin rosette. Many will offer that distinctive Provençal dish, *bouillabaisse*, for which everybody claims to have the only authentic recipe. As a general rule; if it is genuine, it must be expensive.

La Canebière, from *chènevière* (hempfield) was originally the rope-makers' street, and is now the boulevard of departure and return for the visitor. It is *the* place to go, for shops, cafés and bars.

Marseille is a big enough city to have a book all to itself, so this will necessarily be a brief introduction, with an attempt to point out the things that are worth seeing in the town, both in a cultural and a more general sense.

Places of Interest in Marseille

La Vieille-Charité
Seventeenth-century hospice by the architect Pierre Puget who was also responsible for the fine chapel.

Cantini Museum
Renowned for its collection of local pottery. The museum, housed in a seventeenth-century house, also has frequent temporary exhibitions.

Fine Arts Museum
Housed in a Baroque palace. The galleries include work from the sixteenth and seventeenth centuries, and a collection of work by Pierre Puget, the local artist and architect.

History of Marseille Museum
A recent addition to the museums of Marseille, this museum includes part of the remains of the old Roman town — in the Jardin des Vestiges — and items from the excavations. There are also items from other sites.

Museum of Old Marseille
Housed in an interesting sixteenth-century house and including a collection of prints of Old Marseille. Also an exhibition by a local firm of playing-card makers of the techniques of their trade.

Museum of Natural History
Good collection of zoological and geological specimens. Especially good are the section on Provençal wildlife and plants and the fine aquarium.

Gallery of Transport
A history of transport — chiefly within the city — using old photographs, drawings and postcards.

Borély Museum
The museum concentrates on the archaeology of the Mediterranean with Etruscan, Greek, Egyptian (especially good) and Roman exhibits. There is also a good collection of paintings including work by Tiepolo and Titian.

Maritime Museum
Housed in the old Stock Exchange, this museum extends the history of the port through to more modern developments and also looks at Marseille as a trading centre.

Museum of Popular Traditions
Items on local folk history and an exhibition (hopefully permanent) of Marseille during the Revolution.

Grobet-Labadié Museum
The house of the musician Louis Grobet, restored to the way it was in his lifetime but now including collections of paintings, porcelain and musical instruments.

Roman Docks Museum
Museum devoted to the history of the port of Marseille from Roman through to medieval times.

Loubière Caves
A fine set of show caves with beautiful formations and colours.

Château d'If
The fortress was built in the sixteenth century and is famous as the setting (in part) for *The Count of Monte Cristo* by Alexander Dumas. The island and fort are interesting, but the trip is particularly worthwhile for the view the island offers of Marseille.

There are several very fine parks within the city, the best of which is, perhaps, Pharo Park, to the west of the Old Port, on its southern edge.

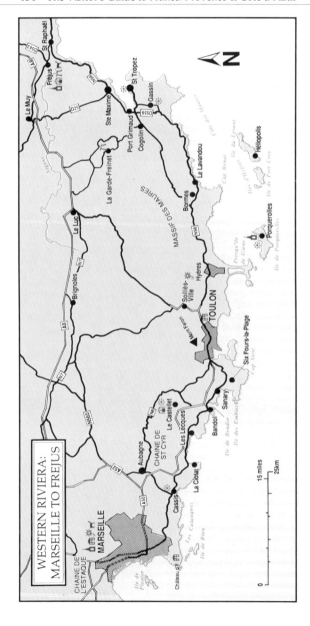

Marseille

Marseille harbour

The city was founded here, on the eastern edge of the Rhône Delta by Greek settlers in the seventh century BC, and was called *Massalia*. It was primarily a trading port, with trade both along the coast and inland with the Ligurians. The coming of the Romans, whose first settlement was at Aix, just inland from Marseille, had little immediate effect on the city. However, the feud between Julius Caesar and Pompey was critical because the town chose the wrong side — that of Pompey. It was captured and had its defences destroyed. For some time after that, the town played a supporting role to the Roman town of Arles.

With the departure of the Romans, the town was passed from one ruler to another as the power pendulum swung in the south of France, a swing that reached its low point in the tenth century when it was destroyed by the Saracens. After being rebuilt, it was at first a free city, then under the rule of the House of Anjou, until 1481 when it was finally made part of France. Its importance as a harbour grew quickly in the early Middle Ages when it was the chief port of embarkation for the Crusades. Much of the defensive work that can be seen today, particularly in the area of the Old Port, and including Château d'If, dates from this period.

At the time of the Revolution, the city had its own 'reign of terror' with the guillotine, installed on La Canebière, working long and bloody hours. Since that time, both the port and the city have expanded, with Marseille playing a leading role in the economic life of France.

A trip around the cultural high spots of Marseille is not easily accomplished as the town, unlike many capitals — Paris, to name the prime example — does not have a compact, harmonious centre. We will start, however, near the heart of the old town, at the archaeological site near the Centre Bourse, not far from the Old Port. There, in addition to a pleasant garden, which is actually situated above an underground car park that is very handy for the visitor, you will find the remains of the ramparts of Old Marseille. Nearby are the History of Marseille Museum, which includes the best finds from the town, and the Maritime Museum, housed in the old *Bourse* (Stock Exchange), which traces the history of Marseille as a port and town from the late Middle Ages to the present day.

Those interested in the port's earlier history should follow the northern edge of the Old Port to the Roman Docks Museum where there is an interesting collection of ancient maritime items. Next to the museum is another, that of Old Marseille. This is housed in a fine sixteenth-century house known as Maison Diamentée because of the stones used to build it. The museum behind the jewelled walls concentrates on Provençal life of the eighteenth and nineteenth centuries, with collections of furniture and kitchen ware, together with some interesting prints of Old Marseille. There is also a fascinating collection on the history and manufacture of playing cards donated by a local company.

To the north-west of this clutch of museums are the old and new cathedrals. The old cathedral, almost destroyed in the last century but now partially restored, is believed to be one of the most beautiful examples of Romanesque architecture in Provence and dates from the twelfth century. By contrast, the new cathedral is as recent as the late nineteenth century, and was the largest cathedral built in France for several centuries. It was built in a style that can be most accurately described as eclectic and looks best when viewed from a boat entering the Old Port. Close to the cathedrals is a fine old hospice from the seventeenth century.

North-east from the centre is Palais Longchamp, a Baroque mansion which has two wings linked by a semi-circular colonnade that faces a superb fountain. The Palais houses the Fine Arts Museum, which has some interesting paintings, including a collection of the work of the artist Pierre Puget, a seventeenth-century Marseille painter and sculptor. Also here is the Natural History Museum which is worth a visit for the items on the wildlife of Provence. Close to the Palais is the Grobet-Labadié Museum, one of the city's foremost, housing a collection of French tapestries and porcelain together with musical instruments from the collection of the musician Louis Grobet. Also close by is a museum of popular tradition whose exhibits include items on Marseille during the Revolution.

If, instead of going west and north, an easterly direction is taken, it leads to the Transport Museum, where there are old photographs of Marseille before the invasion of the car. The Cantini Museum has one of the finest collections of the pottery of Marseille and Moustiers in France. There is also a very good collection of the work of contemporary artists, including Balthus, Bacon and Adami.

To the south, in Borely Park, there is a good museum of the Mediterranean with items from Egypt and and Greece, as well as Roman exhibits and items from the history of the area. There is also a collection of drawings from the eighteenth century, including the

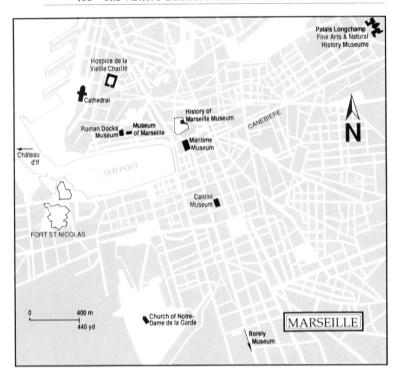

work of Watteau, and some excellent paintings, with work by Titian, Tiepolo and Bruegel.

Going west now, the visitor can reach the basilica of Notre-Dame-de-la-Garde, the Byzantine church that rises like an extended finger from on top of a high rock. The rock is over 150m (500ft) high, the tower of Notre-Dame adding another 46m (150ft) to that height. Inside, the multicoloured marble is particularly impressive. From the basilica, the famous Corniche Président J.F. Kennedy follows the coast southward offering glorious seaward views to Château d'If, and a close up view of Le Corbusier's famed Tower Block, the first example of the design which is now out of favour.

Despite these explorations, it is to the Old Port that the visitor is drawn. Its southern side passes fine old buildings and one of the offices of the Foreign Legion to reach Fort St Nicolas and, beyond, Pharo Park with its *château* and impressive views. The island that

Old Port, Marseille

dominates the seaward view can be reached by a regular boat service from the Old Port, and is worth the journey for its links with *The Count of Monte Cristo* as well as its view of the city.

For the visitor who would like to see the town in action, the Old Port is still the best place, with its ad hoc stalls, roadside bars and cafés. However, nobody should miss La Canebière. The most exclusive shopping areas are Rue de Rome and Rue St Férréol, while the covered shopping area of the Centre Bourse is very attractive for the visitor, concentrating much of general interest into one place. For the most picturesque quarter, go to Le Panier, which lies between Place de Lenche, the cathedrals and Rue de la République.

On the road from Marseille to Cassis, stop at **Col de la Gineste**. Inland is a view of the denuded white limestone Chaîne de St Cyr. Seawards is the inlet of Cassis and, beyond this, the towering Cap Canaille, the highest cliff in France at 399m (1,310ft). Sometimes, on a September evening, the panorama is suffused with intense purple light.

Cassis is a cheerful, busy little port, visited in numbers by the Marseillais. It has a recent casino and holds regattas and watersports events in summer. There is also a small museum of local history. Deep, fjord-like inlets of sheer limestone to the west of Cassis — the Calanques of Port-Miou, Port-Pin and En-Vau — are best seen at close hand by boat excursion from Quai St Pierre. Port-Miou is also accessible by car, a well-marked path leads from the car park. The Calanques are a test of the rock-climber's skill, as a visit on any weekend will show.

Inland from Cassis is **Aubagne** which has a museum that is a must for anyone with even a passing interest in that most romantic of organisations, the French Foreign Legion. The Legion, founded in 1831, was originally housed in Algeria but it moved here in 1962 when the African colony gained its independence. The history of the Legion is explained in a museum near the HQ. Although it is well-known that there was little glamour in the Legion, the legend of men who joined to escape or to forget a lost love is too strong to resist.

Eastwards from Cassis, the Corniche des Crêtes goes over the Pas de la Colle and Cap Canaille (a fine viewpoint) and on to the naval dockyard of La Ciotat. Beyond is **Les Lecques,** whose good, sandy beach makes it popular. At La Madrague is the Tauroentum Museum with Gallo-Roman mosaics and relics, built on the foundations of a Roman villa near the sea.

Bandol, one of the more sophisticated coastal resorts, has bars and discos, as well as a Jardin Exotique et Parc Zoologique, on the way to Sanary-sur-Mer. Pleasant grounds laid out with exotic trees give shelter to a variety of small animals and birds. It also has a superb Romanesque chapel to Notre Dame-du-Bausset-Vieux which contains some fine paintings. The whole hinterland here is attractive for touring. It is worth visiting the villages of La **Cadière-d'Azur** and **Le Castellet**. Just off the N8, the Grand Prix enthusiast will find the Paul Ricard motor racing circuit.

Offshore is Ile de Bendor, to which motor-boats ply frequently from Bandol. Not many years ago it was an empty rock but now there is an imitation Provençal fishing port and an artisanal village. There is an art gallery, an open-air theatre and the remarkable World Museum of Wines and Spirits with more than 7,000 bottles, as well as a nautical club, hotels and restaurants. All of these attract many visitors.

Another island that is only a short distance offshore is the Ile des Embiez which has become well-known through the marine research work conducted there by the biologist Alain Bombard and is funded

Main Sandy Beaches Between Marseille and Fréjus

La Ciotat-Plage — 3km (2 miles) north-east of La Ciotat in a curving bay.

Les Lecques — over 1km ($^1/_2$ mile) long in bay between Les Lecques and La Madrague.

Hyères-Plage — 6km (4 miles) south of Hyères, sheltered, shallow, warm, backed by umbrella pines.

La Capte — 9km ($5^1/_2$ miles) south of Hyères on Gien Peninsula, 3km (2 miles) long, backed by pines.

Le Pellegrin and L'Estagnol — 7 and 8km ($4^1/_2$ and 5 miles) south-east of La Londe-les-Maures in Bay of Hyères. Almost unspoiled, shallow, safe; private, admission charges.

Cabasson — curved bay, shallow.

Le Lavandou - 2km ($1^1/_4$ miles) long, car parking on promenade.

St Clair — east-facing bay, car parking on promenade.

Cavalière — sheltered, backed by pines. One of finest beaches of Maures coast.

Pramousquier and Canadel-sur-Mer — small but safe, sheltered.

Cavalaire — 3km (2 miles) of safe sands north of resort.

Gigaro — 5km (3 miles) south-east of La Croix-Valmer; secluded.

St Tropez — 6km (4 miles) unbroken sands between Plage de Tahiti and south end of Plage de Pampelonne. Some private, a few public.

Ste Maxime — 2km ($1^1/_4$ miles) safe, south-facing sands; shady promenade.

St Aygulf — long, gently shelving; pine forest.

Fréjus-Plage — 1.5km (1 mile) south of Fréjus, extensive, almost joined to St Raphaël.

by Paul Ricard's Fondation Océanographique. As well as an aquarium and museum, the island has a marina, shipyards and hotel.

From Sanary-sur-Mer there is a fine trip inland, following the D11 to Ollioules and then going north, still on the D11 at first, but joining the N8, through the twisting Gorge of Ollioules to reach Ste Anne-d'Evenos. There, go right and follow a narrow road to reach the viewpoint of Mont-Caume where a brisk walk up the final few metres reaches a splendid panoramic view both inland and out to sea. On your return, go right on the D20 after leaving Ollioules to reach the Gros Cerveau, a fine piece of cultivated hillside that also offers extensive views from its high point.

Back in Sanary-sur-Mer, the coast road to Le Brusc can now be taken and beyond here make for Notre Dame du Mai, an early seventeenth-century pilgrimage chapel. This is built on the high point of Cap Sicié and commands extensive views over the Calanques and the islands off Hyères. To the east, reached via the elegantly named Six-Fours-les-Plages, is Toulon.

Like Marseille, the great naval base of **Toulon** is not usually visualised as a holiday centre. However, it holds things of interest in addition to its dramatic setting at the foot of Mont Faron and Mont Caume, both of which are surmounted by forts. In Roman times, local shells were boiled to produce the dye for Imperial purple, though the town is more famous for having been taken from the British in 1793, chiefly as a result of the bravery of a young Corsican officer in the French army; the officer was Napoleon Bonaparte. Equally famous in the annals of warfare is the scuttling of the French fleet in the harbour in 1942.

Make a point of seeing the Naval Museum. Two powerful caryatids, Force and Fatigue, stand at the entrance, the work of Pierre Puget in 1656, master sculptor at Toulon dockyard during the reign of Louis XIV. Many of Puget's drawings of ships are in the museum.

The Fine Arts Museum has Gallo-Roman and oriental exhibits and worthwhile paintings by Provençal artists such as Guigou, Monticelli, Engalière and Van Loo, as well as more modern works by Vlaminck and others. There is also a small natural history museum with a good collection on local geology and wildlife. The Museum of Old Toulon is chiefly devoted to memorabilia of Napoleon but also includes some paintings and drawings, as well as a small collection of arms.

Part of the Old Town which miraculously escaped the Allied bombing of the port is a pedestrian zone of considerable charm. The visitor with little time to spare should make a point of seeing the cathedral and Quai Stalingrad with its shops and cafés.

In July and August the town holds a circus performers' festival, while a covered fish market in Rue Seillon and a vegetable and flower market offer lively entertainment each morning.

From Quai Stalingrad, motorboat trips go round the inner roadstead (Petite Rade) on a trip that includes the arsenal and dry docks. Les Sablettes, St Mandrier and the Iles d'Hyères make short boat

The Opera House, Toulon

excursions while Corsica can be visited between June and September.

The inner roadstead is a good tour on dry land too, visiting Fort Balaguier. This was built in the sixteenth century to protect the

Places of Interest
Between Marseille and Toulon

Cassis
Municipal Museum
Small museum with items on local history and a collection of old town documents.

Aubagne
Foreign Legion Building
The history of the French Foreign Legion, with photographs, arms, uniforms and other memorabilia.

Les Lecques
Tauroentum Museum
The museum is built on the foundations of a Roman villa and displays items from the site, including a first-century mosaic.

Sanary-Bandol
Jardin Exotique et Parc Zoologique
Tropical gardens and zoo of birds and small mammals.

Chapel of Notre Dame-du-Bausset-Vieux
Bandol
Superb Provençal Romanesque chapel with some good paintings.

World Museum of Wines and Spirits
Bendor Island, near Bandol
More than 7,000 bottles illustrating the wines and spirits of fifty countries.

Fondation Océonographique Ricard
Ile des Embiez
An old naval gun battery converted into a marine museum. There are sea water aquaria and a museum of mounted molluscs and fish.
The site has an excellent view.

Boat Trips along the Calanques
Excursions from Quai St Pierre.

harbour on its western side, and now contains some items from the Naval Museum. The eastern side of the harbour was protected by the Royal Tower which can also be visited. It is 'royal' because it was constructed by Louis XII, at the same time as Fort Balaguier, and certainly deserves its alternative name of Great Tower, the walls being more than 6m (20ft) thick.

North of the town, the visitor can use a cable car to reach Mont Faron where there are marvellous views along the coast, a small zoo and the national memorial to the Allied Landings of 1944. The memorial, built around an old fort, is a fine one, impressive yet dignified, the small site museum uses audio-visual techniques to bring the Landings to life.

Places of Interest In and Near Toulon

Museum of Old Toulon
A varied collection of items, including material on Napoleon and local history, as well as old arms, paintings and a number of drawings.

Naval Museum
Housed in an impressive building, appropriately close to the harbour, the museum includes busts and paintings of important figures in French naval history, together with a superb collection of model ships.

Fine Arts Museum
Items from Egypt and Greece as well as the area's Roman past, together with a good collection of paintings including the work of David and Vuillard
Building shared with the Natural History Museum.

Natural History Museum
Good collection of local geological specimens, together with exhibition of local wildlife.

Fort Balaguier
Built at the same time as the Royal Tower on the other side of the bay. Famous for having been captured from the English by Napoleon. The fort has a good collection of model ships and some Napoleonic memorabilia.

Royal Tower
The tower, also known as the Great Tower, was built by Louis XII in the sixteenth century to protect Toulon. The tower walls are over 6m (20ft) thick. The tower houses some material from the Naval Museum.

Boat trips in Toulon harbour

Allied Landings Memorial
Mont Faron
A memorial and museum to the Allied Landings of 15 August 1944, housed in the old Beaumont Tower. Very evocative exhibits. The site's view of Toulon and the coast is magnificent.

Zoo
Mont Faron
Large collection of animals including many of the big cats.

Olive Oil Mill Museum (Costumes)
Solliès-Ville
Not of olive oil, but housed in an old olive oil mill, this museum has a collection of traditional Provençal costumes.

To the north-east lies **Solliès-Ville** where the old oil mill has been converted into a Provençal museum, worth the time of anyone interested in costume as there is a good collection of the traditional local clothing.

To the east of Toulon, about 20km (12$^1/_2$ miles) by way of the coast road, lies **Hyères**, the oldest resort on the Riviera. First admired in the sixteenth century by Catherine de Medici, who thought of building a royal villa at Hyères, and patronised three centuries later by Queen Victoria and Robert Louis Stevenson, its exposed position in winter made it fall out of favour. It lies between the limestone ranges to the west and the Maures Mountains to the east.

It is worth strolling about the Old Town, which is huddled round the hilltop castle ruins. A medieval flavour hangs about the streets, particularly Rue Paradis and Place Massillon where markets are held on weekdays. Broad avenues lined with palms give the new town a sub-tropical look. The Town Museum is interesting for its items from the original Greek settlement of *Olbia*. Some Saracen pottery has also been found at the site, and the lighthouse that stands there today is called L'Almanarre, which is descended from the Arab *Al Manar* (a lighthouse).

The town is also worth visiting for its gardens, especially St Bernard Park which has many tropical plants and the Olbius-Riquier Gardens which also has a large collection of tropical plants and cacti.

The beaches are further south, close to the neck of a 7km (4$^1/_2$ miles) long peninsula, the Presqu'île de Giens, on whose west side are the Presquier saltmarshes and a lagoon where flamingoes are frequently seen. At the peninsula's tip is Tour Fondue from which boats take 15 minutes to reach the island of **Porquerolles**. Porquerolles (*Prote* or 'first' to the Greeks) is the largest of the group of islands known as the Iles d'Hyères or, more romantically, Les Iles d'Or (the Golden Isles). From the miniscule port of Porquerolles — where bicycles can be hired — paths go in various directions through lush vegetation and vineyards. The cyclist or walker can visit the lighthouse and old fort.

Port Cros can be reached in about 90 minutes by motorboats from Port de la Plage d'Hyères. It is called *Mese* or 'middle' by the Greeks, and is more rugged than Porquerolles. The whole of the tranquil, hilly island is a nature reserve which includes the sea fringe. Botanical rambles and underwater viewing tours of the marine life are escorted by guides, and useful booklets explaining the island's natural history can be bought.

The third island, **Ile du Levant**, is reached from Le Lavandou and Cavalaire. Most of it is occupied by the French Navy, only the western tip and the naturist village of Héliopolis can be visited.

East of Hyères is the Côte des Maures, the 'new' Riviera, which

Sunset over Presqu'île de Giens

Flamingoes at Presqu'île de Giens

Places of Interest In and Near Hyères

Hyères

Town Museum
Small museum of Greek and Roman items from the site of *Olbia* (Old Hyères). Also collections of fossils, minerals and birds. Some Louis XVI furniture and a gallery of local artists' work.

St Bernard Park
Excellent flower park around a ruined castle on the high side of the town. Superb views.

The Olbius-Riquier Acclimatisation Gardens
Extensive gardens with many tropical plants, including palms and cacti.

Ile de Porquerolles

Lighthouse
Panoramic view over Iles d'Hyères.

Fort St Agathe
Small exhibition on history of islands, in sixteenth-century fort with huge, round tower.

was discovered as a summer pleasure-ground in the inter-war years. Backing the coast is the Massif des Maures (from the Greek *amauros* and Provençal *maouro*, both meaning sombre, a reference to the dark colour of the pine trees). Stretching some 60km (37 miles) between Hyères and Fréjus, the Maures are rounded by erosion and thickly forested with pines (these are prone to forest fires), cork-oaks and Spanish chestnuts. The crystalline rock contains mica-schist which glints like gold in the sun.

A very good round trip is to take the coast road to St Tropez, and to return over the hills. Just after the coast road has left the Maures, is **Bormes-les-Mimosas**, a beautiful village exquisitely situated, and with a fine collection of the work of a local artist in its small museum. Thereafter, the road reaches Le Lavandou before passing through a string of small resorts, each with its individual character: St Clair, La Fossette, Aiguebelle, Cavalière, Pramousquier, Canadel, Le Rayol and Cavalaire. From here, crossing the promontory of Ramatuelle leads to **St Tropez**. Sandy beaches and coves predominate; the Allied armies landed on these beaches in 1944 to begin the liberation of Provence.

Once the yachts, aspirants to stardom or notoriety, naturists and the crowds who want to share in the dream-world have left, St Tropez reveals itself to be as endearingly attractive as it was when

Matisse painted it long ago. Derain, Braque, Marquet, Bonnard, Dufy and a host of other artists fell under the spell of the white light and immortalised St Tropez in paint, as did Colette in literature.

The work of some of these turn-of-the century masters is housed in the Annunciation Museum in Place Georges Grammont, named after the benefactor. Not only is the exhibition a delight, the building is also pleasing to look at. The other museum in the town is the Maritime Museum in the Citadel; among many other exhibits, there are engravings of Old St Tropez.

Two venerable processions take place every year in St Tropez. They are the *bravades* (literally translated: 'bravados'). One takes place between 16 and 18 May. The gilded bust of St Torpes is carried round the town by a corps of a hundred *bravadeurs* dressed in eighteenth-century costume; they make a prodigious noise with muskets, blank cartridges and music. Bystanders join in the fun and, on the last day, the procession makes its way to the pretty sixteenth-century chapel of Ste Anne, on a rock just south of the town. The ritual celebrates the arrival of the martyred Christian centurion of Pisa's body in an open boat. The second *bravade* is on 15 June. The Fête des Espagnols honours the putting to flight of the Spanish fleet by valiant Tropéziens in 1637 during the Thirty Years' War.

On the quay is the statue of the Bailli de Suffren (1729-88), the admiral who, with only five ships under his command, harrassed the English fleets from the West Indies to the Indian Ocean. Château Suffren, the family home, is in the Old Town, near the town hall. In summer, frequent motorboat excursions can be taken round the Gulf of St Tropez and further afield.

After St Tropez, it would be a pity not to see **Port Grimaud**. You must leave the car at the entrance to the village, for Port Grimaud can be visited only on foot or by boat. It is an elegant, modern holiday village built out into the Gulf of St Tropez, and designed with the yachting community in mind; each front door has its own mooring. In imitation of Provençal fishing villages it has harmonious colours and graceful bridges over canals from one walkway to another. Shops, banks, cafés, church and post-office are grouped around a square which is decked with flowers. Self-drive boats can be hired to tour the canals, and there are sightseeing cruises.

A tour of the Maures begins at **Cogolin** where there is a museum of the local carpet and fabric industry, housed in a factory where hand-weaving is still carried out and can be seen. North of Cogolin

Bormes-les-Mimosas bathed in sunshine

Port Vendour, St Tropez

Moorings, St Tropez

is **La Garde-Freinet,** where there are the interesting remains of a sixteenth-century castle reputedly built on the foundations of a Saracen fortress. North again — and technically out of the Maures — is **Le Luc**, where the historian will find much of interest in a museum in the old chapel of St Anne, while the philatelist will be well-rewarded by a visit to the Stamp Museum.

Back in the Maures proper, it is best to follow the narrow road from La Garde Freinet to the Col du Fourche. GR9 comes this way too, and at several of the high points it is worth leaving the car and following the waymarked trail for a short distance to savour the seclusion of the forest and the occasional surprising viewpoint. After crossing the Col, the road drops down to Collobrières, a centre for the making of *marrons glacés*. From here, there is a road which can only be found by using a local map; any attempt at directions is almost bound to fail. It leads towards the Verne charterhouse, all that remains of a Carthusian monastery, beautifully situated in the middle of the Maures Forest.

South from Collobrières, the road goes to Bormes, passing some excellent viewpoints. Just before Bormes is reached, a left turn onto the N98 allows a drive through the Môle Valley, a mixture of forests and vines. Towards the valley's eastern end, take the D27 over the Col du Canadel, another fine viewpoint, and follow it as it winds back through the forest to Bormes.

Back on the coast, the next town is **Ste Maxime**; a lively resort which is sheltered, unlike St Tropez across the bay, from the *mistral*. Fine beaches — especially at La Nartelle — entertainment at night, a 9-hole golf course at Beauvallon, and plenty of hotels and restaurants (some of which remain open in winter), make it very popular. The town has a small local history museum and an extraordinary museum of mechanical music with a collection of old gramophones, musical boxes and barrel organs. From Ste Maxime, the D25 leads inland towards Le Muy and Draguignan. Side roads, especially those between Col de Gratteloup on the D25, Plan-de-la-Tour on the D44 and Vidauban on N7, provide quiet round trips among the lower Maures Hills.

The N98, continues to follow the coast. **Cap des Sardinaux** is yet another stopping-place for exhilarating views. Tiny resorts are hidden among trees: Val d'Esquières, San Peire-sur-Mer, Les Issambres, and **St Aygulf**, widely known for its excellent camping facilities and separated from Fréjus-Plage by the mouth of the River Argens. A

Places of Interest
Near the Maures Mountains

Bormes-les-Mimosas
Museum of Art and History
A history of the town and area, together with an exhibition of the work of Jean-Charles Cazin, a local artist.

St Tropez
Annunciation Museum
The art collection of Georges Grammont, donated to the town, is housed in the former chapel of the Annunciation. It includes many fine pieces, both painting and sculpture, including work by Seurat, Utrillo and Matisse.

Maritime Museum
Interesting colection of naval memorabilia.

Cogolin
Museum of Carpets and Fabrics
Workshops where pure wool carpets and furnishing fabrics are woven by hand.

La Garde-Freinet
The Saracen's Fortress
Remains of a sixteenth-century castle, though the first castle on the site is attributed to the Saracens, who held the area in the ninth-century.

Le Luc
History Museum
Housed in seventeenth-century chapel of St Anne. Includes the history of the local area, with fossils, minerals, prehistoric and Bronze Age items, as well as medieval sculptures and paintings.

Museum of Stamps
On the second floor of the eighteenth-century Château des Vintimille. A museum of stamps, and a recreation of the studio of the gravurist Albert Ducaris.

Verne Charterhouse
Partially restored Carthusian monastery chapterhouse, dating originally from the twelfth-century. Beautifully situated, deep in Maures Forest. Difficult to reach but very worthwhile.

tour of the Argens Valley is well-worthwhile. It takes in **Roque-brune-sur-Argens** with its picturesque, arcaded houses and a walk to the chapel of Notre-Dame-de-Roquette, well-set among trees and offering fine views over the valley.

Fréjus-Plage has extensive sands which are 1.5km (1 mile) southeast of **Fréjus**. The town is far enough inland not to be a resort, and its chief attractions are its Roman and medieval past. Guided tours of espiscopal Fréjus, which is concentrated at Place Formigé in the

Ste Maxime

town's centre, are organised throughout the year by the Tourist Office.

An austere, early Provençal Gothic cathedral of the thirteenth century is on the right. When you enter, it is clear that it is powerful rather than graceful (Provençal architects had not yet mastered the subtlety of Gothic art). Make a point of seeing a retable on wood by the Nice painter Jacques Durandi (1450), and the fifteenth-century chancel choirstalls. Close by is a fourth- or fifth-century baptistry, octagonal inside, and one of the oldest in France. In the same group of buildings are the restored thirteenth-century cloisters. A garden and ancient well are surrounded by delicate, twin-columned marble pillars; the beams of the arcades were painted in the fourteenth and fifteenth centuries with innumerable creatures and grotesques illustrating the Apocalypse. Adjoining the cloisters is the Archaeological Museum with items from Roman Fréjus.

Two thousand years ago, Fréjus was on the sea and Julius Caesar created a trading post here, *Forum Julii*, on the Aurelian Way in 49BC. A little later, Octavius, the future Emperor Augustus, developed the place into a major naval base and settlement for his retired soldiers. For 200 years, the large harbour was kept skilfully dredged but then its importance diminished, the River Argens silted up the harbour and Fréjus became surrounded by malarial marshes.

While the mind's eye may be able to reconstruct the layout of *Forum Julii* from the widely scattered remnants about the modern town, the remnants themselves are mostly disappointing, with the exception of the Arena. To visit this, park the car in Place Agricola, Rue Général de Gaulle. Fragments of Roman wall support the terrace of the Place, and one tower of the Porte des Gaules survives, as does a small paved section of Via Aurelia. The Arena, the oldest in Gaul, is 300m (980ft) west along Rue Henri Vadon. Its dilapidation through the centuries of pillage was hastened by Roman jerry-building and cheese-paring on the budget. Here, there was none of the refinement lavished on other buildings in Roman Provence. The seating has been restored — bullfights and concerts are held in the amphitheatre in summer.

Keen students of the past will seek out the traces of the only surviving example in France of a Roman naval and civil base. It includes a small theatre, aqueduct, citadel (the *Plate-Form*e), Porte d'Italie, Porte d'Orée (the arch attached to the baths), laundry, and

the Lanterne d'Auguste (a medieval harbour landmark built on the foundations of a Roman lighthouse). The railway line runs over what was the 54-acre harbour.

The more militarily minded can go north-east of the town to the Marine Corps Museum that holds the history of the French Marines from their inception in 1622 to the present day. In the same direction, there is a surprising Buddhist pagoda, built by the Vietnamese to honour their dead of World War I. About 3km (2 miles)

Cathedral Close, Fréjus

Places of Interest In and Near Fréjus

Ste Maxime

Local History Museum
A small museum concentrating on local history and culture.

Museum of Gramophones and Mechanical Music
A pleasant park with a large Provençal country house at its centre which holds a remarkable collection of musical boxes, old gramophones, barrel organs etc. Some are very rare, some quite extraordinary.

Fréjus

The Cathedral Close
The Close is a fortified unit consisting of the cathedral and bishop's palace, cloisters, bapistry and an archaeological museum. The bapistry is fourth- or fifth-century and one of the oldest buildings in France. The thirteenth-century cloisters are superb. The cathedral was built in the tenth-century. The Close Museum has Gallo-Roman items from the Fréjus site. Not to be missed.

The Amphitheatre
The oldest amphitheatre in Gaul, though not well-preserved. Built to hold 10,000 people.

Other Remains of Roman Fréjus
These include a gateway, a theatre and an aqueduct. The tower (Lanterne d'Auguste), restored in the nineteenth century, is now a lighthouse. There is a Roman bridge on the N7, 3.5km (2 miles) north of the town.

Marine Corps Museum
A museum devoted to the history of the French Marines from 1622 until the present day.

The Buddhist Pagoda
Built in 1919 by Vietnamese in memory of countrymen who died in the French Army during World War I.

Chapel of Notre-Dame-de-Jérusalem
Modern chapel with designs by Jean Cocteau.

Esterel Safari Park and Zoo
Fine parkland with pines and olives. Free-roving animals, together with birds and other, caged, animals.

from here, in the grounds of the La Tour de Mare estate, there is a chapel decorated by Jean Cocteau. Nearby, there is Esterel Safari Park which has free-roving animals that can be viewed from the car, as well as caged species.

6

COTE D'AZUR: ST RAPHAEL TO MENTON

Stephen Liégard coined the name 'Côte d'Azur' in a poem of 1887. It applies to the French Riviera between Cannes and Menton. As with all such contrived names — particularly those attached to tourist spots — it has its detractors, but the name does seem to be appropriate. In the strong, overhead sun of the Mediterranean coast, the sea really is azure blue. For the sake of convenience, the coast between St Raphaël and La Napoule is included although, strictly speaking, this should be known as the Côte de l'Esterel.

The Esterel is an ancient and eroded range whose highest point is Mont Vinaigre, rising to 628m (2,060ft). Jagged, rust-red rocks of volcanic porphyry rise dramatically behind the coast, sending out breakwaters into the ultramarine sea. This is the most colourful part of the Riviera coast, for though it is less wooded than the Maures (but as much a prey to forest fires), there are areas of dense shrubby undergrowth called the *maquis*.

The most attractive parts are reached on foot from the small coastal resorts of Agay, Anthéor and Le Trayas on the N98 (the Corniche d'Or). For a thorough exploration, these walks should include the peaks of Mont Vinaigre, Pic d'Aurelle, Pic de l'Ours and Pic du Cap Roux, as well as the Col des Lentisques and the narrow valley of Mal-Infernet. By common consent, the finest viewpoints are Mont Vinaigre, which can be reached in about 45 minutes from the top car park, and Pic de l'Ours which needs more time (allow 3 hours for the return journey) for a climb from the car park at Col Notre-Dame. For a good exploration by car, take the N7 that skirts the north

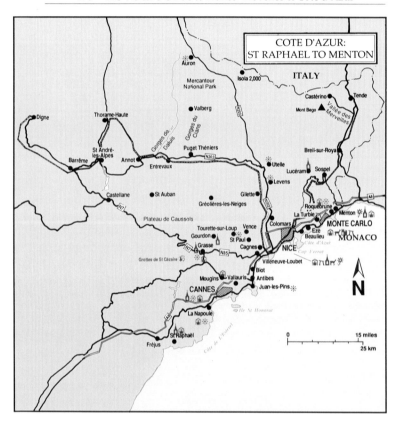

COTE D'AZUR:
ST RAPHAEL TO MENTON

side of the Esterel for 28 winding kilometres (17 miles).

St Raphaël is the beach-half of Fréjus, though to say so in the town would be to risk permanent injury. The town's sedate air attracts the epithet 'the Bournemouth of the Riviera', but that is not really fair, as its marina and casino testify. Its extensive beaches extend into the smart suburb of Boulouris.

Scuba-divers have helped to fill the Museum of Archaeology, in Rue des Templiers, with amphorae and other finds; techniques of underwater archaeology are also on show. There are also some land-based items of local prehistory. Next door is the twelfth-century Templars' fortress-church which defended the people from maritime marauders.

Between St Raphaël and La Napoule lie small resorts — Boulouris, Agay, Anthéor, Le Trayas, Miramar, La Galère and Théoule — tucked into little bays at the foot of the Esterel, some of which are rocky, others sandy. Beyond Anthéor, the Côte de l'Esterel reveals its most impressive scenery as the road skirts the bold mass of Cap Roux 452m (1,480ft). Then, near Le Trayas, rocks, pines and sea unite in an intensity of colour.

La Napoule, with three beaches, a marina and 18-hole golf course, as well as a massive medieval castle, is at the eastern end of the Esterel Range, and is the gateway to the Côte d'Azur proper. Be sure to visit the castle, of which only two huge fourteenth-century towers remain. These were lovingly restored by an American sculptor, Henry Clews, whose work can be seen inside. There is also a glassworks in the town where visitors can watch all aspects of the process.

Now the gently folded east-west ranges which give Provence its 'Classical' ambience begin to be replaced by narrow Alpine valleys running north to south, valleys which run down from 3,000m (9,800ft) peaks in Alpes-Maritimes. These mountain formations protect the coast. Places like Beaulieu (often

La Napoule

referred to as *Petit Afrique*) and Menton, where the average winter temperature is 9.6 °C (50 °F), experience fog, ice or snow as sensational rarities. However, these same mountains confine the warmth, voluptuous colours and exotic plants to a coastal ribbon.

Ironically, most of the eye-catching trees, shrubs and flowers are imported: Bougainvillea, prickly pear, loquat, mimosa, bananas, oranges, lemons and many other varieties of citrus fruits, as well as begonias, palms, aloe, agave and mesembryanthemum. Even the olive tree, which attains its most majestic proportions here, is not strictly indigenous; it was probably planted by the Greeks in the sixth century BC.

The visitor will also notice a cultural difference between the Côte d'Azur and Provence. The former is Italianate, reflecting the long periods in which the County of Nice was part of Italy. Whole streets and squares in Menton, Nice and Villefranche are architecturally Italian. The traditional Nissard cuisine is also orientated towards Italy, and Italian-sounding surnames abound.

A short distance inland, the ground rises quickly and the landscape becomes Alpine; the only thing the area seems to have in common with the Mediterranean is a limpid light. In winter or spring it is possible to bask in warm coastal sunshine, and ski an hour or so later on deep soft snows at Peïra-Cava, Col de Turini, Gréolières-les-Neiges, La Colmiane, La Foux-d'Allos, or at the three major resorts of the Alpes-Maritimes; Valberg, Auron and Isola 2,000 which have extensive pistes, lifts, ski schools and equipment for hire. This rapid and dramatic contrast between coast and hinterland lends exhilaration to an exploration of the region in summer and winter.

Densely populated, the Côte d'Azur is almost a conurbation between Cannes and Menton; driving and parking present familiar difficulties. **Cannes** is reached from La Napoule.

The original fishing port here was called *Canois*, after the reeds that grew in the harbour, and was no more than a fishing village until 1834, when cholera in Nice caused the English Lord Chancellor, Lord Brougham, to stop there rather than to continue to his chosen destination. He liked the village, built a villa, spread the word back in England, and the resort was born.

The Tour Le Suquet in the Old Town is the beacon which identifies it from a distance. Not surprisingly, there is a fine view from the top for all who climb the 21m (70ft) tower. The tower is on the west side of Cannes where the Old Town occupies gently rising ground

Places of Interest In and Near Cannes

Mandelieu-La-Napoule

Henry Clews Foundation
Old *château* bought by an American, Henry Clews, and carefully restored.

Verrerie du Domain de Maure-Vieil
Working glass factory.

St Raphaël

Museum of Underwater Archaeology
Housed in an old presbytery. An interesting museum that exhibits the finds of the local sub-aqua club and includes a collection of diving equipment. The chief exhibit is a very important collection of Roman amphorae, which is nicely displayed with a reconstruction of their loading onto the transport ship.

Church of St Peter
A twelfth-century Romanesque-Provençal church built to double as a fortress in times of pirate attack; hence the thick walls and the watch tower. There is is an ancient pagan altar.

Cannes

Musée Le Castre
Collections of antiquities from Persia, China and the Far East, South America and the Pacific, as well as from the Mediterranean area.

Tour Le Suquet
(Mount Le Suquet or Chevalier Tower)

Twelfth-century tower, 21m (70ft) high. Fine views from the top.

Bellini Chapel
Built in 1880 in Florentine Baroque style by Count Vitali, and then used by the artist Bellini.

Confiserie Blachère
A working sweet factory.

La Californie Observatory
Site includes a panorama dial and telescope. Reputedly the best viewpoint on the Riviera.

Le Cannet Rocheville

Les Ruchers de Dieu
Bee farm.

Cannes-la-Bocca

Europ Mimosa
Mimosa nursery.

Ile de Ste Marguerite

Marine Museum
Set in the oldest part of the island's royal fortress. Collections on marine archaeology, fishing and yachting. The museum includes the cell of the Man in the Iron Mask.

Ile de St Honorat

St Honorat Monastery
Remains of a monastery and church of the tenth and eleventh centuries, fortified to protect it against pirates. The newer monastery includes a museum of Romano-Christian work.

The beach and promenade, Cannes

above the port and the Municipal Casino. Near the tower is the Musée Le Castre, with its fine collections of antiquities from all over the world, including the Mediterranean.

To the east of the town are the sandy beaches and the glittering Boulevard de la Croisette — which no one should miss — with hotels, shops, cafés and marinas. On the Pointe de la Croisette is the Palm-Beach Casino with restaurant, cabaret, disco and swimming-pool under the same roof. In Rue des Belges is the Casino des Fleurs. You will need to find Rue d'Antibes for smart shops and discos, while Rue Meynadier has food shops. There are morning markets in Rue Louis Blanc, and the sweet tooth of many a visitor has been satisfied by a visit to the working Confiserie Blachère.

On the heights is the observatory at La Californie. Lifts will take you to the top of the tower for one of the finest coastal views in Europe. See the sun setting behind the Esterel and you will understand why Kipling said this was the most beautiful coast in the world.

At Le Cannet Rocheville, the visitor can watch all aspects of bee-keeping and buy honey from the bee farm, while the mimosa

Tour Le Suquet, Cannes Old Town

nurseries at Cannes-la-Bocca are open to the public.

From Cannes, boats go to the Iles de Lérins reaching Ile Ste Marguerite in 15 minutes and Ile St Honorat in half an hour. Sightseeing of the historical buildings on the two islands combines with woodland walks to make this an attractive half-day excursion. The monastery of St Honorat on the island of the same name is worth visiting to see the fortifications necessary to protect churches in the tenth century; the marine museum on the larger island is interesting for its fishing items, and for the Man in the Iron Mask's cell. The mask was velvet not iron, but that has not diminished the romantic legend of the man imprisoned on the island from 1687 to 1698, and then in the Bastille until his death in 1703. The rightful king of France, brother of the king, illegitimate son of the king, great-grandfather of Napoleon — all these and more have been suggested as possible identities for the prisoner but the story remains a pleasing enigma.

Juan-les-Pins started life in the 1920s so has little history, but it is blessed with fine sands. Its noisy night-life falls silent at the end of the season. For a contrast, walk along the sea walls of **Antibes** and about the Old Town's narrow and bustling streets. This is a town with a very ancient history, having been a Greek port. In his early years as a general, Napoleon defended the Mediterranean coast from the town, and it was near here that he landed after his escape from Elba. Expecting to be greeted by noisy crowds, the Emperor was surprised when the town threw his envoys into prison.

The Picasso Museum in Château Grimaldi is tastefully laid out in a handsome building and does justice to the diversity of the genius who spent much of his long life in the South of France. In addition, the town has an archaeological museum with exhibits on the Greek town of *Antipolis*. There is an art gallery with work by local and foreign artists and a Napoleonic museum which includes exhibits on the escape from Elba and a fine bust of the Emperor by Canova. There is also a museum devoted to the curious drawings of Peynet, the French 'cartoonist' who drew the *Lovers* series of sentimental pictures.

In Juan-les-Pins itself, still a draw for its jet-set image, there is a guarantee of peace at the Thuret Gardens. These are owned by the State and open to the public; they were among the first gardens to acclimatise tropical trees and plants. There is a guarantee of fine views from the lighthouse and Pointe Beacon. It is also worth visiting the chapel of La Garoupe, next to the lighthouse, for its collection of sailors' ex-voti. As a complete contrast, north of Antibes is Marineland, Europe's first marine zoo.

West of Antibes, at **Vallauris**, is the National Picasso Museum, built around his mural *War and Peace*, which is on the wall of an old chapel. Also in the town is a marvellous Renaissance castle housing many collections including one of Picasso ceramics. Just north of the A8 is **Mougins**, with a photographic museum that consists of portraits of Picasso by the world's leading portraitists. There are frequent exhibitions of the work of leading photographers. There is also a car museum — which, appropriately, can also be entered from a service area on the A8 itself — with a collection of over 200 cars.

North of Antibes, but a little inland, is **Biot**, surrounded by acres of carnations and roses destined for the Riviera flower markets. The ubiquitous and handsome terracotta vases that adorn many gardens once formed the main industry of Biot. Today the visitor can watch glass-making in the village, the factory being famous for Biot bubble glass.

Outside the village is the Fernand Léger Museum; its huge, garish mosaic façade looks out of place in this setting. Works by this

Places of Interest In and Near Antibes

Antibes
Picasso Museum
Château Grimaldi
Sixteenth-century castle on site of older castle and Roman fort. Once held by the Grimaldi family of Monaco. Picasso stayed here for a time in the late 1940s and all his work of the period is displayed, together with that from other modern artists. Frequent exhibitions of contemporary art.

Archaeological Museum
Devoted to the history of the town, including a section on the Greek town of *Antipolis*, housed in part of the seventeenth-century town fortifications.

Art Gallery
Bastion St Andre
Monthly exhibitions of work of local as well as more internationally famous artists. Housed in part of the old town fortifications.

Napoleonic and Naval Museum
Housed in the Battery of Le Grillon on Cap d'Antibes. Exhibits detail Napoleon's escape of Elba and include Canova's bust of the Emperor. Display of naval equipment. Magnificent views from site.

Peynet Museum
Collection of the sentimental but curiously affectionate work, *Lovers* by Peynet, housed in a nineteenth-century house, suitably painted pink.

Marineland
Antibes-Biot
The first marine zoo in Europe. Performing dolphins and orca. Sea elephants and sea lions, seals and penguins.

Juan-les-Pins
Thuret Gardens
Collection of rare shrubs and trees around a fine villa.

Lighthouse
Set inland on a high plateau. The powerful beam carries over 80km (50 miles). There are excellent views from the site.

Cap d'Antibes
Pointe Beacon
Fine viewpoint.

Vallauris
National Picasso Museum
Housed in a chapel of the sixteenth-century town castle. The chapel is a remnant of an older twelfth-century monastery. Over a 7 year period from 1952, Picasso painted his *War and Peace* on the crypt wall, and this is the centrepiece of the museum. The Municipal Museum, on the same site, has other work by the master as well as that of other modern artists.

Town Museum
Superb Renaissance castle on the foundations of twelfth-century Norman castle. Artwork includes collection of Picasso ceramics.

Mougins
Photography Museum
Exhibition of portraits of Picasso by contemporary photographers. Frequent exhibitions of the work of French and foreign photographers.

Automobile Museum
Near Mougins
Two hundred old and new cars.

Fernand Léger Museum, Biot

robust northern artist (1881-1955), interpreter-in-chief of the factory age, fill the museum built by his widow. The town's other museum, which is of local life, includes a restored kitchen.

Cagnes-sur-Mer is a sprawling mass which has engulfed the chic racecourse, l'Hippodrome de la Côte d'Azur. In Cagnes-Ville is the Renoir Museum, Avenue des Collettes, the house and garden where Renoir (1841-1919) spent the last 12 years of his life. The overall impression is that everything has been left much as it was. There are the tools of his trade in the studio, a painting, some drawings and sculptings — including his bronze Venus in the garden surrounded by ancient olive trees — correspondence, photographs and momentos. The museum is a moving tribute to an artist who expressed his love for the freshness of life.

At Haut-de-Cagnes, which is the prettiest part of the town, the handsome Château-Musée houses an exhibition devoted to the olive tree, that veritable symbol of Provence. Also in the *château* is a museum of modern Mediterranean art, including works by some of the many painters who have been profoundly influenced by the light of this coast which is often called the 'Mecca of Modern Art'.

Close to Cagnes is **Villeneuve-Loubet**, with an excellent culinary art museum housed in the home of the Escoffiers, the most famous family in the history of 'cooking-as-art'. There are all the things you would imagine in the world's most famous kitchen, together with exhibitions of sugar and chocolate work. There is also a military museum here.

Inland from here are the twin towns of St Paul and Vence. **St Paul** has always been a little too far from the sea to share in much of the general prosperity, but it was discovered by artists in the 1920s and has been an artistic, rather than jet-set, centre ever since. For proof of this, the visitor need look no further than the Maeght Foundation, a modern art museum set in a suitably designed building constructed in 1964. Some of the art on view is pleasantly displayed outdoors. Artists represented in the museum include Braque, Miro, Chagall and Kandinsky, and the work includes not only paintings, but sculptures and stained glass as well. The museum is one of the most important collections of modern art for many miles.

Vence also has much to occupy the tourist. Though originally a Ligurian town, Vence was important in Roman times, and equally important in the early years of Christian France. In the Wars of Religion, the town was besieged by Huguenots but did not fall, a fact commemorated each Easter with a festival. The visitor should definitely not miss the Old Town, which still has part of the original defensive wall and the remains of an old castle. The old cathedral is early Romanesque, while in the Place du Peyra, a very pretty square, there is a splendid fountain.

Like St Paul, Vence has artistic connections, in this case with Henri Matisse, who designed and then decorated a chapel at the town between 1947 and 1951. Matisse was impressed by the outcome; it was, he said, his masterpiece. Elsewhere in the town there is a museum to the local perfume industry which is housed in an old monastery,

Close to Vence is **Tourette-sur-Loup**, at the start of the Loup Valley. The town has an impressive town hall, but is more famous as the start of a fine journey up the valley which is worthy of time spent away from the coast. The valley has some good viewpoints and waterfalls in its lower reaches, near Pont-du-Loup, where the visitor can visit a working *confiserie*. However, it is the upper section that attracts the most attention, together with the mountains of Haute-Provence beyond.

Places of Interest In and Around Vence

Biot
Verrerie de Biot
A working glass factory. Various processes of glass making. Biot bubble glass is made here.

Fernand Léger Museum
Museum to the artist Léger housed in late 1960s building. Photographic record of the artist's life together with a large collection of his work.

Local History Museum
Exhibits on the history of the town and area. Includes a reconstructed peasant kitchen.

Cagnes-sur-Mer
Château Musée
Housed in a Grimaldi *château* which is mostly thirteenth-century but includes a superb seventeenth-century Renaissance courtyard. Includes a history of the olive tree and oil processing; the Suzy Solidar collection of modern art; a collection of contemporary local artists' work and a banqueting hall with a ceiling by Carlene.

Renoir Museum
Les Collettes is where Renoir spent the last 12 years of his life. He bought it to save some 1,000-year-old olive trees which still flourish.

Villeneuve-Loubet
Culinary Art Museum
In the house where Auguste Escoffier was born. Large collection of photography, books and utensils of the culinary arts. Exhibits of sugar and chocolate work.

Military Museum
Constructed around the collection of M. Christian Vialle. It includes memorabilia from both World Wars, Indo-China and North African campaigns.

St Paul-de-Vence
Maeght Foundation
A modern building by José-Luis Sert, a pupil of Le Corbusier, in a fine setting on top of a wooded hill. The red brick and white concrete building is a good setting for paintings and sculptures by modern artists including Miro, Kandinsky, Chagall and Braque.

Vence
The Rosary Chapel
Chapel designed by Henri Matisse and built between 1948 and 1951. Matisse was also responsible for the interior decoration which is a contrast between the very simple furnishings and the more elaborate murals.

Museum of Perfume and Liqueurs
Housed in a Benedictine monastery dating from the eleventh century. The grounds of the *château* are planted with perfume-producing plants, and all aspects of perfume production are covered. Both perfume and liqueurs are on sale.

Emile Hugues Foundation
Villeneuve Castle
Lovingly restored, fifteenth-century castle. Now houses the Carzou Museum dedicated to the work of the artist-in-residence.

Chapel of the White Penitents
Restored chapel from the early seventeenth century. Interesting dome with coloured mosaic.

Tourette-sur-Loup
Town hall
Built in the fifteenth-century as a fortified mansion. Exhibitions of art and music in the summer.

Pont-du-Loup
Confiserie des Gorges du Loup
A real-life sweet factory.

As a reasonable itinerary, go up the Loup Valley to Gréolières, and then head west on the D2 and then the D5 to the Col de Bleine. Continue northwards on the D5 and then take the D2211 to Briançonnet. From here, take the D2211A and the D17 eastwards to Roquesteron and there take the D1 southward. There is a fine viewpoint south of Le Broc from where the road leads back to Vence.

Westward from St Paul-de-Vence is **Grasse**, a town of great charm, spreading out over shallow hills as though relaxing in the sun or, perhaps, to make it easier to guard the perfume meadows that have made it famous.

In the very early Middle Ages the town was a republic, despite its size, with links to the Italian city-state of Pisa. The bigger state of Provence soon put an end to this independence of spirit. The city is also famous as the home of the great Provençal artist, Fragonard, and for having been virtually on Napoleon's route north after his landing at Antibes. The Emperor, fearful of the reception he might receive, went round the town, only staying locally for an hour to rest his men on what is now known as Napoleon's Plateau.

Since the start of perfume-making as an industry rather than a small time job for a few locals, Grasse has been a leading perfume town. Fields of perfume-bearing flowers lie all around, and the visitor can watch the process of manufacture in several perfumeries in the town — there is also a museum to the industry. Other museums include the Local Art and History Museum, a Marine Museum with a collection from the Comte de Grasse (an admiral in the French Navy) and Villa Fragonard, the house where the artist lived which houses a collection of his work.

Close to the town are the caves of St Cézaire. These lie close to a fine mountain drive that links Grasse with Fayence, which has an excellent Roman aqueduct and St Vallier-de-Thiey, where there are more show caves. Between Grasse and the Loup Valley is Gourdon, worth visiting for its thirteenth-century castle. The hills near Grasse are criss-crossed with routes and, as no one route stands out, it is worth choosing a circular path of your own.

And so to the 'Queen of the Riviera', as **Nice** styles itself. There is some justification for this claim, even though its enormous beach is exposed and pebbly. Like Cannes and Menton, Nice used to be something of an English preserve. Until World War II, that purely English seaside phenomenon, the pier, had a representative, complete with a casino at the end of it, suspended over the Mediterranean

Places of Interest In and Near Grasse

Grasse

Parfumerie Fragonard
Parfumerie Galimard
Parfumerie Molinard
Three perfumeries that accept
visitors.

Provençal Art & History Museum
Situated in an eighteenth-century
townhouse decorated, in part, as it
would have been at the time. Also
craft items from all over Provence
— earthenware, glass, religious
and folklore pieces.

Villa Fragonard
Seventeenth-century villa occupied by Jean-Honoré Fragonard
during the Revolution and
containing his work, together with
that of his son, Alexandre-Evariste,
and grandson, Théophile.

Marine Museum
Interesting collection of models of
eleventh-century ships and
memorabilia of Comte de Grasse,
a French admiral at the time of the
American War of Independence.

International Perfume Museum
New museum set up in an old
perfumery. The techniques of
perfume-making explained.

St Cézaire Caves
Near Grasse
Show caves with good formations
and colours.

Fayence
Roman Aqueduct
Roche Tailée, near Fayence
The ruins of the Roman aqueduct
that took water from Mons to
Fréjus. Nicely situated.

St Vallier-de-Thiey
Baume Caves
1km ($\frac{1}{2}$ mile) of underground
galleries. Collection of plants that
grow in semi-darkness.

Gourdon Castle
Thirteenth-century castle built
over old Saracen fortress. The
castle museum has a fine
collection of arms and armour, as
well as some good paintings.

waters of Nice. Now, the Promenade des Anglais — named, in
gratitude, by the city fathers — is the reminder of that *Belle Epoque*.

Nice is ebullient and noisy; it does not depend solely on tourism,
having a richly varied life of its own. The visitor can take part in the
exhibitions, fêtes, galas, concerts. For many, a walk along the Promenade des Anglais is entertainment enough. It passes that Edwardian
'museum', Hôtel Negresco, whose public rooms contain works of art
and whose lavatories are more lavishly ornamented than many other
hotel lounges.

The beach at Nice

Red stucco arcaded buildings line one side of the harbour, Port Lympia ('port of limpid waters') from which the boats for Corsica leave. The place where Garibaldi was born (in 1807) is marked by a plaque on the house at the corner of Quai Papacino.

Old Nice lies between the sea, Boulevard Jean Jaurès and the 'Castle' — as the hill just west of the port is known, even though the castle was blown up in 1706; there is a lift to the top. There is plenty of sightseeing to do in this area, including the town hall, Baroque church of St François-de-Paul, opera house, cathedral of Ste Réparate, and the Chapellé de la Miséricorde of 1736; the latter has an outstanding retable painted by Jean Miralhet early in the fifteenth century. There are also a number of Genoese buildings, particularly Palais Lascaris, a remarkable Malacological Museum with exhibits of shells and a Natural History Museum (Musée Barla). Flower, fruit and vegetable markets take place in Cours Saleya (go in the mornings from Tuesday to Sunday). Food shops, bistros and an antiques market give Italian vivacity to the Old Town.

Of all the annual festivities held in Nice, the Carnival, started in 1878, is the most hilarious. For a fortnight before Lent, King Carnival

Places of Interest in Nice

Art and History Museum
Masséna Palace
The palace was built towards the end of the nineteenth century by Victor Masséna and is worth a visit for the interior, decorated in First Empire style. The artwork includes Chinese pottery, European paintings and collections of French and German arms.

Library of the Chevalier de Cessole
Collection of old and rare books.

Fine Arts Museum
Housed in a nineteenth-century villa built by a Russian princess. The villa has one gallery devoted to the work of the Van Loo family and others that include works by Rubens and Caravaggio. The Impressionist works include Monet, Sisley and Renoir.

Archaeological Site and Museum
Visitors can view the excavated remains of the old Roman town of *Cemenelum* (Cimiez). The remains of baths and town houses can be seen. The site museum holds finds from the excavations. A new museum was opened on the site in 1989. This holds not only items from the site, but uses audio-visual techniques to bring the old Roman site alive.

Matisse Museum
A superb museum devoted to the work of Henri Matisse. All aspects and periods of his work are covered. There is a room of drawings, many paintings and over 50 bronzes. The museum also holds many of Matisse's personal possessions.

Franciscan Museum and Monastery
Cimiez
The museum, housed in a finely frescoed seventeenth-century convent, charts the work of the Franciscan order in Nice. There are guided tours of the monastery cloisters and sacristy.

Palais Lascaris
Built by the Lascaris-Vintimille family in the mid-seventeenth-century. Classified as a Historic Monument in 1946, the palace was completely restored in period style. Decorations include some Flemish tapestries. There are occasional exhibitions of contemporary art.

Terra Amata Museum
A replica of a 400,000-year-old elephant-hunter's camp excavated near the town. Site sometimes has exhibitions on other aspects of prehistory.

Renoir Gallery
A new gallery, dedicated to Renoir but holding the work of contemporary artists.

appears, followed by costumed processions, floats, grotesque masks, confetti showers and fireworks. King Carnival (called *Caramantran* or *Mardi Gras*) is burned in effigy on Shrove Tuesday. On

Marc Chagall Museum

The most important museum of the artist Chagall's works. Built to house the *Biblical Message*, seventeen canvases painted over the 13 year period from 1954 to 1967. The museum also has other works by the artist, including sculptures and mosaics. There is also a library of books on the history of art and religion. Not to be missed.

International Museum of Naïve Art

The museum comprises Anatole Jakovsky's donation of many hundreds of paintings of the Naïve school from many countries.

Museum of Natural History

The Musée Barla has rooms for the study of birds, minerals, fossils, fish and fishing. There is also the J.B.Barla collection of casts of fungi, over 7,000 specimens in all.

Malacological Museum

A museum of shells, with some beautiful shapes and colours and including some very rare specimens.

Naval Museum

Housed in the Tour Bellanda (Bellanda Tower), an enormous sixteenth-century bastion. Entry is by going past two fine Portuguese bronze cannons. The museum includes collections of arms and armour, and also a series of prints of Old Nice.

Contemporary Art Gallery

A gallery dedicated to the work of modern day artists, chiefly, but not exclusively, French.

Villa Arson

An eighteenth-century villa that is mainly an Institute for the Arts, but has a number of small galleries for the work of contemporary artists.

The Priory of the Old Abode

The creation of a Dominican friar, Father Lemerre, the museum, which is housed in a sixteenth-century house, replicates a medieval house. Also includes collections of old ironwork and stained-glass windows.

Russian Orthodox Cathedral

Built in the early years of this century with money from Czar Nicholas II. A very beautiful building in red brick and grey marble with six onion-shaped domes.

Confiserie du Vieux Nice

Working sweet factory.

Martin Fleurs

Carnation fields.

St Michel Plateau

Viewpoint to the east of the town just north of Beaulieu-sur-Mer. A fine view of the coast and the Esterel Range.

Ash Wednesday there is the frenetic Battle of Flowers.

Place Masséna is the hub of the more modern part of Nice. There ✳ is a spacious pedestrian zone with elegant shops and cafés. Further

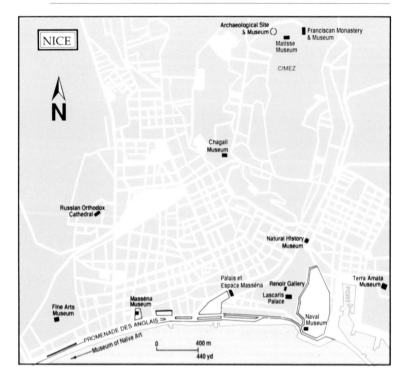

west, towards the airport, there are large shopping complexes and hypermarkets.

 Do not miss going to the suburb of **Cimiez** in the hills overlooking Nice. On the way up is the Marc Chagall Museum in Avenue Dr Ménard, specially built to house his seventeen canvases, *The Biblical Message*, as well as many other examples of the artist's work.

 At Cimiez itself you can inspect the Archaeological Museum and the remains of Roman *Cemenelum*. Henri Matisse (1869-1954) lived in Nice for much of his later life and his art revelled in the light. He is buried close by. In the same building as the Archaeological Museum, the Matisse Museum reveals the successive influences movements in art had on his work. The church (containing three important paintings of the Nice School of 500 years ago), adjoins public gardens which look precipitously over Nice and the sea.

Before leaving Nice, a note about the origin of its name may not

An exhibit in the Matisse Museum, Nice

come amiss. Most books say it comes from the Greek *Nikaîa* (victory). It is more likely that the Greeks called it *Nîkaia* from naiad, a water sprite.

From Nice, several journeys northwards enter the fine country of Haute-Provence. Perched villages, characteristic of Provence, are even more spectacular above the Côte d'Azur. At a distance they look grey, aloof, even distrustful; they were built for protection against incessant invasion. Their thick walls, narrow, steep, twisting cobbled and arcaded streets, their tiny squares and fountains, clustering towards an ancient church, are a delight to explore. Many houses are now workshops for artist and artisans where paintings, ceramics, woven cloths, jewellery or olivewood carvings can be bought.

There is too much country to the north to cover each village, so a small number of excellent itineraries will be suggested.

Our first trip will be by the justly famous autorail scenic journey by the Chemins de Fer de la Provence from Gare de Provence in Nice, Place de la Libération. It takes in the Valleys of the Var, Vaïre, Verdon and Asse, and goes to the stations of Puget-Théniers, Entrevaux, Annot, Thorame-Haute, St André-les-Alpes and Digne. It covers 151km (94 miles) and takes 3hr 20min in each direction; the return can be made on the same day.

Places of Interest North of Nice

Gorge de Daluis
Fine, wild gorge.

Colmars
Fort de Savoie
Fourteenth-century castle built at a time when Colmars defended the border between Savoy and Provence (France). Fort de France, at the other end of the town, is ruined.

Auron
Funivia to Las Donnas
Excellent views to French and Italian Alps.

Gorge du Cians
Magnificent and wild gorge.

Levens
Museum of Butterflies and Other Insects
Museum and collection of butter-flies and other insects. Breeding species and live insects as well as mounted ones.

Mercantour National Park
Offering good walking and scenery.

Merveilles and Roya Valleys
Rock Engravings
The area at the foot of Mont Bégo is an open-air museum of the area's pre-Roman period. The hillside boulders were worn smooth by glacial action about 15,000 years ago, following which Bronze Age Man (Ligurian culture) used the surface for carvings and inscriptions. The carvings continued until the Romans arrived and there are around 100,000 of them on 'Magic Mountain'.

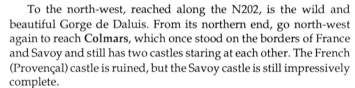

To the north-west, reached along the N202, is the wild and beautiful Gorge de Daluis. From its northern end, go north-west again to reach **Colmars**, which once stood on the borders of France and Savoy and still has two castles staring at each other. The French (Provençal) castle is ruined, but the Savoy castle is still impressively complete.

North of Daluis but reached only by travelling east and north, **Auron** is reached. This is a village with a cable car that leads to high ground where there is superb walking and magnificent views over the French and Italian Alps. To reach Auron, the visitor will cross the head of the Gorge du Cians. Note its position and take it on the return journey. It, too, is wildly beautiful.

Off the N202 is **Levens** where there is an excellent 'museum' of butterflies. The site has a breeding programme so the visitor can see

Places of Interest
Between Nice and Monaco

La Turbie
The Alpine Trophy
Erected by the Roman Emperor
Augustus to celebrate victory
over the local tribes. The site
museum includes a model of
how the monument would have
looked when first completed.

Laghet
The Sanctuary of Notre-Dame
Built in the mid-seventeenth
century on a pilgrimage site and
full of votive offerings and
stained glass.

Eze
Parfumerie Galimard

Exotic Garden
Fine collection of cacti and
succulent plants in the parkland
around a fourteenth-century
castle slighted in the early
eighteenth century. The view
from the garden is among the
finest in the area, with Corsica
visible on clear days.

Villefranche
Volti Museum
The Citadel
Collection of bronzes and
ceramics by the sculptor Volti,
housed in a sixteenth-century
castle. The Citadel also houses
the Roux collection of ceramic
figures illustrating daily life in
Medieval times; the Goetz-

Boumeester collection of
paintings, including works by
Picasso; and an exhibition on the
history of the Citadel and the
town.

St Peter's Chapel
Ancient chapel decorated with
frescos by Jean Cocteau. The
frescos are of scenes from St
Peter's life.

St Jean-Cap-Ferrat
Fondation Ephrussi de Rothschild
Superb villa, built in 1900 and set
in magnificent grounds. Fine collection of work with sixteenth-
century Flemish tapestries,
eighteenth-century furniture,
Chinese vases and Impressionist
work including that of Monet,
Renoir and Sisley. Not to be
missed.

Zoo
Tropical garden with interesting
collection of animals and birds.

Lighthouse
Go up 164 steps to find an
excellent, panoramic view.

Beaulieu-sur-Mer
Villa Kerylos
Reconstruction of a Greek villa by
the archaeologist Theodore
Reinach. Original work is mixed
with historically accurate repro-
ductions. Not to be missed.

live insects as well as mounted ones. North of Levens, the visitor is heading for the Mercantour National Park. The Park offers magnificent scenery and excellent walking; one site that should be visited is the Merveilles Valley where, at the foot of Mont Bégo, ('Magic Mountain') there are thousands of rock engravings spanning the years from Bronze Age to Roman times.

Lastly, go north-eastward to **Lucéram** which, as well as being a fine perched village, has a church with a number of altarpieces by Bréa and others, even though part of the Ste Marguerite retable is lodged in Masséna Museum in Nice. Lucéram had been a major centre from which the poor, itinerant artists, commissioned by Penitent Brotherhoods and overshadowed by Italian Renaissance artists, carried their paints and brushes over mountain tracks from church to church.

East from Nice, there is a choice of four roads: the A8 Autoroute, and the three famous Corniche roads. The Grande Corniche (D2564), built by Napoleon, is the 31km (19 mile) high route between Nice and Menton. Use this road for the impressive views and for visiting the majestic Roman Trophy of the Alps at **La Turbie**. It also offers fine views from Hotel Vistaëro and at Roquebrune. The Moyenne Corniche (N7) also provides viewing lay-bys; it is the direct route to Eze. The Corniche Inférieure (N98) winds along the coast to go through Villefranche, Beaulieu, Eze-Bord-de-Mer, Cap d'Ail, Monaco, Cap Martin and Menton. Side roads connect all three Corniches.

From La Turbie there is a road to **Laghet** with its fine chapel, while **Eze** has a perfumery that can be visited and a very fine garden.

Turn off at Villefranche for a drive round **St Jean-Cap-Ferrat** which offers glimpses of the beautiful private estates on the peninsula. **Villefranche** has a well-set Citadel that contains a Fine Art collection, and a chapel decorated by Jean Cocteau. On Cap Ferrat be sure to see the lighthouse, the zoo, and the Musée Ile de France (Fondation Ephrussi de Rothschild) which has many treasures and is set in ornamental gardens. St Jean is a fishing village from which one can walk round the Point St Hospice or along Promenade Maurice Rouvier; both provide lovely views of the coast to the east.

The next village is **Beaulieu-sur-Mer** where there is a wonderful Greek villa, reconstructed faithfully by an archaeologist specialising in the period. All the correct materials were used — some, like Carrrara marble and alabaster, being rare and expensive. The mosaics and furniture are all faithful copies of real objects or made after a

Hills rising from the sea, near Monaco

Cap Ferrat

careful study of drawings and writings; do not miss this staggering piece of work.

The **Principality of Monaco**, covering an area of under 200 hectares and with a population of only 25,000, is a sovereign state enclave surrounded by the *département* of Alpes-Maritimes. However, there are no frontier formalities even though the police uniform is different and distinctive.

The state consists of the capital town, Monaco, from whose Royal Palace it is administered, the resort of Monte-Carlo, and the commercial centre of La Condamine — not that much open space is available to separate one from another. So precious is land that, in 30 years, the Principality has transformed itself into tier upon tier of skyscrapers, and reclaimed strips of land from the sea to create something by way of imported sand beaches.

Monaco's name derives from a temple to *Monoïkos* (Hercules) erected on the rock by Phoenicians. In 1308, the Grimaldis acquired Monaco from the Genoese and have ruled ever since. Their fidelity to France won them other territories along the coast. A turbulent history has seen the Principality occupied by Spaniards and French or protected by the Kingdom of Sardinia. It was incorporated into the County of Nice (roughly, the Alpes-Maritimes) into France in 1793, when the Revolutionaries renamed it Fort Hercule.

Independence returned at the end of the Napoleonic Wars. The rest of the Alpes-Maritimes were ceded to Italy, to return to France by the plebiscite of 1860. Later, Monaco was on the verge of bankruptcy and Menton and Roquebrune were sold off to France by Charles III. He struck on the lucrative idea of catering for Europe's gamblers and the casino was built on the rock named after him (Monte-Carlo). So successful was the enterprise that Monaco's wealth was drawn from it until World War II.

Today, Monaco is a highly efficient centre of business and commerce. It comes as a surprise to many to learn that gambling yields only 3 per cent of the state's revenue. The legend of glamour is still cultivated through the image of lavish, year-round programmes of entertainment, of galas, operas, Grand Prix (in May), and opulent yachts in the harbour. Such events are financed out of VAT as there is no personal taxation for Monégasques.

Still wearing its Second Empire pride, the sumptuous casino (and its gardens) sees tourists gamble in a modest way. To gamble you will need to show your passport.

Places of Interest in Monaco

The Prince's Palace
The Grands Appartements are open only when the Prince is away. Visits can include the sixteenth-century Hercules Gallery, conceived in grand style; the Court of Honour, surrounded by superb arcaded galleries; the Throne Room and the York Bedroom.

The Napoleon Souvenir Museum and Palace Archives
The collection of Napoleonic memorabilia was amassed by Prince Louis II, the current Prince's grandfather, and includes many interesting and odd objects (including earth from the Emperor's grave on St Helena). The archives include a complete collection of Monégasque coins.

The Waxworks
Life-size wax figures in scenes from the Grimaldi family history. Figures include Princess Grace.

Oceanographic Museum
Superb museum in huge, impressive building dating from the turn of the century. Collections include aquaria with over 4,000 species of fish from all over the world and fixed exhibits covering the rich fauna of the sea. Interesting collection of diving equipment. Not to be missed.

Tropical (Exotic) Garden/ Museum of Prehistory
The site includes excellent fine rock gardens with cacti and succulents; museum on the evolution of man with varied and interesting items; and a cave in the dolomitic limestone with fine formations.

The Galea Collection
The world's finest collection of dolls and automatons (some opened for a view of the drive mechanisms) The collection, built around that of Madeleine de Galea and donated by her grandson, has over 2,000 items.

Zoo
La Condamine
Large collection of animals, especially monkeys, birds and reptiles.

Place the Oceanographic Museum high on the list of things to see in Monaco. Its aquarium, displays of marine life, and submarine exploration equipment betray the expert enthusiasm of Jacques Cousteau. Equally fascinating — and certainly not to be missed by the enthusiast — is the Galea Collection of dolls and automatons.

Roquebrune, reached from the Grand Corniche, is a skilfully restored hill-village. Medieval houses and steep, arched-over alleys

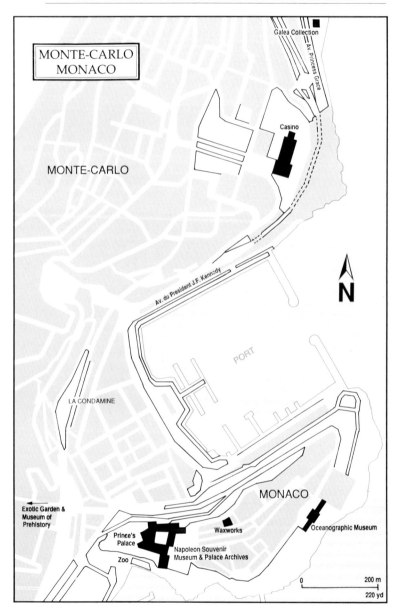

Beach and harbour, Monte-Carlo

Marina, Monte-Carlo

lead up to the tenth-century castle, one of the oldest in France. It is a fine sight when floodlit at night and deserves to be visited for the furnished apartments and primitive kitchen on the third floor. Above is a terrace from which Cap Martin can be seen, 300m (985ft) below.

On the afternoon of August 5, the visitor to Roquebrune can witness scenes from the Passion enacted between the village and the chapel of La Pausa. It is a 500-year-old tradition, fulfilling a vow made in 1467 by villagers who survived the plague.

A second traditional procession takes place on the evening of Good Friday, when some villagers dress as Roman soldiers, with others dressed as disciples and carrying a statue of Christ. The windows of Roquebrune are decorated with flowers and upturned empty snail shells holding lighted wicks. The procession is known in Provençal as *Proucessioun dei Limassa*, (the Procession of the Snails); its religious name is Procession of the Entombment of Christ. Some say the ritual dates back to 1316, the snails being a Christian symbol of resurrection.

On the Menton road, 200m (660ft) beyond Roquebrune, there is an olive tree thought to be 1,000 years old. Although many modern buildings have been built outside the Old Town, **Menton** remains a picture-postcard, Italianate town. Tall, honey-coloured houses rise gracefully from near the sea to the church of St Michel. Outside the church, a prestigious chamber-music festival is held under flood-lights during the first half of August.

Menton's setting is idyllic. The mountains stand well back, respectfully, yet give the town its enviable winter climate which allows lemon crops to ripen. The annual lemon festival is held in February.

Compared with other resorts along the coast, Menton retains a more leisurely atmsophere. Clamber about the old town, particularly Rue Longue, and stroll along the Promenade du Soleil past the casino to the harbour and the Cocteau Museum. The lover of Cocteau's work should also visit the Salle des Mariages, the wedding room in the town hall that the artist decorated with fine murals. Even those who are not familiar with the artist's work will find the murals delightful.

Elsewhere, the cemetery is interesting for the well-known English names, Menton having first been used as a health resort for the treatment of tuberculosis on the initiative of the English specialist, Dr

Places of Interest In and Near Menton

Roquebrune-Cap Martin

Castle Museum
Believed to be the oldest castle in France, dating, in part, from the tenth century. The walls of the keep are up to 4m (13ft) thick and show the full range of medieval defensive architecture. The keep is on four floors, each illustrating a different aspect of life in a medieval castle. The view of Cap Martin and Monaco from the top is excellent. Not to be missed.

Thousand-Year-Old Olive Tree
Said to be one of the oldest in the world. Though obviously considerably younger than the Bristlecone Pines, this tree is a great age considering the regional climate.

Menton

Museum of Local Prehistory
Interesting museum using audio-visual techniques to reconstruct the arrival of Man on the Côte d'Azur.

Carnoles Palace
A former summer residence of the Princes of Monaco, built in the eighteenth century. Museum collections include fine paintings from the seventeenth and eighteenth centuries as well as the work of contemporary artists.

Cocteau Museum
Housed in a seventeenth-century bastion in the old harbour, the museum is exclusive to the work of Jean Cocteau, the painter-poet. Works include an impressive mosaic salamander.

Salle des Mariages
In the Hôtel de Ville, a seventeenth-century building in Italian style. The marriage room has walls and ceiling decorated by Jean Cocteau. There is a fisherman in the traditional fisherman's hat of Menton, and a girl in the traditional Nice bonnet.

Palais de L'Europe
The palace has a continous programme of exhibitions of contemporary art.

The Exotic Gardens
Garavan, near Menton
Laid out around the Villa Val Rimeh, by the Museum of Natural History in Paris, the gardens concentrate on Mediterranean species, although there are also some tropical plants.

Henry Bennet, in the 1860s. The Carnoles Palace is also worth visiting. It is a former palace of the Princes of Monaco built in elegant Italian style in the eighteenth century. There is a Fine Art collection inside. Finally, it is worth going to the Colombières Gardens, where

Bridges spanning the gorge, La Condamine, Monaco

The Prince's Palace, Monaco

Menton

there is a collection of Mediterranean shrubs, and watch the sun go down into the azure sea.

France: Tips for Travellers

Planning Your Visit

Finances

All major credit cards (Access, Visa, American Express etc) are taken at most large restaurants, hotels, shops and garages. Eurocheques and traveller's cheques are also accepted.

Banks are normally open from 8.30am-12noon, 1.30-4.30pm, Monday to Friday only.

Currency Regulations

The French unit of currency is the French franc. There are no restrictions on the import of French or foreign currency. The export of currency valued at up to 5,000 French francs in any currency (including French francs) is permitted. Amounts worth in excess of 5,000 French francs may be exported, providing that the money has been declared on entry.

Entry into France

No visa is required for holders of British, American and Canadian passports.

Customs Regulations

Normal EEC customs regulations apply for those travelling from Britain. Normal European regulations apply for those travelling from North America.

Health Care

British travellers have a right to claim health services in France by virtue of EEC regulations. Form E111 — available from the Department of Health and Social Security — should be obtained to avoid complications.

American and Canadian visitors will need to check the validity of their personal health insurances to guarantee they are adequately covered. For emergency assistance, dial 19 in all towns. In country areas it may be necessary to phone the local *gendarmerie* (police).

Pharmacies, clearly marked with a green cross, can usually deal with minor ailments or advise people where to go if any additional help is needed.

Weather Information

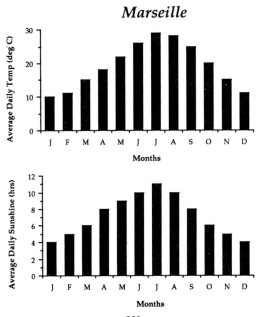

Marseille

Nice

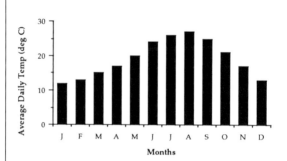

How To Get There

Travel

By Air

Provence is served by the international airport of
Marseille-Provence, situated to the north-west of the city
on the shore of the Etang de Berre, north of the town of
Marignane. There is an excellent, direct road connection
with the A7 autoroute.

The Côte d'Azur is served by the international airport of
Nice-Côte d'Azur, situated above the Mediterranean at

the south end of the town.
Both of these airports are served by international flights and also have regular services to Paris.

There is an airport served by domestic flights to the south-east of Hyères. There are also smaller airports served by more infrequent flights at Nîmes and Fréjus-St Raphaël.

Finally, there is a helicopter link between Nice-Côte d'Azur airport and Monaco.

By Rail
SNCF (Systéme National de Chemin-de-Fer), the French national railway company, has both fast and express trains linking Provence and the Côte d'Azur with other parts of France and the Channel ports. Of particular interest to the traveller keen to cut down on travel time is the TGV (pronounced Tay-Jay-Vay) service, a very fast 250kph (155mph) bullet-shaped train that speeds between Paris and the South. The TGV offers only first class accommodation but does cut journey time considerably.

SNCF also offer motorail services to those not wishing to spend a part of their holiday gazing at the ribbon of the Autoroute du Soleil. These services are available from the Channel ports, but not to Marseille, the most desirable destination for the traveller who has just crossed to France. To use the service to reach Marseille — or to reach Avignon, Toulon, Fréjus-St Raphaël or Nice — the traveller must first reach Paris. The service is not cheap but the journey is overnight, which does have the advantage of extending the holiday by a day if travelling is not considered to be part of the holiday. Night-time accommodation is in a *couchette* — six berths, in three tiers, to a compartment, with blanket and pillow supplied — or in T1, T2 or T3 cabins. As the names imply, these offer one (first class ticket only), two or three berths. Breakfast at the destination is included in the price of the ticket.

By Road

Coaches and Buses

France has an extensive, long-distance coach system and good local bus services. Not surprisingly, the majority of long-distance coach services head for Paris.

Cars

France has an excellent network of autoroutes backed up by a good system of 'ordinary' routes. The south of the country is served by the Autoroute du Soleil, the A7, that links it with Paris and the Channel ports. The A7 follows the Rhône Valley to Orange, where the A9 leaves it to reach Nîmes, continuing to Avignon and Salon-de-Provence. To the south of Salon, the A8 heads off east to Cannes and Nice, while the A7 continues south to Marseille and Toulon. French autoroutes are toll roads but they do offer a much quicker and, for those not used to driving on the right, safer way to travel. Quicker they may be, but it is still over 1,100km (700 miles) from the Channel to the South, so several days should be taken over the journey.

When You Are There

Car Hire

Car hire is available from many companies, including all the well-known major European ones, and from all the big towns, the airports and all large railway stations.

The speed limits currently applied to French roads are:

	In dry conditions	In the wet
Autoroutes	130kph(81mph)	110kph (68mph)
National (N) roads	110kph (68mph)	90kph (56mph)
Other roads	90kph (56mph)	80kph (50mph)
In towns	60kph (37mph)	60kph (37mph)

Please Note:

There is a new minimum speed limit of 80kph (50mph) for the outside lane on *autoroutes* during daylight, on level ground and with good visibility.

No driving is permitted on a provisional licence and the minimum age to drive is 18. Stop signs mean exactly that — the vehicle must come to a complete halt.

It is compulsory for front seat passengers to wear seat belts and children below the age of 10 are not allowed to travel in the front seats. All vehicles must carry a red warning triangle and a spare headlamp bulb.

There are strict — and very strictly interpreted — laws on speeding and drink-driving. The former will usually result in an on-the-spot fine, while the latter will usually result in confiscation of the car.

In built-up areas, the motorist must give way to anybody coming out of a side-turning on the right. This is indicated by the sign, *priorité à droite*. However, this rule no longer applies at roundabouts which means vehicles already on the roundabout have right of way (*passage protégé*). All roads of any significance outside built-up areas have right of way.

Car Parking

Car parking is no easier in French towns than it is in most other large European cities. The by-laws vary from town to town and, occasionally, from day to day. To be safe it is best to use car parks. Check before leaving your parked car: it is common practice to take your ticket with you, to pay as you return and to use the stamped ticket or token to raise the exit barrier. If you drive to an exit and then discover this rule, it is likely that you will have a queue of cars behind you when you are trying to work out what has gone wrong or are trying to reverse. Since tokens are time-limited, the queue is unlikely to be sympathetic.

Post and Telephone Services

Stamps (*timbres*) are available from post offices, which are normally open from 8am-7pm Monday to Friday and 8am-12noon on Saturday. In some smaller towns and villages, the post office may be shut for lunch, both the timing and the duration of the break being a local custom.

Telephones in France take coins rather than tokens. The dial codes from France are:

Great Britain	19	44
Canada	19	1
USA	19	1

Remember to leave out the first zero of your home country number — eg to dial the French Government Tourist Office in London (071 491 7622) from France, dial 19 44 17 491 7622. Many telephone booths now take phonecards; buy the *télécarte* from post offices and where advertised on telephone booths. Calls can be received at phone boxes where the blue bell is shown.

Tipping

Tips (*pourboires*) are given as in your home country but in France they also apply to guides at both *châteaux* and museums.

Electricity

220v ac, 50 Hertz (cycles/sec) in most places. Some small areas are still at 110v ac. Adaptors will be needed by those people who do not use continental two-pin plugs at home.

Holidays

France has the following national holidays:

New Year's Day
Easter Monday
May Day
Ascension Day
V.E. Day — 8 May
Whit Monday
Bastille Day — 14 July
Assumption Day — 15 August
All Saints' Day — 1 November
Armistice Day — 11 November
Christmas Day

FURTHER INFORMATION FOR VISITORS

Annual Events

Only the main events are given here. It is worth checking with the local Tourist Office as new events are constantly being added to the programmes of the major, and many minor, resorts.

Aix-en-Provence
Mid-July to mid-August, music festival.

Antibes
Sunday after 29 June, Festival of St Peter, procession to Harbour.

Apt
Whit Sunday and Monday, cavalcade, music festival.
Last week in July, pilgrimage of Ste Anne.

Arles
Easter Friday to Monday, bullfight festival.
Last Sunday in April, *Fête des Gardians*.
July, international festival of music, dance and drama in Roman theatre.
July, international photography festival.
Mid-December to mid-January, *Santons* trade fair.

Avignon
Last 3 weeks of July, international drama festival, mainly in Great Courtyard of Palais de Papes.
14 July, fireworks display.
15 July, jousting on Rhône.

Barjols
16 January every 4 years, *Fête du St Marcel*.

Les Baux
24 December, midnight mass in St Vincent church and pageant of Nativity.

Beaucaire
End July to early August, *fête* to commemorate medieval fair.

Le Beausset
Early April, 'Moto Journal 200' motor race.
Mid-September, *Bol d'Or* motor race.

Bollène
Last Saturday in June, *Fête du Papagaî*.

Boulbon
1 June, Bottle Procession of St Marcellin, and blessing of wine.

Cairanne
July, wine festival.

Cannes
February, mimosa festival.
March, photography and amateur cinema festival.
May, international film festival.
July-August, *Nuits des Leirins*.
August, fireworks festival.
September, international yachting festival; royal regattas.
September, festival of vintage cars.
October-November, international golf championships.

Carpentras
July, festival of Notre-Dame de Santé.

Cavaillon
First Monday in September, traditional festival.

Châteaunauf-du-Pape
24 and 25 April, festival of St Marc.
1 May, lily of the valley festival.

Courthézon
End June, vine-stock festival.

Cucuron
Saturday after 21 May, procession with poplar tree in honour of Ste Tulle.

Digne
First Sunday in August, lavender festival.

Entrevaux
Weekend nearest 24 January, festival of St John the Baptist.
Two weeks in August, sixteenth- and seventeenth-century music festival.

Fontaine-de-Vaucluse
Mid-June to mid-September, *son-et-lumière*.

July, *Festival de la Sorgue*.

Fréjus
Third Sunday after Easter, *bravade* costume procession.

Grasse
Last two weeks of July, international amateur music, folk and drama festival.

Graveson
Last Sunday in July, festival of St Eloi.

Ile Ste Marguerite
1 June to 15 September, *son-et-lumière* at fort.

Istres
First Sunday in August, *Fête de St Pierre*, jousting, bullfighting.

Lagarde-Paréol
May, international moto-cross.

Lagnes
Mardi Gras, *Fête du Caramentran*.

Marseille
Two weeks from first Sunday in November, *santons* fair on La Canebière.

Martigues
First Saturday in July, nocturnal cavalcade of jousting boats.

Menton
Week before Shrove Tuesday, lemon festival.
First two weeks of August, international festival of chamber music in floodlit Place de l'Eglise.

Monaco

27 January, Monte-Carlo motor rally.

27 January, festival of Ste Dévote.

February, international television festival.

April, international tennis championships.

May, Monaco Grand Prix.

July to August, international fireworks festival.

August to September, world amateur theatre festival.

November, Monégasque National Festival.

December, international circus festival.

Mondragon

May, *Fête du Drac*.

Monteux

Sunday after 15 May, festival of St Gens.

Tuesday after last Sunday in August, fireworks display.

Nice

Two weeks before Lent, Carnival, fireworks display (Shrove Tuesday), Battle of Flowers (day after Ash Wednesday).

April, international dog show.

Each Sunday in May, *Fête des Maïs* in Cimiez Gardens.

May, spring music festival.

July, grand jazz parade in Cimiez Gardens.

July, international folklore festival.

August, wine festival in Cimiez Gardens.

October, autumn music festival.

Orange

Last two weeks in July, international music festival in Roman theatre.

Pernes-les-Fontaines

May, international moto-cross.

Piolenc

End of August, garlic festival.

Roquebrune-Cap Martin

Good Friday evening, procession of the Entombment of Christ.

Afternoon of 5 August, procession of the Passion.

St Paul-de-Vence

Second fortnight in July, *Nuits de la Fondation Maeght*.

St Tropez

16-18 May, *Bravade de St Torpes*.

15 June, *Fête des Espagnols*, the Spanish *bravade*.

Once a month in July and August, classical concerts in Citadel.

La Ste Baume

21-22 July, festival of Mary Magdalene and midnight mass.

Ste Cécile-les-Vignes

1 May, moto-cross.

Les Ste Maries-de-la-Mer

24-25 May, *Pèlerinage des Gitanes*, Gipsy celebrations.

Sunday nearest 24 July, *Fête Virginenco*.

Weekend nearest 22 October, gipsy pilgrimage.

Séguret

April to September, ethnological exhibition.

Second fortnight in August, Provençal festival.

July to August, and December to January, exhibition of *santons* (clay figurines).

Third Sunday in August, *bravade.*
24 December, mystery play.

Signes
Sunday nearest 24 June, festival of
St Eloi.

Sisteron
Mid-July and mid-August, festival
of drama, music and dance.

Tarascon
Last Sunday in June,
Fête de la Tarasque.

Toulon
April, flower festival.
July to August, festival of circus
artistes.
November, *santons* fair.

Vaison-la-Romaine
Early July, international folklore
festival.
Mid-July to mid-August, theatre
and music festival in Roman
theatre.
First Sunday after 15 August,
Provençal mystery play.

Valréas
23 June at 10.15pm, nocturnal
procession of 'Petit St Jean'
(500 years old).
July and August, musical evenings,
theatre.
First Sunday and Monday in
August, lavender fair.
Christmas to January, *santons* cribs.

Vence
Easter Sunday and Monday, Battle
of Flowers, Provençal dancing.

Ventabren
24 December, Nativity play.

Villeneuve-lès-Avignon
End April, festival of St Marc.
July, international summer festival
of music, dancing, theatre,
poetry, art and cultural exhibitions, workshops.

1 — The Rhone Valley to Avignon

Ardèche Gorge

Mas de la Vignasse
Auriolles
Open: May to September Daily
except Tuesday 9am-12noon,
2-6pm
☎ 75.396507

Grotte de la Madeleine
Open: April to October
April to June, September Daily
9.30am-12noon, 2-6pm; July,
August Daily 9.30am-6pm; October
Sunday 9.30am-12noon, 2-6pm
☎ 75.987091

Aven du Marzal and Musée du
Monde Souterrain
Open: March to November
Mid-April to September Daily 9am-
6pm; March to mid-April and
October to November Saturday
and Sunday 11am-6pm
☎ 75.041245

Also at the site is:-
Zoo Préhistorique
Open: March to November
April to October Daily 10am-6pm;
March and November Saturday
and Sunday 10am-6pm
☎ 75.987091

Aven d'Orgnac
(Orgnac Aven)
25km (16 miles) north-west of
Bagnols-sur-Cèze
Open March to mid-November
April to September Daily 9am-
12noon, 2-6pm; March, October to
mid-November 9am-12noon,
2-5pm
☎ 75.386167

Avignon

Le Palais des Papes
Place du Palais
Open: All year
June to September Daily 9am-6pm;
October to Easter Daily 9-11am,
2-4pm; Easter to May Daily
9-11.30am, 2-5.30pm
Guided tours available (in French)
approximately every hour
Closed on official holidays
☎ 90.860332

Chapelle St Nicolas
Pont St Bénézet
Open: All year
May to September Daily 9am-
12noon, 2-6.30pm; October to April
Daily 2-6pm
Closed on official holidays
☎ 90.826511

Musée du Petit Palais
Place du Palais
Open: All year
April to September Daily except
Tuesday 9.30-11.50am, 2-6.15pm;
October to March Daily except
Tuesday 9.15-11.50am, 2-6pm
Closed on official holidays
☎ 90.864458

Musée Lapidaire
Rue de la République
Open: All year

Daily except Tuesday 10am-
12noon, 2-6pm
Closed on official holidays
☎ 90.826511

Musée Requien
Rue Joseph-Vernet
Open: All year
Tuesday to Saturday 9am-12noon,
2-6pm
The library is open Monday to
Friday 9am-12noon, 2-6.30pm
☎ 90.863384

Musée Calvet
Rue Joseph-Vernet
Open: All year
Daily except Tuesday 10am-
12noon, 2-6pm
Free entry on Sundays in winter
☎ 90.863384

Chapelle des Pénitents-Gris
Rue des Teinturiers
Open: All year
Monday, Wednesday to Saturday
8am-12noon, 2.30-7pm; Tuesday
8.30-9.30am, 3.30-7pm
Sunday and holidays 8am-12noon

Musée Louis Vouland
Rue Victor Hugo
Open: All year
July to September Tuesday to
Thursday 10am-1pm, 3-6pm,
Friday 10am-1pm, 3-8pm; October
to June Tuesday to Friday 2-5pm.
Closed on official holidays
☎ 90.860379

Musée Théodore Aubanel
Near Eglise St Pierre
☎ 84.844626

Musée Municipale
Villeneuve-lès-Avignon
Open: All year
April to September Daily 10am-
12.30pm, 3-7.30pm; October to

March Daily 10am-12noon, 2-5pm
☎ 90.254203

La Chartreuse du
  Val-de-Bénédiction
Villeneuve-lès-Avignon
Open: All year
April to September Daily 9am-
12noon, 2-6pm; October to March
Daily 10am-12noon, 2-5pm
☎ 90.250546

Carpentras

Musée Lapidaire
234 boulevard Albin-Durand
Open: All year
June to September Daily except
Tuesday 10am-12noon, 2-6pm;
October to May Daily except
Tuesday 10am-12noon, 2-4pm
☎ 90.630492

Musée Comtadin-Duplessis
234 boulevard Albin-Durand
Adjacent to the Musée Lapidaire
Open: All year
June to September Daily except
Tuesday 10am-12noon, 2-6pm;
October to May Daily except
Tuesday 10am-12noon, 2-4pm
☎ 90.630078

Musée Sobirats
Rue du Collège
Open: All year
April to October Daily except
Tuesday 10am-12noon, 2-6pm;
November to March Daily except
Tuesday 10am-12noon, 2-4pm
☎ 90.630492

La Synagogue
Place de l'Hôtel de Ville
Open: All year Monday to Friday
10am-12noon, 3-5pm

Châteauneuf-du-Pape

Musée du Père Anselme
Open: All year Daily 9am-12noon,
2-6pm
☎ 90.837108

Comtat Plain (near Avignon)

Grotte de Thouzon
3km north of Le Thor on the D16
Open: All year except December
May to September Daily 9am-7pm;
October, November, January to
April, Monday to Saturday 9am-
7pm, Sunday 2-6pm

Musée National d'Histoire
L'Harmas
Village near Serignan-du-Comtat
on the N976
Open: All year
May to September Daily except
Tuesday 9am-11.30pm, 2-6pm;
October to April Daily except
Tuesday 9am-11.30pm, 2-4pm
☎ 90.700044

Grignan

Le Château
Open: All year except November
Thursday to Sunday 9.30-11.30am,
2.30-5.30pm, Wednesday 2.30-
5.30pm
☎ 75.465156

Mont Ventoux

Musée des Vieux Outils
(Museum of Old Tools)
Caromb
Open: All year Daily 9am-12noon,
2-6pm
☎ 90.624024

Le Château
Aulan
Open: July to mid-September Daily
except Tuesday 10am-12noon,
2-6pm. ☎ 75.288000

Orange

Théâtre Antique
Open: All year
April to September Monday to
Saturday 9am-6.30pm, Sunday
9am-12noon, 2-5pm; October to
March Daily 9am-12noon, 2-5pm
Closed on official holidays
☎ 90.347088

Musée Municipal
Open: All year
April to September Daily 9am-
12noon, 2-6.30pm; October to
March Daily 9am-12noon, 2-5pm
Closed on official holidays
☎ 90.347088

Uzès

Musée Gide
The Bishop's Palace
Open: All year
July to August Daily 9am-12noon,
2-6pm; September to June Saturday
and Sunday 2-6pm
☎ 66.226899

Le Duché
Open: All year
June to September Daily 9am-
12noon, 2-7pm; October to May
Daily 9.30am-12noon, 2.30-5pm

La Crypt
Open: April to December
June to September Daily 10am-
12.30pm, 2.15-7pm; October,
November, April and May Daily
10am-12noon, 3-5pm

Vaison-la-Romaine

Quartier du Puymin
Open: All year
June to September Daily 9am-7pm;
October, November Daily 9am-
6pm; December to February Daily
9am-5pm; March to May Daily
9am-6pm
☎ 90.360211

Château de Simiane
Valréas
10km north-west of Vaison-la-
Romaine on the D541 off the D538
Open: All year Monday to Friday
10am-12noon, 3-7pm
☎ 90.360211

2 — Upper Provence and the Durance Valley

Allemagne-en-Provence

Château de Castellane
Open: June to September Daily
2.30-6.30pm
☎ 92.744161

Cavaillon

Musée Archéologique
Grand Rue
Open: All year Daily except
Tuesday 10am-12noon, 2-6pm
☎ 90.713201

La Synagogue
Rue Hèbraïque
Open: All year
April to October Daily except
Saturday 10am-12noon, 3-6pm;
November to March Daily except
Saturday 10am-12noon, 2-4pm
☎ 90.713201

Cucuron

Musée Marc Deydier
Open: July to September Daily
10am-12noon, 3-7pm
☎ 90.772502

Digne

Musée Municipale
Rue de la Grande Fontaine
Open: All year
Daily except Monday 10am-
12noon, 2-6pm
☎ 92.310067

Musée de la Guerre 39-45
Place Paradis
Open: All year
Daily except Monday 10am-
12noon, 2-6pm
☎ 92.314529

Fondation Alexandra David-Néel
27 avenue du Mal-Juin
Open: All year
Daily for 1hr guided tours only at
3pm and 5pm
☎ 92.313238

Le Centre de Géologie
4km north of the town
Open: All year
Monday to Friday 9am-12noon,
2-5pm
☎ 92.315131

Durance Valley

L'Abbaye de Silvacaine
On the D561 north-west of Aix
Open: All year
Daily except Tuesday 10am-
12noon, 2-5pm
☎ 42.504169

Chartreuse de Bonpas
10km north-west of Cavaillon on
the D973
Open: Gardens only — all year
Daily 10am-5pm

Tour du Griffon
Châteaurenard
Open: February to November Daily
10am-12noon, 2-6pm
☎ 90.940727

Fontaine-de-Vaucluse

Le Monde Souterrain de Norbert
Casteret
Open: February to October, April
to September Daily 10am-12noon,
2-6.30pm; March, October Wednesday to Sunday 10am-12noon,
2-6.30pm
☎ 90.203413

Le Centre Artisanal de Vallis
Clausa
Open: All year
June to September Monday to
Saturday 9am-12.30pm, 2-7pm,
Sunday 10.30am-12.30pm; April,
May, October, November Monday
to Saturday 9am-12.30pm,
2-6.30pm, Sunday 10.30am-
12.30pm; December to March
Monday to Saturday 9am-12.30pm,
2-6pm, Sunday 10.30am-12.30pm
☎ 90.203414

Musée des Restrictions
Open: Easter to mid-October Daily
2-7pm
☎ 90.203179

Tour Ferrande
Pernes-les-Fontaines
5km north of Fontaine on the D938
Open: By request only — inquire at
the Tourist Office (☎ 90.613104)

Forcalquier

Le Couvent des Cordeliers
Open: May to September
July and August Daily 10.30am-
12noon, 2.30-6pm; May, June and
September Sunday and holidays
2.30-6pm
☎ 92.751002

Le Château de Sauvan
Near Forcalquier
Open: All year Daily except
Saturday 3-6pm
☎ 92.750564

Observatoire de Haute Provence
Near Forcalquier
Ask at the Tourist Office in
Forcalquier (Hôtel de Ville, Place
du Bourguet, ☎ 92.751002) for
details of visiting times.

Gordes

Musée Didactique Vasarely
Le Château
Open: All year Daily except
Tuesday 10am-12noon, 2-6pm
☎ 90.720289

Village de Bories
2km south of Gordes on the D15
Open: All year 9am-Dusk (10am-
Dusk on Saturdays and Sundays,
November to January)
☎ 90.720348

Musée du Vitrail Frédérique Duran
(Duran Stained-Glass Window
Museum)
4km south of Gordes on the D103
off the D2/D15
Open: All year
April to October 10am-12noon,
3-7pm; November to March by
request
☎ 90.722211

L'Abbaye de Sénanque
8km from Gordes on th D177 off
the D15
Open: All year
July and August 9am-12noon, 1.30-
7pm; September to June 9am-
12noon, 2-6pm
☎ 90.720205

Luberon

Musée de la Boulangerie
Bonnieux
Open: April to December
June to September Daily 10am-
12noon, 3-6.30pm; March, April,
October to December Saturdays,
Sundays and holidays 10am-
12noon, 3-6.30pm
☎ 90.758834

Château de Lacoste
Lacoste
Open: By request
☎ 90.758039

L'Abbaye St Hilaire
Near Lacoste
Open: By request
☎ 90.722131

Château de Lourmarin
Lourmarin
Open: All year
July to September Daily except
Tuesday 9.30-11.45am, 2.30-
6.15pm; October to June Daily
except Tuesday 9-11.45am,
2-5.45pm
☎ 90.681523

Château Sabran
Ansouis
Open: All year Daily except
Tuesday 2.45-5.45pm
☎ 90.792099

Musée Extraordinaire de Georges
Mazoyer
Ansouis
Open: All year
June to September Daily except
Tuesday 2-7pm; October to May
Daily except Tuesday 2-6pm
☎ 90.792088

Manosque

Prieuré de Ganagobie
North of Manosque on the D30 off
the N96
Open: All year Daily 9.30am-
12noon, 2.30-5pm

Riez

Musée d'Histoire Naturelle de
Provence
Open: All year
Daily except Tuesday 10am-
12noon, 3-6.30pm
☎ 92.744113

Sisteron

La Citadelle
Open: April to October 8am-Dusk
☎ 92.611203

Musée de Sisteron
Off the Place de la République
No official opening hours. Ask at
the Tourist Office (Hôtel de Ville,
Avenue de la Libération,
☎ 92.611203) for permission to visit.

3 — Arles and the Camargue

Aigues-Mortes

Tour de Constance
Aigues-Mortes
Open: All year
April to September Daily 9am-
12noon, 2-6pm; October to March
Daily 10am-12noon, 2-5pm
Closed on official holidays

Arles

A combined ticket is available for
the Amphitheatre, the Classical
Theatre, Constantine's Palace, the
Alyscamps, the St Trophime
Cloisters, the Pagan and the
Christian Art Museums, the Réattu
Museum and the Arlaten
Museum.
    All the sites except the Arlaten
Museum are open as below. The
Arlaten Museum is closed on
Mondays with the exception of
those Mondays in July and August.

Open: All year
January, February Daily 9am-
12noon, 2-4.30pm; March Daily
9am-12noon, 2-5.30pm; April Daily
8.30am-12noon, 2-6pm; May Daily
8.30am-12noon, 2-7pm; June to
mid-September Daily 8.30am-
12.30pm, 2-7pm; mid-September to
mid-October Daily 8.30am-
12.30pm, 2-6pm; mid-October to
November Daily 8.30am-12.30pm,
2-5.30pm; December Daily 8.30am-
12.30pm, 2-4.30pm
Closed on official holidays

Arènes
(Roman Amphitheatre)
☎ 90.969337

Théâtre Antique
(Roman Theatre)
☎ 90.969330

Thermes de la Trouille
(Constantine's Palace)
Rue de Maïsto

Allée des Sarcophages
(The Alyscamps)
Follow Avenue des Alyscamps
south-east from the old town centre
☎ 90.968317

St Trophime, Church and Cloisters
Place de la République
☎ 90.493636

Musée Lapidaire Païen
Place de la République
☎ 90.493636

Musée Lapidaire Chrétien
Rue Balze
☎ 90.493636

Musée Arlaten
Palais du Félibrige
Rue Mistral
☎ 90.960823

Musée Réattu
Rue du Grand Prieuré
☎ 90.963768

Espace Van Gogh
Rue de la République
☎ 90.493672

L'Abbaye de Montmajour
On the D17 north-east of Arles
Open: All year
April to September Daily except
Tuesday 9am-12noon, 2-6pm;
October to March Daily except

Tuesday 9am-12noon, 2-5pm
Guided tours on Sundays at
4.30pm and Daily (except Tuesday)
at 10am and 3pm from April to
September. The chapel of St Pierre
is only open during guided tours.
☎ 90.546417

Beaucaire

Le Château de Beaucaire
Open: All year
April to September Daily except
Tuesday 10am-12noon, 2.15-
6.30pm; October to March Daily
except Tuesday 10.15am-12noon,
2-5.30pm
Guided tours (in French) available
☎ 66.591006/594761

Musée du Vieux Beaucaire
27 rue Barbés
Open: All year
April to September Daily except
Tuesday 10am-12noon, 2.15-
6.30pm; October to March Daily
except Tuesday 10.15am-12noon,
2-5.30pm
☎ 66.592657

L'Abbaye de St Romaine
5km west of Beaucaire off the D999
Open: All year
July to mid-October Monday to
Wednesday, Friday 10am-7pm,
Saturday and Sunday 3-6pm; mid-
October to June Daily except
Thursday 3-6pm

Les Baux-de-Provence

Musée d'Art Moderne
Hôtel des Porcelets
Open: Easter to October Daily 9.30-
12noon, 2-6.30pm
☎ 90.543403/973439

Fondation Louis Jou
Hôtel Brion
Open: April to October Daily
10am-1pm, 2-7pm
☎ 90.973417

La Cité Morte
(The Deserted, or Upper, Village)
Open: Easter to October Daily 9.30-
12noon, 2-6.30pm
The old village is illuminated at
night all year as follows: April to
October Wednesday, Saturday,
Sunday and holidays; November to
March Saturday and Sunday
☎ 90.543403/973439

Cathédrale d'Images
On the D27, 500m north of the
village
Open: mid-January to mid-
November; mid-January to mid-
March Daily 2-6pm; mid-March to
June Daily 10am-7pm; July, August
Daily 10am-8pm; September Daily
10am-7pm; October to mid-
November Daily except Tuesday
10am-6pm
☎ 90.543865

Moulin de Daudet
15km south-west of Baux, off the
D33 from the D78
Open: All year except January;
May to October 9am-12noon, 1.30-
6.30pm; November, December
February to April 10am-12noon,
2-4pm
☎ 90.976078

Camargue

Musée Camarguais
Albaron
Arles
At Mas du Pont Rousty, 8km
south-west of Arles on the D570

Open April to September; April to
June, September Daily except
Tuesday 9am-12noon, 2-6pm; July
and August Daily except Tuesday
9am-12noon, 3-7pm
☎ 90.971082

Centre d'Information et d'Anima-
tion de Ginès
On the D570 5km north of Stes-
Marie-de-la-Mer
Open: April to September Daily
except Friday 9am-12noon, 2-6pm
☎ 90.978682

Parc Ornithologique
    de Pont de Gau
Near the Information Centre
Open: All year Daily 8am-Dusk
☎ 90.478262

Musée de Cire du Boumain
2km north of Stes-Marie-de-la-Mer
Open: April to October Daily
10am-12noon, 2.30-7pm
☎ 90.978472/978265

Musée Baroncelli
Stes-Marie-de-la-Mer
Open: All year Daily 10am-12noon,
2-6pm
☎ 90.978245/978255

Marsillargues

Château Teillan
Off the D265 a little to the north-
east of the town
Open: Mid-June to mid-September
Daily except Monday 2-6pm
☎ 67.404243

Martigues

Musée Ziem
Ferrières
Open: All year

July, August Daily except Tuesday
10am-12noon, 2.30-6.30pm;
September to June Wednesday to
Sunday 2.30-6.30pm
☎ 42.806606

Musée du Vieil-Istres
Rue du Portail-Neuf
Istres
Open: June to October Daily except
Tuesday 3-7pm
☎ 42.550497

Les Fouilles
St Blaise
North-west of Martigues
Open: June to March
June to mid-September Daily 9am-
12noon, 3-7pm; Mid-September to
March Monday, Wednesday and
Friday 2-5pm, Saturday and
Sunday 9am-12noon, 2-5pm
☎ 42.803072

Nîmes

The Roman monuments (the
Amphitheatre, the Maison Carrée,
Temple of Diana and the Magne
Tower) are open all year as follows:
June to September Daily 9am-
12noon, 2-7pm (Amphitheatre
open 9am-7pm); October to May
Daily 9am-12noon, 2-5pm
Information can be obtained from
the Tourist Centre, Rue Auguste
☎ 66.672911

Musée d'Archeologie et Histoire
Naturelle
Grand'Rue
Open: All year
June to September Monday to
Saturday 9am-12noon, 2-6pm,
Sunday 2-6pm; October to May
Wednesday to Saturday 9am-
12noon, 2-6pm, Sundays 2-6pm
☎ 66.672557/673914

Musée des Beaux Arts
Rue de Cité-Foulc
June to September Monday to
Saturday 9am-12noon, 2-6pm,
Sunday 2-6pm; October to May
Wednesday to Saturday 9am-
12noon, 2-6pm, Sundays 2-6pm
☎ 66.673821

Musée du Vieux Nîmes
Place aux Herbes
June to September Monday to
Saturday 9am-12noon, 2-6pm,
Sunday 2-6pm; October to May
Wednesday to Saturday 9am-
12noon, 2-6pm, Sundays 2-6pm
☎ 66.360064

St Rémy-de-Provence

Musée des Alpilles
Hôtel Mistral de Mondragon
Open: All year
March to October Daily except
Tuesday 10am-12noon, 2-6pm;
November to February Saturday
and Sunday 10am-12noon, 2-4pm
☎ 90.920810

Centre Archéologie
Hôtel de Sade
Open: March to September
Saturday and Sunday
Guided tours at approximately
hourly intervals
☎ 90.921307

Glanum
1km south of St Rémy-de-Provence
following La Route de Maussane
Open: All year
April to September Daily 9am-
12noon, 3-7pm; October to March
Daily 9am-12noon, 2-5pm
☎ 90.922379

Salon-de-Provence

Château de l'Empéri
Open: All year
Mid-April to September Daily
except Tuesday 10am-12noon,
2-6pm; October to mid-April Daily
except Tuesday 10am-12noon, 2.30-
6.30pm
☎ 90.562236

Musée de Salon et de la Crau
Avenue de Pivasis
Open: All year Saturday and
Sunday 10am-12noon, 2-5pm
☎ 90.562837

Maison de Nostradamus
Off rue de l'Horloge
Open: June to September Daily
except Tuesday 10am-12noon, 2.30-
6.30pm
☎ 90.539000

Château de la Barben
10km east of Salon-de-Provence off
the D572
Open: All year
April to September Daily 10am-
12noon, 2-6pm; October to March
Daily 10am-12noon, 2-5pm
☎ 90.551912

Tarascon

Château du Roi Réne
Open: April to September
Guided tours only. Tours Daily at
approximately hourly intervals
from 9am until 6pm.
☎ 90.910193

L'Abbaye de St Michel-de-Frigolet
10km north-east of Tarascon on the
D81 off the N570
Open: All year
Guided tours only. Tours Daily at
approximately hourly intervals

from 9am until 6pm.
☎ 90.957007

Le Château
Barbentane
5km north of L'Abbaye de St
Michel-de-Provence on the D35e
Open: All year
July to September Daily except
Wednesday 10am-12noon, 2-6pm;
October to June Sunday 10am-
12noon, 2-6pm. On other days by
request.
☎ 90.955107

Musée Mistral
Maillane
10km east of Tarascon on the D32
Open: All year
June to September Daily except
Monday 10am-12noon, 2-6pm;
October Daily except Monday
10am-12noon, 2-5pm; November to
March Daily except Monday 10am-
12noon, 2-4pm; April, May Daily
except Monday 10am-12noon,
2-5pm
☎ 90.910352

4 — Central Provence

Aix-en-Provence

Musée du Vieil Aix
17 rue Gaston-de-Saporta
Open: All year
April to September Daily except
Monday 10am-12noon, 2.30-6pm;
October to March Daily except
Monday 10am-12noon, 2-5pm.
Closed on official holidays
☎ 42.214355

Musée de Tapisseries
L'Archevêche

Place de la Résistance
Open: All year
July, August Daily except Tuesday
9.30am-12noon, 2.30-6.30pm;
September to June Daily except
Tuesday 9.30am-12noon, 2-6pm.
Closed on official holidays
☎ 42.210578

Musée Paul Arbaud
2a rue du 4-Septembre
Open: All year
Daily except Sunday 2-5pm
Closed on official holidays
☎ 42.383895

Musée Granet
Place de St Jean-de-Malte
Open: All year
Daily except Tuesday 10am-
12noon, 2-6pm.
Closed on official holidays
☎ 42.381470

L'Atelier Cezanne
9 avenue Paul Cezanne
Open: All year
June to September Daily except
Tuesday 10am-12noon, 2-6pm;
October to May Daily except
Tuesday 10am-12noon, 2-5pm
☎ 42.210653

Hôtel-de-Ville
Place Hôtel-de-Ville
Open: All year, but very variable
hours. Ask, or call the Tourist
Office (2 place du Général de
Gaulle, ☎ 42.260293) for details

Hôtel Boyer d'Eguilles
Rue Espariat
Open: All year
Monday to Friday 10am-12noon,
2-6pm. Closed on official holidays
☎ 42.262367

Le Pavillon Vendôme
34 rue Célony

Open: All year
Daily except Tuesday 10am-
12noon, 2-5pm
☎ 42.210518

Fondation Vasarely
4 km west of the town. Follow
Avenue Marcel Pagnol
Open: All year
Daily except Tuesday 9.30am-
12.30pm, 2 -5.30pm
☎ 42.210109

Entremont
3km north of Aix off of the D14
Open: All year Daily 9am-12noon,
2-6pm
☎ 42.233573

Aups

Fondation Simon-Segal et Donation
Bassano
Rue Albert
Open: June to mid-September
Daily 10am-12noon, 3-6pm
☎ 94.701298

Les Grottoes
Parc Municipale
Villecroze
Open: mid-June to September
Daily 9am-12noon, 2-7pm
☎ 94.706306

Brignoles

Musée du Pays Brignolais,
Brignoles
Open: All year June to September
Wednesday to Saturday 9am-
12noon, 2.30-6pm, Sundays and
Holidays 3-6pm; October to May
Wednesday to Saturday 10am-
12noon, 2.30-5pm, Sundays and
holidays 3-6pm
☎ 94.694518

L'Abbaye de la Colle
on the D405 4km south-west of
Brignoles
June to September by request only
☎ 94.690844 in season, ☎ 94.690904
out of season

Draguignan

Musée Bibliothèque
9 rue de la République
Open: All year Tuesday to
Saturday 10am-12noon, 2-6pm,
Monday and Sunday 2-6pm
☎ 94.689287

Musée des Arts et Traditions
Populaires
Rue de la Motte
Open: All year Tuesday to
Saturday 9am-12noon, 3-6pm
☎ 94.470572

Tour de l'Horloge
Open: All year Monday to
Saturday 9am-12noon, 2-6pm
Apply to Tourist Office
(☎ 94.686330) for key

Chapelle Ste Roseline
5km south-east of the town,
off the N555
Open: All year June to mid-
September Wednesday and Sunday
3.30-6.30pm; Mid-September to
May Wednesday and Sunday 2.30-
5pm

L'Abbaye du Thoronet,
Open: All year March, April Daily
except Tuesday 10am-12noon,
2-5pm; May to September Daily
except Tuesday 10am-12noon,
2-6pm; October Daily except
Tuesday 10am-12noon,
2-5pm Daily; November to
February Daily except Tuesday

10am-12noon, 2-4pm
☎ 94.738713

Entrecasteaux

Le Château
Entrecasteaux
Open: All year April to September
Daily 10am-8pm; October to March
Daily 10am-6pm
☎ 94.044395

Verdon Gorge

Musée de la Faïence
Place du Presbytère
Moustiers-Ste Marie
Open: April to October Daily
except Tuesday 9am-12noon,
2-6pm
☎ 94.746619

Musée des Tourneurs
Aiguines
Open: All year July, August Daily
10am-12noon, 2-6pm; September to
June by request only
☎ 94.702129/702175

5 — Western Riviera:
Marseille to Fréjus

Aubagne

La Légion Etrangère
1km east of the town on the D44a
off the D2
Open: All year June to September
Daily except Monday 10am-
12noon, 3-7pm; October to May
Wednesday, Saturday and Sunday
10am-12noon, 2-6pm
☎ 43.030320

Bandol

Wine and Spirit Exhibition
Bendor Island, near Bandol
Open: All year Daily except
Wednesday 10am-12.30pm, 2-6pm
☎ 94.294434

Zoo and Gardens
Sanary-Bandol
3km north on the D559
Open: All year Daily except
Sunday 8am-12noon
☎ 94.294038

Chapelle Notre Dame-du-Bausset-
Vieux, Bandol
8km north, off of the N8
Open: All year July to 1st week
September Sunday to Friday
2-5pm, Saturday 8am-6pm; 2nd
week September to June Saturday
8am-5pm, Sunday 2-5pm
☎ 94.294135

Bormes-les-Mimosas

Musée Arts et Histoire,
Bormes-les-Mimosas
65 rue Carnot
Open: All year Mid-June to mid-
September Wednesday to Sunday
10am-12, 3-5pm; Mid-September to
mid-June Wednesday and Sunday
10am-12noon
☎ 94.711508

Cassis

Musée Municipal des Arts et des
Traditions Populaires
On the first floor of the Tourist
Office, Place Baragnon
Open: All year Wednesday and
Friday to Sunday 3-5pm
☎ 42.017117

La Ciotat

Musée de Tauroentum
Open: All year June to September
Daily except Tuesday 3-7pm;
October to May Saturday and
Sunday 2-7pm
☎ 94.263046

Cogolin

Les Tapis et Tissues de Cogolin
(Museum of Carpets and Fabrics)
98 Boulevard Louis-Blanc
Open: All year Monday to Friday
8.30am-12noon, 2-6pm (5.30pm on
Fridays).
Closed on official holidays
☎ 94.563652

Ile des Embiez

Ricard Oceanographic Foundation
Ile des Embiez
Open: All year except November
Thursday to Tuesday 9am-
12.30pm, 1.30-5.45pm, Wednesday
1.30-5.45pm
☎ 94.250249

Fréjus

Le Groupe Episcopal
Open: All year April to September
Daily except Tuesday 9.30am-
12noon, 2-6pm; October to March
Daily except Tuesday 9am-12noon,
2-4.30pm
A single ticket covers the cathedral,
bapistry, cloister and museum.
Tickets are available from the
cloister.
☎ 94.512630

L'Amphithéâtre
Open: All year April to September
9am-12noon, 2-4.15pm; October to
March 9am-12noon, 2-4.30pm
☎ 94.513431

La Pagode Bouddhique
Follow Avenue du XVe Corps
(the N7) for 2km north of Fréjus
Open: June to mid-September
3-5pm. At other times by appointment.
☎ 94.810377

Safari de l'Estérel et Parc Zoologique de Fréjus
Open: All year June to September
Daily 9.30am-7pm (Park open until
8pm); October to May Daily 10am-
5pm (Park open until 6pm)
☎ 94.407065

Musée des Troupes de Marine,
5km north of the town on the D4
Open: All year June to September
Daily except Tuesday 10am-
12noon, 2-5.30pm; October to May
Daily except Tuesday 2-5.30pm
☎ 94.523445

La Chartreuse de la Verne
In the Maures Mountains 20km
south-west of Fréjus. Follow the
D558 and the D14, leaving the
latter to reach the site.
Open: All year March to September
Daily except Tuesday 11am-6pm;
October to February Daily except
Tuesday 10am-5pm
☎ 94.432291

Hyères

Musée Municipale
Place Théodore-Lefévre
Open: All year Monday, Wednes-
day to Friday 10am-12noon, 3-6pm,

Saturday and Sunday 10am-
12noon. Closed on official holidays
☎ 94.651207

Exposition Florale du Parc St-
Bernard
Open: All year May to September
Daily 8am-8pm; October to April
Daily 8am-5pm
☎ 94.651855

Jardin d'Acclimatation
   Olbius-Riquier
Avenue Ambroise-Thomas
Open: All year May to September
Daily 8am-8pm; October to April
Daily 8am-5pm
☎ 94.651855

Lighthouse, Ile de Porquerolles
Open: All year June to September
Daily 10am-12noon, 2-6pm;
October to March Daily 10am-
12noon, 2-4pm; April, May Daily
10am-12noon, 2-5pm
☎ 94.651855

Fort St Agathe, Ile de Porquerolles
Open: June to September Daily
9am-12.30pm, 3-6pm
☎ 94.651855

Les Lecques

Musée de Tauroentum
Open: All year June to September
Daily except Tuesday 3-6pm;
October to May Saturday and
Sunday 2-7pm
☎ 94.263046

Le Luc

Musée Historique du Centre Var
Open: March to October; July and
August Wednesday to Sunday

10am-12noon, 3.30-7pm, Tuesday
10am-12noon; September, October
and March to June Wednesday,
Saturday and Sunday 10am-
12noon, 2.30-5pm
☎ 94.608821

Musée Régional du Timbre et de la
Philatélie
Open: All year Monday, Wednesday to Sunday 10.30am-12noon,
2.30-6pm
☎ 94.479616

Marseille

Centre de la Vieille-Charité
2 rue de la Charité
Open: All year Monday to Friday
12-7pm, Saturday and Sunday
10am-7pm
☎ 91.562838

Musée Cantini
19 rue Grignan
Open: All year Thursday to Sunday
10am-12noon, 2-6.30pm, Wednesday 2-6.30pm
☎ 91.547775

Musée des Beaux-Arts
Palais Longchamp
Open: All year Daily except
Tuesday 10am-12noon, 2-6.30pm
☎ 91.622117

Musée D'Histoire de Marseille
Centre Bourse
Open: All year Tuesday to
Saturday 10am-7pm
☎ 91.904222

Musée du Vieux-Marseille
Rue de la Prison
Open: All year Daily except
Tuesday 10am-12noon, 2-6.30pm
☎ 91.551019

Musée D'Histoire Naturelle
Palais Longchamp
Open: All year Daily except
Tuesday 10am-5pm
☎ 91.623078

Galerie des Transports
Place du Marché-des-Capucins
Open: All year Tuesday to
Saturday 10.30am-5.30pm
☎ 91.541515

Musée Borély
Château Borély
Avenue Clot-Bey
Open: All year Daily except
Tuesday 9.30am-12.15pm,
1-5.30pm
☎ 91.732160

Musée de la Marine et de
l'Economie de Marseille
Palais de la Bourse
Open: All year Daily except
Tuesday 10am-12noon, 2-6pm
☎ 91.919151

Musée des Arts et Traditions
Populaires du Terroir Marseillais
5 place des Héroes
Open: All year Saturday to
Monday 2-6pm
☎ 91.681438

Musée Grobet-Labadié
140 boulevard Longchamp
Open: All year Thursday to Sunday
10am-12noon, 2-6.30pm
☎ 91.622182

Musée des Docks Roman
Place Vivaux
Open: All year Daily except
Tuesday 10am-12noon, 2-6.30pm
☎ 91.912462

Les Grottes Loubière
500m from Château-Gombert

Open: May to October Daily except
Tuesday 10am-5pm
☎ 91.681502

Château d'If
Reached by boat from Marseille
Times of boats vary, but they
generally run Daily from 9am-5pm
during the summer months (May
to September) and from 10am-4pm
in winter.

Ste Maxime

Musée des Traditions Locales
Open: All year except November
Daily except Tuesday and Sunday
10am-12noon, 2-4pm
☎ 94.967030

Musée du Phonographer et de la
Musique Mécanique
Parc de St Donat
8 km north of Ste Maxime, on the
D25
Open: Easter to September Daily
10am-12noon, 2.30-6.30pm
☎ 94.965042

St Tropez

L'Annonciade
Rue de la Nouvelle Poste
Open: All year except November;
June to September Daily except
Tuesday 10am-12noon, 3 -7pm;
October, December to May Daily
except Tuesday 10am-12noon,
2-6pm. Closed on official holidays
☎ 94.970401

Musée de la Marine
Citadelle
Open: All year except mid-
November to mid-December; mid-
June to mid-September Daily

except Thursday 10am-6pm; mid-
September to mid-November Daily
except Thursday 10am-5pm; mid-
December to mid-June Daily except
Thursday 10am-5pm
☎ 94.970653

Solliès-Ville

Musée du Moulin d'Oli
Rue de la Marseillaise
10km north-east of Toulon on the
D67 off the N97.
Open: All year Wednesday and
Saturday 4-6pm
☎ 94.288897/273850

Toulon

Musée du Vieux Toulon
69 Cours LaFayette
Open: All year Daily except
Sunday 3-6pm.
Closed on official holidays
☎ 94.922923

Musée Naval
Place Monsenergue
Open: All year Daily except
Tuesday 10am-12noon, 1.30-6pm.
Open on Tuesdays in July and
August. Closed on official holidays
☎ 94.020201

Musée des Beaux Arts
Avenue Général Leclerc
Open: All year Daily 1-8pm.
Closed on official holidays
☎ 94.931554

Musée d'Histoire Naturelle
Avenue Général Leclerc
Open: All year Daily 9.30-11.45am,
2-5.45pm
☎ 94.931554

La Tour Royale
5km south of the town, along
Avenue de l'Infanterie de Marine
Open: All year except March
June to mid-September Daily
except Monday 2-6pm; Mid-
September to October Daily except
Monday 3-6pm; November to
February, April, May Daily except
Monday 2-5pm

Musée Mémorial du Débarque-
ment en Provence
Mont Faron
Reached by road — go north of the
town along Avenue de Valbourdin
— or by *téléphérique* from Boulevard Amiral de Vence.
Open: All year June to September
Daily 9.30am-12noon, 2.30-7pm;
October to May Daily 9.30am-
12noon, 2.15-4.30pm
☎ 94.934101

Parc Zoologique
Mont Faron
Near Toulon
Reached by road — go north of the
town along Avenue de Valbourdin
— or by *téléphérique* from Boule-
vard Amiral de Vence.
Open: All year June to mid-
September Daily 10am-12noon,
2-7pm; mid-September to May
Monday, Wednesday, Saturday
and Sunday 10am-12noon, 2pm-
Dusk.
☎ 94.923529

Fort de Balaguier
West of the town on the N559
Open: All year mid-June to mid-
September Tuesday, Thursday to
Sunday 10am-12noon, 3-6.45pm;
mid-September to mid-June
Tuesday, Thursday to Sunday
10am-12noon, 2-5.45pm
☎ 94.948472

6 — Côte d'Azur:
St Raphaël to Menton

Antibes

Musée d'Archéologie
Bastion St André sur les Ramparts
Open: All year except November
May to October Daily 9am-12noon,
2-7pm; December to April Daily
except Tuesday 9am-12noon,
2-6pm
☎ 93.344801

Musée Grimaldi Picasso
Place du Château
Open: All year except November
June to September Daily except
Tuesday 10am-12noon, 3-7pm;
December to May Daily except
Tuesday 10am-12noon, 2-6pm.
Closed on official holidays
☎ 93.349191

Musée Naval et Napoléonien
Batterie du Grillon
Avenue John Kennedy
Open: All year except November
Daily except Tuesday 9am-12noon,
2-6pm
☎ 93.614532

Galerie du Bastion
Galerie d'Art Municipal du Musée
du Bastion
St André sur les Ramparts
Open: All year except November
Daily except Tuesday 9am-12noon,
2-6pm
☎ 93.344801

Musée Peynet
Place Nationale
Open: All year except November
Daily except Tuesday 10am-
12noon, 2-6pm
☎ 93.343664

Marineland
Carrefour (Junction) RN7/Route
de Biot
Open: All year Daily 11am-6pm
☎ 93.334949

Auron

Funivia to Las Donnas, Auron
Open: July, August and December
to April only; July to August Daily
9am-12.15pm, 2-4.30pm; December
to April 9am-4.30pm
☎ 93.808484

Beaulieu-sur-Mer

Villa Kerylos
(Fondation Théodore Reinach)
Avenue Gustave Eiffel
Open: All year except November
July, August Daily except Monday
2-6.30pm. All other months Daily
except Monday 2-6pm
☎ 93.01014

Biot

Musée National Fernand Léger
Signposted off the D4 south-east of
the village
Open: April to September Daily
except Tuesday 10am-12noon,
2-6pm; November to March Daily
except Tuesday 10am-12noon,
2-5pm
☎ 93.656349/656361

Musée d'Histoire Locale
Place de la Chapelle
Open: April to September Daily
except Monday 2.30-6pm; November to March Thursday, Saturday
and Sunday 2.30-6pm
☎ 93.650585/651179

Verrerie de Biot
Chemin des Combes
Open: All year Monday to
Saturday 8am-6pm, Sunday 2.30-
6.30pm
☎ 93.650300

Cagnes-sur-Mer

Château Musée
Haut-de-Cagnes
Place Grimaldi
Open: All year except mid-October
to mid-November; July to September Daily 10am-12noon, 2.30-7pm.
All other times Daily except
Tuesday 10am-12noon, 2-5pm
☎ 93.208557

Musée Renoir du Souvenir
La Maison de Renoir
'Les Collettes'
Open: All year except mid-October
to mid-November; June to mid-
October Daily except Tuesday
10am-12noon, 2-6pm; mid-
November to May Daily except
Tuesday 2-5pm. Closed on official
holidays
☎ 93.206107

Cannes

Musée de la Castre
Château da la Castre
Le Suquet
Open: All year April to June Daily
except Tuesday 10am-12noon,
2-6pm; July to September Daily
except Tuesday 10am-12noon,
3-7pm; October to March Daily
except Tuesday 10am-12noon,
2-5pm
☎ 93.385526

La Californie
Super Cannes
Open: All year Daily 2-6pm
☎ 93.391555

Chapelle Bellini
Parc Fiorentina
67 bis avenue de Vallauris
Open: All year Daily 2-6pm.
At other times by appointment
☎ 93.391555/386180

Confiserie Blachère
6 rue Pasteur
Open: All year May to mid-October
Daily 9.30am-7pm; mid-October to
April Daily 9.30am-12noon, 2-6pm
☎ 93.945759

Les Ruchers de Dieu
Chemin de l'Aubarède
Le Cannet Rocheville
Open: All year afternoons only.
Any reasonable time on request
☎ 93.450068

Europ Mimosa (Mimosa)
44/46 rue de Cannes
Cannes-la-Bocca
Open: All year any reasonable time
☎ 93.471969

Musée de la Mer
Ile Ste Marguerite (in the enclosure
of the Royal Fortress)
Open: All year except January and
February; June to September Daily
except Tuesday 9am-12noon,
2-6pm. At other times Daily except
Tuesday 10.30-11.45am, 2-3.45pm.
Closed on official holidays
☎ 93.689192

Monastère de St Honorat
Ile de St Honorat
Open: All year June to September
9.40am-4.40pm; October to May
10.40am-3.30pm.

Closed Good Friday
☎ 93.388282

Colmars-les-Alpes

Le Fort de Savoie
Open: June to September Daily
2.30-6.30pm. At other times by
request at the Information Centre.
☎ 92.834192

Eze

Jardin Exotique
Open: All year May to September
Daily 8am-7pm; October to April
Daily 9am-12noon, 2-5pm
☎ 93.410303

Parfumerie Galimard
Place de Gaulle
Open: All year May to mid-October
Daily 9.30am-7pm; mid-October to
April Daily 9.30am-12noon, 2-6pm
☎ 93.411070

Gourdon

Musée du Château de Gourdon
Open: All year June to September
Daily 11am-1pm, 2-7pm; October
to May Daily except Tuesday
11am-1pm, 2-6pm
☎ 93.425013

Grasse

Musée d'Art et d'Histoire de
Provence
2 rue Mirabeau
Open: All year except November;
June to September Monday to
Friday 10am-12noon, 2-6pm; Also
first and last Sunday of each
month, times as above; October,

December to May Monday to
Friday 10am-12noon, 2-5pm; Also
first and last Sunday of each
month, times as above.
Closed on official holidays
☎ 93.360161

Musée de la Marine Amiral de
Grasse
2 boulevard Jeu de Ballon
Open: All year except November;
June to September Tuesday to
Saturday 2.30-6pm; October,
December to May Tuesday to
Saturday 2.30-5pm.
Closed on official holidays
☎ 93.091071

Villa Musée Fragonard
23 boulevard Fragonard
Open: All year except November;
June to September Monday to
Friday 10am-12noon, 2-6pm; Also
first and last Sunday of each
month, times as above; October,
December to May Monday to
Friday 10am-12noon, 2-5pm; Also
first and last Sunday of each
month, times as above.
Closed on official holidays
☎ 93.360161

Musée International
   de la Parfumerie
8 place du Cours, Grasse
For opening hours, telephone or
ask at information office in Place de
la Foux (☎ 93.360356)
☎ 93.360161

Parfumerie Fragonard
Boulevard de Fragonard
Open: All year May to mid-October
Daily 9.30am-7pm; mid-October to
April Daily 9.30am-12noon, 2-6pm
☎ 93.092000

Parfumerie Galimard
Route de Cannes
Open: All year May to mid-October
Daily 9.30am-7pm; mid-October to
April Daily 9.30am-12noon, 2-6pm
☎ 93.092000

Parfumerie Molinard
60 Boulevard Victor Hugo
Open: All year May to mid-October
Daily 9.30am-7pm; mid-October to
April Daily 9.30am-12noon, 2-6pm
☎ 93.360162

Les Grottes de St Cézaire
On the D613 north of St Cézaire-
sur-Siagne, to the west of Grasse
Open: March to October; June to
September Daily 10.30am-12noon,
2-6pm; March to May, October
Daily 2.30-5pm. Guided tours
(in French) available
☎ 93.602235/602287

Laghet

Madonne-de-Laghet
Sanctuaire de Laghet
La Trinité
(Reached from A8, exit at La
Turbie)
Open: All year Daily 3-5pm

Levens

Musée des Papillons et d'Insectes
Levens (20 km north of Nice)
Open: June to September, Wednes-
day to Sunday 4-7pm; Monday and
Tuesday by appointment only.
Guided tours (in French) by
request
☎ 93.797012

Mandelieu-La-Napoule

Fondation Henry Clews
06210 Mandelieu-La-Napoule
Open: All year but very variable
hours. Telephone for up-to-date
information
☎ 93.499505

Verrerie du Domaine
 de Maure-Vieil
(Verrerie d'Art Artisand)
Mandelieu
Open: All year Monday to
Saturday 8.30am-12.30pm; 2-7pm;
Sunday 4-6pm
☎ 93.498258

Menton

Musée Cocteau
Bastion du Vieux Port
Open: All year Mid-June to mid-
September Daily except Tuesday
10am-12.30pm, 3-7pm; mid-
September to mid-June Daily
except Tuesday 10am-12noon,
2-6pm. Closed on official holidays
☎ 93.577230

Cocteau's 'Salles des Mariages'
Mairie
Rue de la République
Open: All year Monday to Friday
8.30am-12.30pm, 1.30-5pm.
Closed on official holidays
☎ 93.578787

Musée du Palais Carnolès
3 avenue de la Madonne
Open: All year Mid-June to mid-
September Daily except Tuesday
10am-12.30pm, 3-7pm; mid-
September to mid-June Daily
except Tuesday 10am-12noon,
2-6pm. Closed on official holidays
☎ 93.354971

Musée de Prehistoire Régionale
Rue Lorédan Larchey
Open: All year mid-June to mid-
September Daily except Tuesday
10am-12.30pm, 3-7pm; mid-
September to mid-June Daily
except Tuesday 10am-12noon,
2-6pm. Closed on official holidays
☎ 93.358464

Palais de l'Europe
Avenue Boyer
Open: All year Mid-June to mid-
September Daily except Tuesday
10am-12.30pm, 3-7pm; mid-
September to mid-June Daily
except Tuesday 10am-12noon,
2-6pm. Closed on official holidays
☎ 93.575700

Le Jardin Botanique Exotique
Avenue St Jacques
Garavan, near Menton
Open: All year Daily except
Tuesday 10am-12noon, 3-6pm or
Dusk.
☎ 93.575700

Monaco

Musée d'Anthropologie et Jardin
Exotique
Boulevard du Jardin Exotique
Monaco
Open: All year May to September
9am-7pm; October to April 9am-
Dusk
☎ 93.303365

Musée Océanographique
Avenue St Martin
Monaco
Open: All year Daily 9.30am-7pm.
Closes at 12.30pm on the day of the
Grand Prix
☎ 93.301514

Musée de Cires (Waxworks)
27 rue Basse
Monaco
Open: All year February to October
Daily 9.30am-7pm; November to
January Daily 10.30am-5pm
☎ 93.303905

Le Palais Princier
Place du Palais
Monaco
Open: June to October; June to
September Daily 9.30am-6.30pm;
October Daily 10am-5pm. Guided
tours (in English) available
☎ 93.506088

Musée du Souvenir Napoléonien et
des Archives
Place du Palais
Monaco
Open: All year except November;
June-September Daily 9.30am-
6.30pm; October Daily 10am-5pm;
December-May Daily except
Monday 10.30am-12.30pm, 2-5pm
☎ 93.301831

Centre d'Acclimation Zoologique
La Condamine
Open: All year October to June
Wednesday, Thursday, Saturday to
Monday 2-6pm; Sundays and
Holidays 10am-12noon, 2-6pm;
July to September Wednesday,
Thursday, Saturday to Monday
10am-11.30pm, 2-6.30pm
☎ 93.301831

Musée National Collection de
Galea
17 boulevard Princesse Grace
Monte-Carlo
Open: All year Mid-March to mid-
September Daily 10am-6.30pm;
mid-September to mid-March
Daily 10am-12.15pm, 2.30-6.30pm
☎ 93.309126

Mougins

Musée de l'Automobiliste
(Autoroute A8 Nice-Cannes)
Les Hautes Bréguirès
772 Chemin de Font-de-Currault
Open: All year except mid-
November to mid-December Daily
10am-7pm
☎ 93.692780

Musée de la Photographie
Porte Sarrazine
Mougins-Village
Open: All year July and August
Daily 2-11pm. Other months
Wednesday to Sunday, 1-7pm
☎ 93.758567

Nice

Musée des Beaux Arts Jules Cheret
33 avenue des Baumettes
Open: All year May to September
Daily except Monday 10am -
12noon, 3-6pm; October to April
Daily except Monday 10am -
12noon, 2-7pm.
Closed on official holidays
☎ 93.445072

Musée Renoir
8 rue de la Loge
Open: All year Tuesday to
Saturday 2-6pm.
Closed on official holidays
☎ 93.134046

Musée d'Art Naïf Anatole
Jakovsky
Château Ste Hélène
Avenue Val Marie
Open: All year May to September
Daily except Tuesday 10am-
12noon, 2-6pm; October to April
Daily except Tuesday 10am-
12noon, 2-5pm.

Closed on official holidays
☎ 93.717833

Musée National Marc Chagall
Avenue du Docteur Ménard
Open: All year July to September
Daily except Tuesday 10am-7pm;
October to June Daily except
Tuesday 10am-12.30pm, 2-5.30pm
☎ 93.817575

Musée d'Histoire Naturelle
60 bis, boulevard Risso
Open: All year except mid-August
to mid-September Daily except
Tuesday 9am-12noon, 2-6pm.
Closed on official holidays
☎ 93.551524

Musée International
de Malacologie
3 cours Saleya
Open: All year except November,
Tuesday to Saturday 10.30am-1pm,
2-6pm. Closed on official holidays
☎ 93.851844

Musée Naval
Tour Bellanda
Parc du Château
Open: All year except mid-
November to mid-December; June
to September Daily except Tuesday
10am-12noon, 2-7pm; October to
May (except as above) Daily except
Tuesday 10am-12noon, 2-5pm.
Closed on official holidays
☎ 93.804761

Musée Matisse
164 avenue de Cimiez
Open: All year except November;
May to September, Tuesday to
Saturday 10am-12noon, 2.30-
6.30pm; Sunday 2.30-6.30pm;
October, December to April,
Tuesday to Saturday 10am-12noon,
2-5pm; Sunday 2-5pm

☎ 93.571770

Musée d'Archéologie
160 avenue des Arènes
Telephone and opening as below

Musée d'Archéologie
(City archaeological site and old
museum)
Avenue Monte Croce
Open: All year except November;
May to September Tuesday to
Saturday 10am-12noon, 2-6pm;
Sunday 2-6pm; October, December
to April Tuesday to Saturday
10am-12noon, 2-5pm; Sunday
2-5pm
The archaeological site is open on
Mondays, times as weekdays
above.
☎ 93.815957

Musée Masséna
Palais Masséna
65 rue de France and 35 Promenade des Anglais
Open: All year May to September
Daily except Monday 10am-
12noon, 3-6pm; October to April
Daily except Monday 10am-
12noon, 2-5pm.
Closed on official holidays
☎ 93.881134/880622

Library of the Chevalier de Cessole
Palais Masséna
65 rue de France
Open: All year Monday to Friday
9am-12noon, 2-6pm
☎ 93.881276

Palais Lascaris
15 rue Droite
Open: All year except November
Every day except Monday 9.30am-
12noon, 2.30-6pm
☎ 93.620554

Terra Amata
25 boulevard Carnot
Open: All year except first two
weeks of September
Every day except Monday 10am-
12noon, 2-6pm
☎ 93.555993

Villa Arson
20 avenue Stéphane-Liégard
Open: All year May to September
Daily except Tuesday 12-7pm;
October to April Daily except
Monday and Tuesday 12-7pm
☎ 93.844004

Musée Franciscain et Monastére de
Cimiez
Place du Monastère
Open: All year
Every day except Sunday 10am-
12noon, 3-6pm. Closed on official
holidays
☎ 93.815541/810004

Musée d'Art Contemporaire
59 quai des Etats-Unis
Open: All year Tuesday to
Saturday 10.30am-12noon, 2-6pm;
Sunday 2-6pm. Closed on official
holidays
☎ 93.623711

Prieuré du Vieux Logis
59 avenue Barthelemy
Open: All year Wednesday,
Thursday, Saturday and first
Sunday of the month 3-5pm. At
other times by prior appointment
☎ 93.884474

Confiserie du Vieux Nice
14 quai Papacino
Open: All year May to mid-October
Daily 9.30am-7pm; mid-October to
April Daily 9.30am-12noon, 2-6pm
☎ 93.554350

Martin Fleurs (Carnations)
23 route de Grenoble
Open: All year
Any reasonable time
☎ 93.720880

Pont-du-Loup

Confiserie des Gorges du Loup
Pont-du-Loup
Open: All year May to mid-October
Daily 9.30am-7pm; mid-October to
April Daily 9.30am-12noon, 2-6pm
☎ 93.593291

Roquebrune-Cap Martin

Château Musée
Roquebrune Village
Open: All year except mid-
November to mid-December; May
to September Daily 10am-12noon,
2-7pm; October to mid-November,
mid-December to April Daily
except Friday 10am-12noon, 2-5pm
☎ 93.350722

St Jean-Cap-Ferrat

Fondation Ephrussi de Rothschild
Jardins et Villa Ile-de-France
Open: All year except November;
July and August Daily except
Monday 3-7pm; September,
October, December to June Daily
except Monday 2-6pm
☎ 93.013309

Parc Zoologique
Open: All year Daily 9am-Dusk
☎ 93.013156

St Paul-de-Vence

Fondation Maeght
Route Passe-Prest
St Paul
Open: All year July to September
Daily 10am-7pm; October to June
Daily 10am-12.30pm, 2.30-6pm
☎ 93.328163

Musée d'Archéologie et de
Préhistoire
Next to the church of St Pierre
St Paul-de-Vence
Open: All year Daily except
Sunday 11am-12noon, 2-5pm.
Closed on official holidays

Chapelle du Rosaire ou Matisse
Avenue Henri Matisse
Vence
Open: All year except November to
mid-December; Tuesday and
Thursday 10-11.30am, 2.30-5.30pm.
At other times by prior appoint-
ment. July to September may be
open more frequently from 1990,
telephone as above or 93.580638
(Tourist Office) for details
☎ 93.580326

Fondation Emile Hugues
Château des Villeneuve
Place du Frêne
Vence
Open: All year except November;
July to October Daily 10am-
12noon, 3 -7pm; December to June
Daily 2-6pm. Guided tours on
Thursdays at 4pm
☎ 93.242423

Musée Carzou
Château des Villeneuves
Place du Frêne
Vence
Open: All year except November;
July to October 10am-12noon,

3-7pm; December to June 2-6pm
☎ 93.242423

Chapelle des Pénitents Blancs
Rue des Poilus
Vence
Open: Easter to November Daily
10am-12noon, 3-7pm
☎ 93.580638

Musée du Parfum et de la Liqueur
2618 route de Grasse
Vence
Open: All year Monday to
Saturday 10am-12.30pm, 2-6pm;
Sunday 2-6pm
☎ 93.580600

St Raphaël

Eglise St Pierre
Open: All year Daily except
Sunday 11am-12noon, 2-5pm.
Closed on official holidays
☎ 94.951687

St Vallier-de-Thiey

Les Grottes de la Baume
Open: June to September Monday
to Friday 10am-6.30pm, Saturdays,
Sundays and Holidays 10am-
12noon, 2-5pm
☎ 93.360356

La Turbie

Le Trophée des Alpes
Site museum
Open: All year April to September
Daily 9am-7pm; October to March
Daily 9am-5pm
Closed on official holidays
☎ 93.411010

Vallauris

Musée National Picasso
Place de la Libération
Open: All year April to September
Daily except Tuesday 10am-
12noon, 2-5pm; October to March
Daily except Tuesday 2-6pm.
Closed on official holidays
☎ 93.641805

Musée Municipal
Place de la Libération
Open: All year Daily except
Tuesday 10am-12noon, 2-5pm
☎ 93.641605

Villefranche-sur-Mer

Fondation Volti
Citadelle St Emile
Open: All year except November;
June to September Monday,
Wednesday to Saturday 10am-
12noon, 3-7pm, Sunday 3-7pm;
October, December to May
Monday, Wednesday to Saturday
10am-12noon, 3-7pm, Sunday
3-7pm
☎ 93.554512

Musée Goetz-Boumeester
Citadelle St Emile
Open: All year except November;
June to September Monday,
Wednesday to Saturday 10am-
12noon, 3-7pm, Sunday 3-7pm;
October, December to May
Monday, Wednesday to Saturday
10am-12noon, 3-7pm, Sunday
3-7pm
☎ 93.554512

Musée Roux
Citadelle St Emile
Open: All year except November
Monday to Friday 10am-12noon,
2-5.30pm
☎ 93.554512

Chapelle St Pierre
Port de Villefranche
Open: All year except mid-
November to mid-December; July
to September Daily except Friday
9.30am-12noon, 2.30-7pm; October
to mid-November Daily except
Friday 9am-12noon, 2-6pm; mid-
December to March Daily except
Friday 9.30am-12noon, 2-4.30pm;
April to June Daily except Friday
9am-12noon, 2-6pm
☎ 93.017368

Villeneuve-Loubet

Musée d'Art Culinaire
(Fondation Auguste Escoffier)
3 rue Escoffier
Open: All year Daily except
Monday 2-6pm.
Closed on official holidays
☎ 93.208051

Musée Militaire
Place de Verdun
Open: All year April to October
Tuesday to Sunday 10am-12noon,
2-5pm; November to March
Tuesday to Saturday 10am-12noon,
2-5pm, Sunday 2-5pm.
Closed on official holidays
☎ 93.220156

Sports

The South of France has one of the
highest concentrations of sporting
facilities in Europe and more are
being added all the time. The
opportunities available cover the

whole spectrum of sport. They range from water sports — at their best here in the warm waters of the Mediterranean — through to hang gliding, rock climbing, and skiing in the mountains of the pre-Alps.

It would be impossible to provide a comprehensive glossary of the sports available in the area. However, one facility does bear special mention; the walking available on the superb French system of waymarked footpaths, the *Sentiers de Grande Randonnée*. Five routes of varying difficulty cross some of the region's most striking scenery. They are part of a network covering the whole country, and their Provençal sections are marked on Michelin maps 81 and 84 (1:200,000) by broken lines together with their identification numbers (GR4, GR5 etc).

Detailed illustrated guides, known as *Topo-guides*, can be bought at local bookshops. More information can be obtained from Comité National des Sentiers de Grande Randonnée (CNSGR), 92 rue de Clignancourt, 75018 Paris. ☎ 259 60 40.

The footpaths in the area link the following places:

GR4 Méditerranée — Océan

Vaison-la-Romaine — Malaucène — Sault — Simiane-la-Rotonde — Oppedette — Céreste — Manosque — Gréoux-les-Bains — Riez — Moustiers — Gorges du Verdon by the Sentier Martel — Castellane — Entrevaux — St Cassien — Gréolières — Cipières — St Lambert — Grasse.

GR5 Hollande — Méditerranée

Larche — St Etienne-de-Tinée — Auron — Roya — St Sauveur-sur-Tinée — Rimplas — St Dalmas-Valdeblore — Utelle — Aspremont — Nice.

GR52

St Dalmas-Valdeblore — Boréon — La Madone de Fenestre — Pas du Mont Colomb — Refuge Nice — Refuge des Merveilles — Sospel — Menton.

GR9 Jura — Côte d'Azur

Brantes — Mont Ventoux — Sault — St Saturnin-d'Apt — Buoux — Vaugines — Cucuron — Beaumont-de-Pertuis — Trets — Hôtellerie de la Ste Baume — Signes — Belgentier — Pignans — La Garde-Freinet — St Paul-les-Mûres.

GR6 Alpes — Océan

St Paul-sur-Ubaye — Barcelonnette — Seynes-les-Alpes — Sisteron — Forcalquier — Vachères — Oppedette — Viens — Rustrel — Roussillon — Eygalières — Les Baux — Tarascon.

Useful Addresses

Consulates-General

Great Britain

24 Avenue du Prado
Marseille
☎ 91.534332

United States of America

9 Rue Armeny
Marseille
☎ 91.549200

1 Rue du Maréchal-Joffre
Nice
☎ 93.888955

Canada

24 Avenue du Prado
Marseille
☎ 91.371937/371940

French Government Tourist Offices

Great Britain

178 Piccadily
London W1V 0AL
☎ 071 491 7622

United States of America

610 Fifth Avenue Suite 222
New York NY 10020-2452
☎ 212 757 1683

Canada

1981 Avenue McGill College
Tour Esso Suite 490
Montreal
Quebec H3 A2 W9
☎ 514 288 4264

Tourist Offices in France

Almost all towns and many villages have their own *Syndicats d'Initiative* and these will supply local information and maps. The main offices are listed below.

Aix-en-Provence
2 Place du Général de Gaulle
☎ 42.260293

Arles
Esplanade des Lices
☎ 90.962935

Avignon
41 Cours Jean-Jaurès
☎ 90.825629

Cannes
Palais des Festivals
Esplanade President-Georges-Pompidou
☎ 93.392453

Marseille
4 Le Canebière
☎ 91.549111

Monaco
2 Boulevard des Moulins
☎ 93.506088

Nice
Gare SNCF
Avenue Thiers
☎ 93.870707

Toulon
8 Avenue Colbert
☎ 94.220822/926335

INDEX

A Note to the Reader

We hope you have found this book informative, helpful and enjoyable. It is always our aim to make our publications as accurate and up to date as possible. With this in mind, we would appreciate any comments that you might have. If you come across any information to update this book or discover something new about the area we have covered, please let us know so that your notes may be incorporated in future editions.

As it is MPC's principal aim to keep our publications lively and responsive to change, any information that readers provide will be a valuable asset to us in maintaining the highest possible standards for our books.

Please write to:
Senior Editor
Moorland Publishing Co Ltd
Free Post
Ashbourne
Derbyshire
DE6 9BR